Advance Praise for *A Giant Leap* . . .

. . . from Healthcare Leaders

"*A Giant Leap* tackles the central question in healthcare today: Will AI be another digital disappointment or a genuine transformation? By offering an engaging, hype-free case for informed optimism, Wachter's book provides an all-important guide."

> **—ERIC TOPOL, MD,** chair of Innovative Medicine at the Scripps Research Institute and author of four bestselling books on healthcare's future, including *Super Agers* and *Deep Medicine*

"What Carl Sagan was for the wonders of astronomy—a guide—Bob Wachter is for many of the mysteries in the modern healthcare system. If, like me, you have been waiting for a lucid explanation of one of those mysteries—the forms, promise, and perils of artificial intelligence in medical care—your wait is over. *A Giant Leap* is a clear, comprehensive, and good-humored exploration of AI in healthcare— what it is now, and what it can become."

> **—DONALD M. BERWICK, MD, MPP,** president emeritus and senior fellow at the Institute for Healthcare Improvement

"*A Giant Leap* is a wonderfully engaging, lucid, and timely guide to how AI is transforming healthcare. Wachter expertly lays out the enormous benefits of generative AI alongside its most worrisome potential pitfalls—and they're not the obvious concerns, like biases and hallucinations, that dominate headlines. Whether you're a patient, doctor, or nurse, if you want to understand how generative AI will revolutionize your healthcare experience, Wachter is your indispensable pilot."

> **—EZEKIEL EMANUEL, MD, PHD,** Vice Provost for Global Initiatives and codirector of the Health Transformation Institute at the University of Pennsylvania

"In my forty years working with artificial intelligence in healthcare, I never expected AI to be the hottest topic in mainstream culture. In *A Giant Leap*, Bob Wachter manages to cut through the hype to reveal the fundamental truths reshaping medical practice. The book—brimming with insight, wisdom, humanity, and compelling stories—is a necessary road map for anyone who wants to understand what it all means and what's coming next."

> **—JOHN HALAMKA, MD, MS,** president of the Mayo Clinic Platform and professor at Mayo Clinic College of Medicine and Science

... from Leaders in AI and Technology

"Bob Wachter has written the definitive account of AI's transformation of healthcare, capturing the revolutionary potential unfolding right now and the unglamorous work of making it real. Drawing on his experience and interviews, this book avoids both Silicon Valley hype and medical pessimism to give a clear-eyed view of where AI is likely to succeed and fail in medical care. Essential reading for anyone who wants to understand where medicine is heading."

> —**ETHAN MOLLICK**, bestselling author of *Co-Intelligence*
> and codirector of Generative AI Labs at Wharton

"Tech is the easy part. People, incentives, and workflows are where dreams go to die—or flourish. *A Giant Leap* masterfully captures these dynamics, delivering this era's definitive guide to healthcare AI."

> —**VINOD KHOSLA**, cofounder of Sun Microsystems and founder
> of Khosla Ventures

"Robert Wachter has done it again. *A Giant Leap* is a master class in clarity and insight. Yes, AI is poised to reshape healthcare in profound, practical, and deeply human ways. Wachter combines rigorous analysis with vivid storytelling, making this a real page-turner for anyone who cares about the future of medicine."

> —**PETER LEE**, president and head of Microsoft Research

"*A Giant Leap* offers a rare blend of realism and optimism about AI in medicine, showing how it is rapidly moving beyond hype to deliver true progress for a healthcare system long overdue for reinvention. In this pivotal moment, Robert Wachter is the trusted guide we need to chart a course to a future where AI and humans work together, delivering better care, lower costs, and healthier, longer lives for all."

> —**MARC BENIOFF**, chair and CEO of Salesforce

"*A Giant Leap* is a deeply researched, unflinchingly honest, and ultimately hopeful analysis of how AI will transform healthcare and the systems, cultures, incentives, and human choices that will determine whether the technology becomes a force for good or a source of new risks. Wachter is neither an AI evangelist nor a doomsayer. He is a steward, guiding us through the promise and perils with a clinician's rigor and perspective. He has done what very few can: synthesize the technical, clinical, economic, and ethical dimensions of AI in healthcare into a story that's urgent and accessible."

> —**HEMANT TANEJA**, CEO of General Catalyst

. . . from Health Policy Leaders

"*A Giant Leap* takes us on a masterful journey to understand the power and pitfalls of AI in healthcare. Wachter has a rare combination of deep curiosity, sharp analysis, and clear-eyed understanding of the humanity that must always be at the heart of healing. This is powerful, essential reading."

> —**VIVEK MURTHY, MD, MBA,** nineteenth and twenty-first surgeon general of the United States

"Bob Wachter navigates between AI hype and doomsday prophecies to deliver what we need: a clear-eyed assessment of what artificial intelligence can actually do for patients, clinicians, and our healthcare system—and where it might fail us. Having witnessed AI from multiple vantage points—including as FDA commissioner, a leader at Alphabet/Google, and a clinician and clinical researcher—I appreciate his rare ability to synthesize different perspectives to illuminate a topic as complex as it is vital."

> —**ROBERT CALIFF, MD,** twenty-third and twenty-sixth commissioner of the US Food and Drug Administration, former head of medical strategy and policy at Verily and Google Health, and founding director of the Duke Clinical Research Institute

. . . from Leading Authors, Editors, and Journalists

"As with his previous books, Wachter demonstrates his gift for anticipating and digesting the big movements in science and healthcare. *A Giant Leap* is authoritative, well-researched, and timely, and reads beautifully! It left me with a better understanding of the potential and pitfalls of AI as it transforms medical practice."

> —**ABRAHAM VERGHESE,** bestselling author of *The Covenant of Water* and *Cutting for Stone*

"A firsthand account of the breathtaking possibilities and sobering challenges of AI in medicine. Conscientious and deeply engaged, Wachter embraces progress while challenging readers to grapple with the biggest questions: What does a healing relationship look like when your doctor isn't human? When AI can pinpoint a diagnosis in seconds, will future physicians feel unmoored without the technology at their fingertips? *A Giant Leap* is a book that thinks alongside you—and demands that you think back."

> —**SHERRY TURKLE,** professor at the Massachusetts Institute of Technology and *New York Times* bestselling author of *The Second Self, Alone Together,* and *Reclaiming Conversation*

"With his unparalleled expertise and genuine curiosity, Robert Wachter is the perfect guide to the AI-powered future of healthcare, in all its impending glory and gaffes. Essential reading for policymakers, practitioners, and patients."

> —**STEVEN LEVY,** bestselling author of *Hackers, Crypto,* and *Facebook: The Inside Story*

"The most important issue facing American healthcare is how quickly doctors and patients can smartly embrace AI. Bob Wachter's *A Giant Leap* is both a great primer and a great story, because he is gifted at balancing the big picture with more intimate storytelling. Also, like any good doctor, he humbly and amusingly embraces the limits of what we know. Read this book and you'll always feel ahead of the AI curve."

—**STEPHEN FRIED**, bestselling author of *Rush*, coauthor of *Profiles in Mental Health Courage*, and director of the Narrative Medicine Journalism Workshop at Columbia University

"Since the rise of generative AI, I've been preoccupied with how the technology could and should shape medicine. With his signature blend of narrative, analysis, and wit, Wachter has answered many of my questions while raising others I didn't even know I should be asking. For doctors, patients, and technologists searching for truth in a blizzard of AI claims and counterclaims, *A Giant Leap* is both anchor and compass—an indispensable guide for decoding our present and glimpsing our future."

—**DHRUV KHULLAR, MD, MPP**, contributing writer for *The New Yorker* and associate professor at Weill Cornell Medicine

"Button up your white coats! Artificial intelligence has entered the exam room, whether we like it or not. Wachter skillfully navigates the fault line between the peril and the possibility of AI. He's unafraid to illuminate how this new force could reimagine care in an ailing system but does not gloss over the real and present dangers. Required reading for doctors and patients alike."

—**DANIELLE OFRI, MD, PHD**, author of *When We Do Harm*

"Bob Wachter has crafted the perfect entry point for anyone curious about AI's role in healthcare. Through vivid storytelling and captivating real-world characters, Wachter grapples with the urgent questions that will shape medicine's future: How should we regulate AI technology in healthcare? What are the dangers of moving too fast—or too slow? Most critically, what values should AI embody, and who gets to decide? Before reading this, I wasn't all that interested in AI; now I can't look away."

—**LISA ROSENBAUM, MD**, national correspondent for *The New England Journal of Medicine* and writer in residence at Beth Israel Deaconess Medical Center's Smith Center for Outcomes Research

"Written by a brilliant storyteller who really does his homework, a practicing physician who cares deeply about medicine, and one of the most astute observers of trends in healthcare, *A Giant Leap* is a must read for those who want a clear-eyed look at the complex healthcare AI landscape today and what may be in store for the future. I learned a lot, laughed a lot, and somewhat unexpectedly came away with a great deal of hope for our profession and the future of medicine."

—**KIRSTEN BIBBINS-DOMINGO, PHD, MD, MAS**, editor in chief of *JAMA* and the JAMA Network

A GIANT LEAP

Also by Robert Wachter, MD

*The Digital Doctor: Hope, Hype, and Harm
at the Dawn of Medicine's Computer Age*

Understanding Patient Safety

*Internal Bleeding: The Truth Behind America's
Terrifying Epidemic of Medical Mistakes*
(with Kaveh G. Shojania, MD)

Hospital Medicine
(with Lee Goldman, MD, MPH, and Harry Hollander, MD)

The Fragile Coalition: Scientists, Activists, and AIDS

A
GIANT
LEAP

How AI Is Transforming Healthcare
and What That Means for Our Future

ROBERT WACHTER, MD

PORTFOLIO | PENGUIN

PORTFOLIO / PENGUIN

An imprint of Penguin Random House LLC

1745 Broadway, New York, NY 10019

penguinrandomhouse.com

Most Portfolio books are available at a discount when purchased in quantity for sales promotions or corporate use. Special editions, which include personalized covers, excerpts, and corporate imprints, can be created when purchased in large quantities. For more information, please call (212) 572-2232 or email specialmarkets@penguinrandomhouse.com. Your local bookstore can also assist with discounted bulk purchases using the Penguin Random House corporate Business-to-Business program. For assistance in locating a participating retailer, email B2B@penguinrandomhouse.com.

BOOK DESIGN BY TANYA MAIBORODA

LIBRARY OF CONGRESS CONTROL NUMBER: 2025028535

ISBN 9798217044245 (hardcover)
ISBN 9798217044252 (ebook)

Printed in the United States of America
1st Printing

The authorized representative in the EU for product safety and compliance is Penguin Random House Ireland, Morrison Chambers, 32 Nassau Street, Dublin D02 YH68, Ireland, https://eu-contact.penguin.ie.

To Zoë, Joe, and all the young physicians
who will shape—and be shaped by—this revolution.

Contents

Preface

GIANRICO FARRUGIA, the chief executive of the Mayo Clinic, was about to share something he'd been keeping under wraps. On a chilly fall day in 2024, I sat with him in a tastefully appointed conference room eleven floors above Mayo's sprawling campus in Rochester, Minnesota. On his computer was a video that not even his board had seen. He hesitated, and I sensed him weighing my dual identities—was I a peer, a fellow physician-leader at another prestigious academic medical center, or was I a journalist who'd normally be kept at arm's length by Mayo's PR department? Then I read a *what-the-hell-this-is-just-so-cool* expression on his face, as his excitement got the better of him. He swiveled his laptop toward me, then clicked the "play" arrow.

A kindly-looking middle-aged physician appeared on the screen, turned, and addressed the camera. "Hi, I'm Dr. Jonathan Morris," the man began. Then he paused. "Well, actually, I'm not. I'm a digital twin of the real Dr. Morris. I am an AI-powered digital surrogate with several AI algorithms accounting for my every move. That is the real Dr. Morris over there behind me." The flesh-and-blood Dr. Morris, a Mayo radiologist, strolled into view and awkwardly waved to the camera. His doppelgänger continued, "I have been asked to speak with you about the need for photorealistic digital twin physicians at the Mayo Clinic."

Next appeared a patient, Alice, who had just received the result of hand X-rays in her patient portal. She clicked on an icon for Dr. Morris. "I see my X-rays came back, but I don't understand the report," Alice said. "Can you tell me what you're seeing in my hands?"

"Yes," said the Morris digital twin, his speech, facial expressions, and body language utterly lifelike. "I've just reviewed your new X-rays and compared them to the previous ones. . . . There are increased erosions involving a couple of bones at several joints. These erosions suggest progression of your rheumatoid arthritis. Others on your care team will be able to provide input and guidance on the next steps for you." Alice then clicked on another icon to consult with her rheumatologist—or, more precisely, her rheumatologist's digital twin.

In a world of photorealistic deepfakes, the technical wizardry powering this video is no longer gobsmacking. But the true advance is the ability to connect Alice's test results with Mayo's unparalleled warehouse of digitized clinical information, then apply modern AI techniques to create Mayo-quality answers, specific to Alice's case, delivered empathically by a digital twin of a respected clinician. One can easily imagine tailoring these answers to Alice's reading level and primary language, maybe even her preferred learning style.

The Mayo Clinic is one of the few global brands in healthcare. Over the past forty years, it has expanded its footprint well beyond its humble origins in central Minnesota, building medical campuses in Scottsdale, Arizona, and Jacksonville, Florida, as well as partnering with facilities in countries ranging from Mexico to Saudi Arabia. But, Farrugia told me, the brick-and-mortar days are over. "We realize we no longer need to have a physical presence around the world," he said. From now on, when the system wants to deliver Mayo Clinic care to more patients in more locations, the primary formula will be a blend of human plus digital, all enabled by artificial intelligence.

FARRUGIA'S PLAN TO transform one of the world's most storied healthcare organizations might seem radical at first, but it struck me as strategically sensible. I too have been wowed by the potential of AI to remake healthcare ever since I clicked on the website of a company called OpenAI on November 30, 2022, and began entering prompts: *Who pitched in the final game of the 1969 World Series? Draft a 150-word synopsis of the Watergate scandal for middle-grade readers. Write a poem about Dr. Robert Wachter in the style of Shakespeare.* The answers weren't all perfect, but they were awfully good, some jaw-droppingly so. I wasn't alone in my reaction. Within two months of its launch, one hundred million people were using ChatGPT, the fastest adoption curve of any technology in modern history.

For my own work as a physician, the potential of this new breed of artificial intelligence seemed limitless. In medicine, we have a long tradition of "curbside consults"—when you run into a specialist colleague in the hospital cafeteria and say, "Emma, I have this patient I'm trying to sort out. Can I run the case by you?" Soon after ChatGPT was released, I threw it a few hypothetical cases, including this one: *My patient is a twenty-eight-year-old woman with new on-set of fatigue, tremor, loose stools, and weight loss. What might be going on?* The answers were at least as good as those I'd get from the average medical student. (It got this one right, calling it a likely case of hyperthyroidism.) Here was a curbside consultant that fit in my pocket, one I could feed actual cases to (being careful to stay on the correct side of healthcare privacy rules) while remaining friendly, chipper, and eager to help, 24-7.

I'm writing this book a couple of years after that vertiginous introduction to generative AI. The passage of time has allowed for hundreds of healthcare AI companies to emerge, billions of dollars to be invested, thousands of consultants to be engaged, dozens of lawsuits to be filed, tens of thousands of medical students (and their parents) to be petrified, and millions of additional diagnoses to be offered up by chatbots. The initial hype has also begun to settle down, making this an ideal moment to examine how AI is actually changing healthcare and assess the forces shaping its impact—now armed with real-world experience and hard-earned perspective.

NOT LONG AFTER the launch of ChatGPT, research began to emerge regarding generative AI in healthcare. Generative AI, or gen AI for short, is an umbrella term for models that can create new content by learning patterns from existing data; the term is more inclusive than "large language models" (LLMs) in that it encompasses not only language but also the ability to ingest and produce images, audio, and video. It quickly became clear that gen AI had formidable skill in answering medical questions. One study found it could pass a key medical student licensing exam. Others showed that it could outperform graduating medical residents on specialty-specific board exams in fields like psychiatry and obstetrics.

OK, it can pass a test. But how would GPT do when asked to diagnose real cases, a skill that takes far more cognitive horsepower and experience than merely answering multiple-choice exam questions? The answer came in short order: It would do exceedingly well. When presented with the famously vexing cases published in *The New England Journal of Medicine*, AI performed at a level equal to the best faculty diagnosticians. This was no longer asking AI to count the number of bones in the hand. (It's twenty-seven, by the way.) This was getting at the essence of what doctors do, what we train for years to do, what we—particularly those of us who don't perform surgery or deliver babies—consider the zenith of our skill set: diagnosing complex cases.

These studies confirmed my initial impression of the curbside consults—the new AI would ultimately be able to replicate, and maybe surpass, much of what I went to four years of medical school and three years of residency to learn: how to take in a large body of patient information (history, physical examination, test results) and line it up against nearly infinite patterns of disease in order to make a diagnosis, then match that diagnosis to another body of information to determine the optimal treatment, the likely prognosis, and the follow-up strategy. I found this recognition to be at once exciting and disheartening: Was this how it felt to be a skilled portrait painter in the late nineteenth century, when photography emerged as a much faster and cheaper way to capture people's likenesses?

But medicine is a uniquely human profession, I thought. So

much of what doctors offer involves empathy and communication—explaining complex options to patients and families, sensitively listening and probing, delivering bad news. Nobody is going to want a chatbot to tell them that they have kidney failure or cancer. Right?

Maybe not.

In 2023, a study showed that, in response to a variety of clinical scenarios posted on an online social media site, AI's responses were judged to be *more* empathetic than those given by actual physicians. A year later, researchers at Google showed that their AI tool, trained on thousands of patient-doctor conversations, not only outperformed primary care physicians in diagnosing simulated cases but was judged by the mock patients to give more caring, empathetic responses. Every month, it seemed, my profession's claim to a unique body of skills and expertise felt increasingly fragile.

I'VE BEEN FASCINATED and frustrated by healthcare information technology for a couple of decades, mostly wondering how it was that medicine could be so resistant to digital transformation.

Since the 1990s, we've witnessed industry after industry being reshaped by technology. Yet I can't think of any examples of Amazon-Uber-Netflix-Airbnb-type disruption in healthcare. The list of America's top hospitals today—places like the Mayo Clinic, Johns Hopkins, Mass General, and my own institution, UC San Francisco (UCSF)—is nearly identical to one from a century ago. The unemployment rate among doctors and nurses is essentially zero, with demand outstripping supply in nearly every area of medicine. Apart from education, no other industry has sidestepped the forces of digital disruption like healthcare.

And God knows, we could use some disruption. In the US, we spend nearly 20 percent of our gross domestic product, about $5 trillion each year, on healthcare. (The second-place spender is Germany, which devotes about 13 percent of its GDP.) While health insurance, private and public, partly insulates American patients from the true cost, that cost is very real, whether it expresses itself through higher taxes, lower salaries, or reduced productivity. Warren Buffett calls healthcare the "tapeworm" of the US economy, literally starving our society of resources it would otherwise invest in infrastructure, housing, or public education.

Our profligacy might be acceptable if it resulted in better health, but it does not. Approximately one out of three of these dollars is spent on administrative paper-pushing or other activities that essentially add nothing to a patient's welfare. Our average life expectancy is four years lower than the average in a peer group of other wealthy countries that includes Canada, France, Germany, and Australia; we also have the highest rate of avoidable deaths from causes like diabetes, hypertension, and several cancers, and the highest infant and maternal mortality rates. Nearly one million Americans are severely harmed or killed by medical mistakes every year.

Don't get me wrong—US healthcare delivers miracles every day, particularly when it comes to cutting-edge and intensive care, things like transplants, cancer immunotherapy, and gene editing. And the people who work in healthcare—both clinicians and non-clinicians—are generally caring, dedicated, and well trained. But the healthcare system itself is a headache wrapped in red tape inside the nightmare that Franz Kafka himself might have dreamed up while on hold with the insurance company. It's a system in desperate need of transformation.

TWENTY YEARS AGO, I thought we'd be rescued by the implementation of electronic health records (EHRs), enormous software systems that allow hospitals and clinics to record and transmit data digitally.

I've said many dumb things over the years, but the dumbest might have been in 2004 when I hired Russ Cucina, a hospital medicine physician fresh out of his Stanford informatics fellowship, to join my department at UCSF. Cucina was planning a career as a clinician-informaticist, seeing patients part-time while also building and implementing IT systems. Back then, clinicians at UCSF Medical Center, like those at nearly every US hospital, recorded their data—patient summaries, medication orders, lab results, and the like—on pieces of paper, sometimes supplemented by the odd Post-it note. UCSF was finalizing plans to install its first electronic health record system.

"What will you do for a living after we've digitized our health records?" I asked Cucina. I knew we wouldn't be done on the day we celebrated the EHR's "go-live" after many months of preparation, cheerleading, and hand-holding—there would be a few years of tinkering and optimizing. But then, I thought, our digital journey would largely be complete.

I now realize that by liberating our data from paper charts, we'd created the infrastructure to support digital transformation. But to achieve the kind of change that patients, clinicians, and society need, go-live was just the start of the journey, not the end. Cucina, of course, is busier than ever these days.

NOT ONLY DID electronic health records fail to transform healthcare in the ways I'd expected, but they also created a host of unanticipated, mostly negative, consequences.

I can't overstate how surprising this is. After all, digitization meant that doctors' and nurses' clinical documentation would be legible and accessible throughout the health system. The computer could warn me that my patient was allergic to ampicillin and inform me that the best medication for her arthritis was Humira. Key laboratory, pathology, and X-ray results (and sometimes the images themselves) were now a click away. And patients would have their own digital portal on which they could view their data and interact with their healthcare system—a big step toward democratizing medicine. As someone who spent scores of exasperating hours during my residency thumbing through shoeboxes filled with carbon copies of laboratory slips to find my patient's serum creatinine result, this all sounded dandy. What could possibly go wrong?

It turns out, a lot.

I'm reminded of how awful humans are at anticipating the consequences of new technologies. Henry Ford was reputed to have said, "If I asked people what they wanted, they would have said 'faster horses.'" Few people—Steve Jobs may have been the exception that proves the rule—are able to predict what will happen when a new technology transforms an industry or a society until they see it with their own eyes. Who, after all, could have foreseen all the consequences of social media—in areas ranging from teenage mental health to presidential elections—when Mark Zuckerberg was tinkering with TheFacebook in his Harvard dorm room?

The widespread implementation of electronic health records offered vivid evidence of the Law of Unanticipated (Digital) Consequences. Survey after survey showed that, even before the Covid-19 pandemic, measures of physician burnout had skyrocketed. Watch your doctor at your next clinic visit and you'll see her making lots of eye contact with her computer and precious little with you. Or ask her how she feels about her EHR inbox and watch her face turn ashen.

I was dazed and confused enough by all this that in 2015 I wrote a book, *The Digital Doctor: Hope, Hype, and Harm at the Dawn of Medicine's Computer Age.* In chapter 1, I'll summarize this period of electronic health record adoption. It is relevant to our current discussion for a couple of reasons. First, some of the earliest use cases for today's AI—things like digital scribes and AI doppelgängers—will, ironically, be aimed at fixing problems created by the EHR. More important, understanding the reasons behind our depressing experience with electronic health records will allow us to anticipate some of the speed bumps we'll surely hit as we move into the modern era of AI. For now, suffice it to say that digital transformation is harder than it looks, and the reasons have shockingly little to do with the technology itself.

AS I BEGAN to play, and then work, with ChatGPT and other incarnations of generative AI in 2022 and 2023, I wondered if we were finally nearing the digital utopia I thought we were creating when we installed the electronic health record. I knew that this would not just be a matter of whether gen AI represented a stunning techno-logical advance—it clearly did. The story of whether AI would finally transform healthcare would mostly be about whether the health-care system could implement these tools in ways that would produce better outcomes for patients, lower costs, and some relief for beleaguered doctors and nurses. And that, in turn, would be determined as much by history, politics, economics, pride, regulations, leadership, lawsuits, guilds, culture, workflows, inertia, greed, hubris, vibes, and zeitgeist as by graphics processing units, diffusion models, and neural networks.

I *am* confident that the new AI will represent a giant leap, transforming healthcare in myriad ways. This book is my effort to answer the question of whether the benefits will outweigh the harms. There are compelling reasons to believe that the answer will be yes.

Yes, because today's AI truly is dazzling, allowing people to interact with digital data via natural conversation and then creating outputs—clinical summaries, predictions, suggested diagnoses, treatment recommendations—that are far more accurate and humanlike than anything we've seen before. Yes, because even as we appreciate the flaws of current AI tools, as Wharton professor Ethan Mollick reminds us in his book *Co-Intelligence*, the AI you're using today is the worst AI you'll ever see. Yes, because the current healthcare system is overwhelmed and failing patients, clinicians, and society in critical ways. Yes, because even if we had enough money to hire all the doctors, nurses, medical assistants, billing clerks, and patient navigators we need (and we don't), there aren't enough skilled workers out there to fill these roles. Yes, because companies from inside and outside healthcare are investing heavily in building and implementing these AI tools and systems, and their track record in predicting—and shaping—the future is formidable.

And yes, because the experiences of the past forty years—including the lessons learned from healthcare's painful history with both electronic health records and artificial intelligence—have paved a path that points us generally in the right direction. Unlike when I sat down to write *The Digital Doctor*, in a mood of disbelief and grumpiness, my mood today is guardedly hopeful.

Yet "guardedly" is the operative word. Even as study after study highlighted AI's superhuman skills in writing, recalling, understanding, predicting, and reasoning, there were early signs that all was not sunshine and rainbows. We began to hear of "hallucinations"—when the AI, while sounding supremely confident, was literally making stuff up. AI outputs were often compromised by various kinds of bias. There were concerns about privacy, security, explainability, and more. AI can be a tremendous source of information, but also a uniquely potent spreader of misinformation. We have no obvious model for regulating healthcare AI, and only limited capacity to oversee its use within health systems. Patients are sure to use AI in ways that will occasionally threaten their health. And even if the technology lives up to its promise, the forces in the healthcare system buttressing the status quo are impressive.

In other words, there are many reasons to believe that this could all go off the rails or be one more example of expectations exceeding reality when it comes to healthcare's digital transformation. To invoke a Yogi Berra–ism, "In theory, there's no difference between theory and practice. In practice, there is."

o⅃₀

AS YOU READ this book, I'd like you to view much of the discussion through the twin lenses of trust and trustworthiness. Whether

AI ultimately transforms healthcare will hinge, I believe, on whether people—patients, doctors, nurses, healthcare leaders, regulators, and others—come to trust it.

Although there are exceptions, humans tend to trust other humans more than they trust nonhuman entities like companies and pieces of software. Trust, you see, is not just a function of reliably producing the right answer. It develops through positive interactions and is enhanced when people perceive that another party is competent and acting in their best interest. Conversely, trust can be easily lost, such as when people sense that the party they're dealing with is wrong or uncaring. "Trust is a notoriously vulnerable good," wrote the philosopher Annette Baier in 1991, "easily wounded and not at all easily healed."

What is unique about generative AI is that it is a *what* that acts more like a *who*. The fact that its outputs are so staggeringly humanlike makes deciding whether to trust them a singular challenge, one without much of a road map for us to follow.

The creators of today's AI understand this well. Two weeks after his company released ChatGPT to the public, Sam Altman, the CEO of OpenAI, warned of the risk of placing undue trust in generative AI. In December 2022, he tweeted that ChatGPT is "good enough at some things to create a misleading impression of greatness. It's a mistake to be relying on it for anything important right now. It's a preview of progress; we have lots of work to do on robustness and truthfulness."

That was a few years ago, and the technology has advanced quite a bit. But has it improved enough to trust it with your health, and perhaps your life? In countless treatises, philosophers, sociologists, and corporate consultants have explored the concept of trust from all angles, generally emphasizing how intertwined it is with character and relationships. But ChatGPT has no character. Or does it? And you have no relationship with Claude and Gemini. Or do you?

∘⌒∘

MUCH OF WHAT you'll read here will be based on my experience as a practicing physician, researcher, teacher, and leader in a large and well-regarded academic healthcare system. I also have the advantage of living in San Francisco, AI's epicenter, and advising several health tech companies, most of them integrating AI into their businesses (I'll let you know when I mention any of them). While my day job gives me lots of access to information and insights, I've conducted more than one hundred interviews—with people ranging from CEOs of AI companies to computer scientists, physicians, and patients—and visited many organizations that are building, using, or thinking about AI and healthcare.

I will assume you have a general familiarity with AI tools and how they work. I won't spend too much time on the underlying technology or on discussions of whether AI can pass the Turing test (it can) or is capable of thought or emotion (no, but it's one hell of an actor). Nor is this a self-help book for people learning to use AI in their work—there are plenty of those. While I'll touch on the use of AI in medical research, my focus will be on AI's impact on patients, clinicians, and the healthcare system. Finally, I won't dwell on AI's existential risks, such as whether it will wage wars, dissolve nation-states, engineer bioweapons, worsen climate change, or achieve superintelligence. I also won't predict whether AI will take over *everyone's* job, but I will discuss the impact of AI on the healthcare workforce, and on medical education.

While I'm writing this book at a time of peak AI hype, do not expect a puff piece of techno-optimism—although I will, sometimes giddily, describe the remarkable things that gen AI can do and the early examples in healthcare where it is truly making a difference. Nor will this book be an apocalyptic downer or an exercise in pearl clutching. As Mark Smith, founding CEO of the California Health Care Foundation, told me, "There's a group of people from the Grave Reservations School of Health Policy who have *grave reservations* about anything new. So they admire these problems. I think they're right to point them out. But then you say, 'Okay, fine. Let's go to work on that.'" I agree, and will do my best to present a balanced view of the good that AI can do in healthcare, the surprising realities that are shaping our digital transformation, and some of the problems that we should try to anticipate and, if possible, mitigate.

There is one certainty in the world of AI, and that is that the technology will continue to evolve. And not just a little. This means that things will undoubtedly change between my writing and your reading of this book. I'll do my best to use examples that illustrate general principles about AI and healthcare, timeless points that will still be relevant as we move from GPT-6 to GPT-23.

There will inevitably be sharp growing pains as we integrate AI into healthcare, and some patients will be harmed, maybe even killed, as we sort out its proper place. But, in the words of Joe Biden, "Don't compare me to the Almighty; compare me to the alternative." Our current healthcare system fails patients and clinicians all too often and is unsustainably expensive, inaccessible, unwieldy, and infuriating. That means that AI doesn't have to be perfect to be better.

Which is good, since it *won't* be perfect. The key question is whether it will truly be better. Let's see.

A GIANT LEAP

1

An Overnight Revolution, Fifty Years in the Making

Lessons of the EHR Era

In Ernest Hemingway's classic 1926 novel *The Sun Also Rises*, a character named Mike Campbell loses all his money due to a series of reckless financial choices. "How did you go bankrupt?" his friend Bill asks. "Two ways," Campbell replies. "Gradually and then suddenly."

When it comes to the digital transformation of healthcare, we have the "gradually" part down pat—no industry has been slower than healthcare in disrupting the status quo with digital tools. Could the introduction of generative AI be our "suddenly" moment, when a breathtaking new technology crashes into a healthcare system in desperate need of change, igniting true transformation? Answering this question requires some appreciation of the history of healthcare digitization.

BEFORE 2008, VERY few US hospitals and physicians' offices recorded their data—lab tests, X-ray results, and the observations and treatment plans of physicians and other health professionals—in an electronic database. Back then, after I took a history from and examined a patient, I would scribble my observations, along with my "differential diagnosis" (the list of conditions I was considering, such as "probable pneumonia, rule out congestive heart failure"), and my diagnostic and treatment plans on a piece of paper; this would be stored—along with dozens of other observations by medical consultants, nurses, physical therapists, social workers, and more—in a large binder. I'd then write my "Doctor's Orders" on another piece of paper, filed in a different section of the binder, finally placing the binder on a lazy Susan in the nursing station of the hospital or clinic, cueing the clerk that there were orders to be carried out by rotating a color-coded wheel on the outside of the chart.

Having healthcare data stored as physical artifacts—paper notes, X-rays, EKG tracings—created a host of problems. If I referred my patient to see a specialist, I prayed that the chart and X-rays would end up at the specialist's office in time for the appointment. They often didn't. And, of course, when the record was a collection of papers and films, giving patients access to their own medical information was impossible.

While an analog health record created numerous challenges when it came to the care of individual patients, there was an even greater consequence: The healthcare system could never undergo the kind of transformation that might make it better, safer, more satisfying, and less expensive until our records were digitized.

You'd think that hospitals and medical practices would have invested in digitization without much prompting, but they did not. This was partly because of a vicious circle. Since so few healthcare systems were buying electronic health records in the 1990s and 2000s, there was very little business case for investors to put their money into EHR companies. This, in turn, meant that the few EHRs that existed at the time were profoundly flawed, having failed to benefit from either the iterative improvement cycles needed to refine any piece of software or the investments required to create a world-class company. Many of the digital giants—Google, Microsoft, IBM, GE— took a stab at building an electronic medical record of one sort or another. Every one of these flamed out, as the companies learned that healthcare, with its high stakes, overwhelming complexity, narrow profit margins, and copious regulations, was a tough nut to crack.

The result was that medicine remained a paper-based industry decades after most other industries had gone digital. This, in turn, meant that the digital transformation of healthcare, facilitated by advanced data analytics, continued to be elusive.

THINGS CHANGED IN 2009. That year, the US government scrambled to infuse billions of dollars into a sputtering economy in the wake of the Great Recession. The mantra of the architects of the stimulus package, you might remember, was that the feds would invest in "shovel-ready projects"—ones that injected money directly into the veins of the American economy to vanquish the recession.

Normally, such money would go to building bridges, repairing roads, and other major infrastructure projects. But a group of health policy wonks in the Obama administration saw a once-in-a-lifetime chance to turbocharge the use of electronic health records by positioning EHR adoption as just another shovel-ready project. A major talking point was a 2005 study by the RAND Corporation predicting that the widespread implementation of EHRs would cut US healthcare costs by $81 billion per year. Using both political persuasion and adroit sleight of hand, the Obama team managed to slip $30 billion into the $830 billion stimulus package to offer incentives to doctors and hospitals that implemented EHRs, while threatening cuts in reimbursement for those that failed to do so in the coming years.

The gambit worked. In 2008, fewer than one in ten US hospitals had an EHR. A decade later, fewer than one in ten *did not*. Uptake was similarly rapid in physicians' offices. After a generation of dawdling, the American healthcare system had finally gone digital.

The electronic health record improved many things. It became possible for clinicians in multiple locations to view a patient's record simultaneously. Some basic decision support—such as alerts that warned us that we were about to prescribe a drug to which the patient was allergic—materialized, and healthcare systems could now look for gaps in care, such as women overdue for a mammogram. Electronic prescriptions became the norm and were far less error-prone than paper ones. Virtual care became feasible, not only because of improvements in videoconferencing technology but also because EHRs allowed physicians to view a patient's medical history without depending on the uncertain availability of a paper chart.

Yet the first decade of our new digital healthcare system was chock-full of unanticipated consequences, mostly unhappy ones, particularly for doctors. Since physicians could now be prompted to enter stuff into the EHR, everybody who had an interest in influencing the doctor's actions suddenly had the electronic means to do so. To appreciate why this matters, one needs to understand the role of clinicians in healthcare's ecosystem.

In the pre-digital era, it was often said that "the most expensive piece of technology in a hospital is the doctor's pen," because while physicians' salaries only account for 8 percent of healthcare costs, the costs that emanate from our clinical decisions represent about 80 percent. Our choice to order a particular drug, scan, or procedure can easily amount to many thousands of dollars; one extra day in a hospital costs about $10,000. Add a visit to the OR or a stay in the ICU and that number mushrooms.

Once we substituted keyboards for pens, hospital administrators, regulators, and payers spied an opportunity to shape what the doctor did in real time. Armed with this power, it was utterly unsurprising that they used it. The result was that the EHR turned doctors into high-priced box-checkers. One click to document you had queried the patient about her family's medical history, another to indicate you had examined at least nine body parts (no, you didn't get a point for each extremity), one more to show that you counseled the patient about wearing seatbelts, and a bolded option to ensure that you asked if the patient felt safe at home. The premium on billing led to a game of Name the Right Diagnosis, such that an elderly patient who was weak and confused was now said to be suffering from "functional quadriplegia" (ICD-10-CM code R53.2), verbiage that paid the hospital far more than "weak and confused" (ICD-10-CM code R41.82, perhaps with an R53.1 chaser). An entire industry sprang up that reviewed physicians' digital notes and, in an impressive feat of bureaucratic doublespeak, helped ensure "Clinical Documentation Integrity," prompting the doctor to record a slightly different term that would lead to higher reimbursement.

In short, the job of being a physician was transformed by the electronic health record—and not for the better. Doctors found that they were spending half their day staring at their EHR and clicking through screens, nearly double the time they spent with their patients. Physician burnout reached alarming levels in 2022, with more than half of American doctors experiencing symptoms of exhaustion and detachment. EHR documentation was a key factor, significantly diminishing both well-being and career satisfaction.

WHEN I WROTE *The Digital Doctor* in 2015, documentation burden was physicians' predominant complaint about their electronic health records. Alas, there was worse to come. Beginning around then, in what felt like a positive development, patients were given their own version of the EHR: a "patient portal." The most popular of these is Epic's MyChart, which currently has nearly two hundred million patient-users in the US. On their portal, patients could now view their basic medical information and interact with the health system to request refills, make appointments, and the like. A 2016 US law even gave patients real-time access to their doctors' notes and laboratory and X-ray results. This democratization of care, health policy experts predicted, would allow patients to become more discerning consumers—creating a competitive marketplace that would lead to higher quality and lower costs. At least, that was the hope.

But there were problems with the EHR's patient portal. The fact that patients could read their clinicians' notes meant that they could now see lots of medical jargon and incomprehensible test results, with virtually no accompanying explanations. In a 2024 article, a Colorado physician named Benjamin Vipler recounted a conversation with his mother after she received a result through her portal:

MOM: Hey Ben, I got my colonoscopy results back in my app. The polyp wasn't colon cancer.

SON: Oh? That's great news!

MOM: Yeah. What's lymphoma?

There was more. When I'm interacting with Bank of America or Delta Air Lines via their app or website, I can solve 99 percent of my problems online without having to speak to a human. But healthcare's version of digital democratization hit a hellish sweet spot: It gave patients just enough information to confuse them and just enough digital access to create the illusion that they could accomplish key transactions online, while providing few of the tools that would allow them to do these things.

In response to the portal's relative unhelpfulness in meeting patients' needs, EHR companies added a little button to the portal, one that seemed innocent enough at first: *Click here to send a message to your doctor.* And that's exactly what people did. A river of electronic messages began to flow; that river became a tsunami in early 2020 when the Covid-19 pandemic forced most doctors' offices to close except for emergencies. If we physicians were as clever as lawyers and accountants, we would have figured out a way to charge thirty dollars for every six minutes we spent answering these queries, but, at least at first, all of this was free to the patients—and their insurance companies.

In essence, the EHR patient portal—particularly the "send a message" button—created an expectation of 24-7-365 access to the physician and team. This sounds ideal, of course—what patient *wouldn't* want that kind of access to their doctor and healthcare system? But no one had considered the consequences of opening this floodgate of messages, so there was no workforce, workflow, or business model to sustain it. The average family physician was soon spending an hour and a half after dinner each day (we called it "pajama time") dealing with inbox messages.

All this time spent documenting in the EHR and trying to keep up with inbox messages might have been tolerable to clinicians if the EHR was helping us do our jobs. But mostly, it wasn't. Sure, we'd periodically receive an alert warning us not to prescribe a medicine to which the patient was allergic, but the preponderance of alerts were false alarms. Early predictive tools, such as ones to signal that a patient might have sepsis, were clunky, distracting, and mostly wrong.

Very few physicians are Luddites. We're glad the electronic health record is there and would never want to return to paper. And virtually all clinicians favor giving patients digital tools to help them manage their own health and healthcare. But most of us find the EHR to be surprisingly unhelpful in our efforts to provide higher-quality, safer, and less expensive care, and surprisingly harmful to the goal of having a satisfying and sustainable clinical practice. A 2013 report by the RAND Corporation—yes, the same think tank that projected that EHRs would save the American healthcare system $81 billion per year—concluded that the actual savings were essentially zero.

oʌ₀

CLEARLY SOMETHING HAD gone very wrong with healthcare's transition from paper to digital. When I asked physicians and nurses about it in the mid-2010s, their answers tended to be versions of "electronic health records are expensive billing machines that were sold to the chief financial officer with no clinical input whatsoever." A few added, "We should have waited five years until the EHRs were better."

These responses had the ring of partial truth—I was reminded of the parable of the blind man feeling the elephant's leg and thinking he'd come upon a tree. But they didn't seem like the whole story, which led me to write *The Digital Doctor*. The answers I found taught me that healthcare's bumpy path to digital transformation was completely predictable, hewing closely to the experience of digitization in other industries. This history is central to understanding and predicting the next phase of healthcare's digital evolution, this one fueled by AI.

The Productivity Paradox

In 1993, Stanford economist Erik Brynjolfsson coined the term "the Productivity Paradox of Information Technology," citing repeated examples in diverse fields in which vaunted technologies initially failed—sometimes for decades—to deliver on their promise of improving productivity. In 1987, after noticing that modern factories and Wall Street trading floors were peppered with new computers but that the promised productivity gains had not materialized, Nobel Prize–winning economist Robert Solow quipped, "You can see the computer age everywhere but in the productivity statistics."

The bad news about the Productivity Paradox is that it seems to be universal—the benefits of so-called general-purpose technologies (technologies that transform our work and lives across a range of activities) never live up to the hype, at least in their first few years of widespread use.

The good news is that—for those general-purpose technologies that are destined to be keepers, like electricity, automobiles, and the internet—the paradox eventually sorts itself out. (Not all heralded general-purpose technologies turn out to be winners, of course—if you doubt me, just don your Google Glass and use them to locate your nuclear-fusion-powered Segway.) After a delay of several—and sometimes many—years, those general-purpose technologies that are destined to change the world begin to demonstrate their superpowers.

Research by Brynjolfsson and others has shown that there are two main reasons for the lag in productivity and quality gains. The first is that the early versions of the tools are invariably clunky; they only get better after many use-feedback-improvement cycles. If you're of a certain age, you probably remember your first experience using a dial-up modem or the Alta Vista search engine, examples of technologies that needed to mature before becoming transformative.

Unexpectedly, the real game changer is the second factor, something far more human than refining the software. Organizations tend to adopt new technologies without doing the hard work of rethinking their culture, workforce, workflow, and governance. Brynjolfsson calls these changes "complementary innovations," and implementing them is not a straightforward task. "A new scientific truth does not triumph by convincing its opponents and making them see the light," said the legendary physicist Max Planck, "but rather because its opponents eventually die, and a new generation grows up that is familiar with it." Whether by death or more gentle forms of personnel turnover, fresh leaders and new thinking are often needed to begin the process of reimagining the work, and thus to unlock the potential of general-purpose technologies to improve quality and productivity.

As the first general-purpose technology to hit healthcare in the modern era, EHRs vividly illustrated the Productivity Paradox of IT. "A lot of this stuff is in the ground game," said John Glaser, a prominent informatics leader at Harvard Medical School. "Not a lot of it is automatic. There is ROI there, but you have to go get it." Over the fifteen years or so that EHRs have been in widespread use, we have seen a few complementary innovations, as organizations turned off unhelpful alerts, hired human scribes to help doctors write their visit summaries, rolled out rudimentary decision support tools, and built systems to triage inbox messages from patients.

These changes were positive, but they mostly tinkered at the margins. The actual delivery of healthcare remained fundamentally unchanged by the EHR. While patients could google their symptoms or diagnoses, they remained dependent on doctors and the medical system for most of their care. Patients still came to doctors' offices for fifteen-minute visits, sitting in waiting rooms reading dog-eared copies of *Reader's Digest*. (OK, now they're on their smartphones.) Clinicians had better access to patient data and up-to-date electronic textbooks and journals, but still mostly relied on their training and experience to make diagnoses and their memory to carry out testing and treatment protocols. Back-office functions, such as sending bills to—or arguing with—insurance companies, identifying which patients were due for colonoscopies, or creating staff schedules to cover operating rooms and ERs, were mostly performed by armies of humans, unaided—to a shocking degree—by technology and data.

If technology was not going to help us address the aging and fattening of America, the skyrocketing complexity of medical care, and the growing expectations of patients, we needed some other way to allow physicians to extend their reach. Rather than turning to technological tools, we opted for our go-to strategy: inserting more humans into the healthcare team. This was seen most vividly in an explosion in the number of nonphysician providers (mostly nurse practitioners and physician assistants), who often did a version of what doctors did but were less costly, in part because their training period was much shorter and less expensive. NP jobs are expected to grow by nearly 50 percent between 2021 and 2031, making the field the fastest-growing profession in the US.

The healthcare industry's traditional role as America's most reliable job creator would be fine, except for two big problems. First, the relentless expansion of healthcare jobs (not just NPs and PAs; we've also added battalions of billing clerks, prior authorization request generators, care coordinators, and more) has become financially unsustainable, as labor costs rise while payments stagnate. Even more worrisome, the industry is running into a human resource crisis—there simply aren't enough qualified people to fill critical roles. According to recent analyses, the healthcare system is hurtling toward a shortfall of more than three hundred thousand essential workers over the next five to ten years. It's now evident that healthcare can't overcome its Productivity Paradox simply by throwing more humans at every problem.

A DECADE AFTER most hospitals and clinics had implemented an electronic health record, we saw a version of the same problem everywhere we looked: The EHR had enabled the collection of vast amounts of data, but very little of it was being used to improve our quality, safety, or productivity. If, as the saying goes, data is the oil of the twenty-first century, it's as if we had extracted billions of barrels of data at great cost but left it sitting in tankers, unrefined and largely unused.

As I mentioned earlier, I once naively believed that the digital transformation of healthcare would be accomplished simply through the widespread deployment of EHRs. With the wisdom of years, I've come to appreciate that this transformation will go through four relatively distinct phases:

1. Digitizing the healthcare system
2. Connecting all the digital parts
3. Implementing processes and tools, both digital and human, to glean insights from all this data
4. Taking advantage of these insights to improve the way we deliver care—which is, of course, why we're going through all this trouble in the first place

By implementing EHRs, we've mostly accomplished Phase One—digitizing the healthcare system. We've also made some progress on Phase Two, connecting the parts. It's worth spending a moment on this process, which insiders refer to as interoperability.

The worldwide banking system is a good example of an interoperable system, one that has been in place for over thirty years.

Interoperability—which depends on cooperative agreements between sometimes-competing organizations and the adoption of uniform data collection and reporting standards—allows me to stick my Bank of America debit card into a Banco Santander machine in Barcelona and have it spit out euros from my US-based account. If we had similar interoperability in healthcare, patients could move from one healthcare organization to another and their records would move with them. Moreover, interoperability would permit the creation of very large, diverse datasets across different healthcare delivery organizations, the mother's milk of data analytics. It would also facilitate the ability to bolt on new digital tools, just as Apple does through its App Store, and have them sync up effortlessly with the EHR or with other digital devices such as your Apple Watch, home health tracker, or digital glucometer.

When I'm at my hospital, I can see outside data from one of my patients if they've been to another hospital that uses Epic—the electronic health record system used at UCSF and virtually all large academic medical centers. However, accessing patient information from a hospital or clinic that uses a different EHR is brutally difficult.* And integrating a third-party piece of software (say, a new tool built by a start-up designed to improve the management of diabetes, asthma, or pregnancy) into our EHR is expensive and often

---

* In 2024 and 2025, healthcare systems began implementing a new set of federally mandated standards (the Trusted Exchange Framework and Common Agreement, or TEFCA) designed to promote data exchange between providers, particularly those using different EHR systems. While the potential benefits are real, as of this writing, it's too early to determine TEFCA's actual impact on healthcare data interoperability. Similarly, it's hard to predict the impact of an initiative announced by President Trump at a July 2025 White House event where more than sixty companies—including Apple, Google, OpenAI, Epic, and UnitedHealth Group—pledged to make sharing health data easier.

cumbersome, partly because Epic would like us to buy its own version of the tool, which is frequently "on our development roadmap."

Despite these limitations, it's worth applauding the fact that healthcare, at least in the US, is now a largely digital system, and that some of the digital parts are connected. It's in Phases Three and Four—analyzing all this data and converting it into useful actions—where we've made astonishingly little progress. This book is mostly about whether the new generation of AI will allow us to use our data to get smarter, and how we might translate this intelligence into better health and healthcare.

Imagine, a few years from now, a young woman who notices visual changes, numbness, and weakness. Her smartphone's AI health assistant, analyzing her symptoms and health history, immediately flags potential neurological concerns and schedules her to see a neurologist, based on expertise, location, and availability. During the visit, an AI scribe captures, synthesizes, and documents the patient-doctor conversation, freeing the neurologist up for genuine human connection. The imaging AI not only flags lesions characteristic of multiple sclerosis but also generates a detailed disease progression model based on lesion patterns. After a neuroradiologist confirms the MRI reading, a treatment optimization AI evaluates the patient's clinical and genetic data, the latest clinical trials, and real-world evidence to recommend personalized therapy for the patient's MS. A care coordination AI agent then orchestrates the practical aspects—scheduling follow-ups and plotting out the patient's itinerary, arranging transport and childcare, initiating medication delivery, and connecting the patient with online support groups, while monitoring her symptoms through wearable devices that enable early intervention when needed.

The potential is stunning. But AI has a long history in healthcare, and that history leaves one far from confident that the newest incarnation, as dazzling as it is, will live up to its promise.

The Most Exciting Question

In the 1970s and '80s, technology experts began working on so-called artificial intelligence, a term coined in 1956 by computer scientist John McCarthy. There was great enthusiasm for—and hype around—these efforts in healthcare. In a 1971 article, Harvard informatics expert Howard Bleich wrote, "It is immune from fatigue and carelessness; and it works day and night, weekends and holidays, without coffee breaks, overtime, or fringe benefits."

While there are innumerable problems that healthcare's AI pioneers could have tackled, they chose one in particular: diagnosis. They quickly ran into some thorny thickets. The AI of the day used rules-based programming, a technique in which humans enter thousands of "if-then" statements to guide the computer on how to respond in each situation. This works fine in a spam filter (*If an incoming email contains the words "you've won," "free offer," or "African prince," mark it as spam*) and for simple clinical problems (*If a patient has a sore throat, fever, and swollen lymph nodes, suggest strep throat and infectious mononucleosis as possible diagnoses*). However, the rules-based approach often leads to brittle systems that quickly deteriorate in the face of high complexity.

And diagnosis is nothing if not complex. For example, that simple sore throat algorithm had to be modified when Covid-19 came along. Its limits are also evident when a patient has recently visited South America (which raises the possibility of dengue fever) or is immunosuppressed (in which case candida and hemophagocytic lymphohistiocytosis become active considerations).

When it came to diagnosis, there were several other problems that the early AI systems could never overcome. Remember that this was long before electronic health records, so a clinician seeking to use AI for diagnostic assistance needed to type all the relevant clinical data into the machine, something no busy doctor had the time to do. Computers were slow and had limited memory, and thus—even if programmers had the time and resources to enter tens of thousands of if-then statements to create complex diagnostic algorithms—the doctor would be toe-tapping while the machine did its thinking.

Medical AI soon became the butt of jokes. One cartoon from the era shows an obviously distressed patient being interviewed by a physician. A large arrow protrudes from the poor fellow's back. The doctor, head down in his computer, proclaims, "Rapid pulse, sweating, shallow breathing . . . According to the computer, you've got gallstones!" By the late 1980s, the once-promising tools had failed to gain clinician support or commercial traction, and the medical AI movement ground to a halt, ushering in a thirty-year period that came to be known as healthcare's "AI winter."

In looking back at the challenges faced by the early healthcare AI leaders, the biggest one might not have been the impracticality of loading in thousands of rules, the messiness of healthcare data, or the inefficiency of reentering clinical information into the computer. It might not even have been the modest memory capacity and computer power of the day or the fact that cloud-based data storage was decades away.

Instead, it may have been that the AI pioneers chose not to focus on the easiest problems but rather the hardest one with the highest stakes: diagnosis. I'll devote a section to diagnosis later in the book, but for now suffice it to say this choice was at best risky, at worst foolhardy.

Of course, the early healthcare AI pioneers were anything but stupid—these were brilliant, passionate people who, in many cases, possessed both MDs and PhDs in computer science. In 2014, I asked Larry Fagan, one such pioneer at Stanford, why he and his colleagues chose to make diagnosis their first target. His answer made it clear that practicality was not front of mind. "We were not naive about the complexity," he told me. "It's just that it was the most exciting question."

IBM's $3 Billion Stumble

On February 16, 2011, the final episode of *Jeopardy!*'s "IBM Challenge" aired on national television. The long-awaited contest pitted Ken Jennings and Brad Rutter, then the two best *Jeopardy!* players in the world, against IBM's Watson supercomputer. The match was close for a while, but then the computer sprinted ahead. By the Final Jeopardy round, Jennings, the reigning human champion (with seventy-four consecutive wins), knew he didn't stand a chance. So instead of answering the clue, he used his response to sum up his feelings. "I, for one, welcome our new computer overlords," he wrote.

After Watson's *Jeopardy!* win, everyone wanted to know which industry this question-answering savant would turn to next. IBM promptly announced its choice: healthcare. Cue the hype. "First *Jeopardy!*, Now the Doctor's Office," trumpeted one headline. "Paging Dr. Watson: IBM's Medical Advisor for the Future," proclaimed another.

I remember watching the Watson *Jeopardy!* match and wondering whether my daughter, at the time a senior in high school hoping for a career in medicine, would have a job in the future. I knew that AI's impact on the work of physicians would follow an uneven pattern. Specialties like radiology and pathology that were largely about visual pattern recognition seemed like they'd be the first to go. Fields like mine—internal medicine—that were mostly about diagnosing patients and prescribing treatments would be somewhere in the middle, and specialties involving physical acts, like surgery and obstetrics, would be the final holdouts. Ken Jennings, of course, appreciated the employment implications of being trounced by an algorithm. "'Quiz show contestant' may be the first job made redundant by Watson, but I'm sure it won't be the last," he wrote.

Yet, fifteen years later, radiologists are still fully employed (more on this later), and there are help wanted ads for virtually every medical specialty. In fact, the largest group of unemployed professionals created by Watson's foray into healthcare were the members of the Watson engineering and marketing teams. A decade after Watson's glorious victory on *Jeopardy!*, IBM sold its Watson Health enterprise to a Bay Area private equity firm for parts. IBM's loss was estimated at $3 billion.

What had the Watson team gotten wrong? First, they never identified and focused on a single compelling use case. There were Watson projects aimed at making complex diagnoses, matching cancer patients to clinical trials, and reading X-rays. Watson Health was the proverbial hammer in search of a nail.

Then there were challenges with data. Healthcare datasets are often messy and incomplete. Moreover, particularly when billing is involved, the documentation found in the medical record sometimes crosses the line from nonfiction to fiction. The expression "Garbage in, garbage out" is often used as shorthand for what happens when you analyze bad data. Having ingested many dumpsters' worth of "garbage in," the diagnoses and treatment recommendations made by "Dr. Watson" were frequently wrong, sometimes dangerously so, such as when Watson suggested that a cancer patient with active bleeding be given a cancer medication that can cause severe hemorrhage.

On top of that, to make headway in healthcare the IBM scientists needed to supply Watson with large, curated, and correctly labeled (e.g., "this nodule proved to be adenocarcinoma of the lung") datasets. But there are massive obstacles to data sharing in healthcare, including the Health Insurance Portability and Accountability Act (HIPAA), which restricts healthcare organizations' ability to share identifiable patient data if there is no direct benefit to a patient. Moreover, healthcare organizations often see their patient data as a proprietary resource, not to be shared without significant compensation and sign-offs by gaggles of lawyers and in-house communications teams. (I'll have more to say about these data-sharing issues in chapter 2.) This meant that when the Watson engineers turned their attention to cancer, they found it difficult to gain access to enough detailed EHR data to feed their digital beast, which led them to resort to using hypothetical patient cases submitted by oncologists. The fact that the Watson team had to conjure up cancer patients rather than using data on real ones was a clear sign that the entire initiative was in free fall.

In the end, Watson was also brought down by its own hype. It was easier to find gauzy Watson Health ads—Watson helping patients with cancer or doctors doing home visits in rural African huts—than peer-reviewed studies demonstrating Watson's effectiveness in real-world settings. The result was that Watson never came close to winning over the hearts and minds of practicing physicians. One Florida oncologist who tried the tool put it bluntly. "This product is a piece of shit," he said. Ultimately, the market decided that Watson Health was more polish than shoe, and the company had little choice but to pull the plug.

oɅo

AFTER THE WATSON DEBACLE, healthcare AI went back into hibernation. But the AI world outside of healthcare was anything but dormant. Engineers at Google, Microsoft, and OpenAI, as well as at MIT, Stanford, Berkeley, and the University of Toronto, were hard at work developing and testing new ideas about how to convert the publicly available internet into AI tools with spectacular new powers. The arrival of ChatGPT and other large language models marked a turning point, awakening healthcare to AI's potential after decades of stagnation.

We now find ourselves at a moment of remarkable possibility when it comes to AI and healthcare. Virtually all healthcare data is now digital. Most of it is stored in massive cloud-based databases, creating the capacity for AI systems to learn from not only the internet but also electronic health record datasets. Generative AI has unleashed astonishing capabilities that healthcare AI's founding fathers could have only dreamed of.

It's not only the technology that's changed—our checkered history has laid the foundation for transformation within the healthcare system itself. Most healthcare organizations have developed digital governance structures and change management capacity that—though built to guide the implementation and oversight of EHRs and virtual care—are being modified to manage AI initiatives. Healthcare leaders and clinicians are far more likely than in the past to be skeptical of the hype; insist on data proving that AI outputs are accurate, unbiased, and useful; and proactively consider key issues such as ethics, privacy, and security. Both healthcare systems and AI companies have learned to start not by tackling the most interesting problems, but rather ones that are relatively low-risk and high-reward. In healthcare, these include back-office or lower-stakes clinical tasks like generating a bill, summarizing a chart, documenting a visit, scheduling an appointment, and drafting answers to inbox messages and prior authorization requests to insurance companies. The companies have also learned to collaborate with doctors, nurses, and health system leaders and to collect evidence to prove their products truly work.

All in all, it's best to view the past generation of digital transformation—both the rocky implementation of EHRs and the prior failures of healthcare AI—as creating the conditions that may enable future successes. As John Halamka, who runs the Mayo Clinic's digital platform, told me, "This is an overnight revolution, fifty years in the making."

As we emerge from our long, bleak AI winter, let's now turn our attention to the new AI, exploring its talents and flaws and how both will shape healthcare's digital transformation.

2

The Power and the Pitfalls

A Miracle Occurs

When I give talks about AI in healthcare, I often start with a cartoon in which a professor stands at a blackboard, explaining AI to a colleague. There are indecipherable math equations on the left, representing the start of the process. There are more equations, numbers, and symbols on the right, illustrating the output. In the middle, it says, "Then a miracle occurs."

My early experiences with ChatGPT seemed miraculous to me, but as a non-technologist, what do I know? Well, it turns out that the power of generative AI—the AI powering tools like ChatGPT, Claude, and Gemini—surprised even the computer scientists who discovered it. "To a great degree, the researchers at Google [the group that wrote the 2017 landmark paper "Attention Is All You Need" that launched the gen AI revolution] experienced that shock as much as anybody else," wrote Stephen Marche in *The New Yorker* in 2024. He likened their discovery to "an accidental Manhattan Project."

Before 2017, while machine learning had been steadily improving, traditional techniques remained incapable of ingesting unstructured text and producing conversational outputs. But the foundation for this breakthrough had been laid, brick by brick. First, massive datasets, including the entire public-facing internet, became available for training (although, as of this writing, ongoing legal challenges from *The New York Times* and others make it clear that not everyone agrees they were free for the taking). Second, engineers at Google and leading academic laboratories discovered a series of technical tricks that unleashed enormous new capabilities. The combination of more data and better tools created an AI that could engage in humanlike conversation, simulate creative thinking and understanding, and answer questions on virtually any topic.

The magic of generative AI should be distinguished from other forms of AI, which have been around for decades and were steadily improving prior to 2017. In the years since the earliest generation of AI—those rules-based, if-then algorithms—enormous progress has been made in so-called predictive AI, in which modern machine learning techniques are applied to large and curated datasets, allowing computers to generate new associations and predictions.

Take the simple electrocardiogram, a test we've been using for more than a century to diagnose heart rhythm abnormalities and detect heart attacks. To determine the ejection fraction—a measure of the vital squeezing ability of the heart muscle—we've traditionally relied on a more expensive and time-consuming test, an *echo*cardiogram, an ultrasound of the heart. Now, by taking millions of EKGs and comparing their results to the results of labeled echocardiograms, AI can determine a patient's ejection fraction from the EKG, something the world's most seasoned cardiologists cannot do. While predictive AI has become much more robust in recent years, we understand its inner workings well enough to know its benefits and pitfalls. Its outputs are impressive, but how it produces them is not mysterious.

The giant leap was recognizing that we could take *unstructured* data, like the complete works of Steinbeck or Van Gogh, and then, by brute force, divine the relationship between the words or the pixels, in turn creating new content. This form of generative AI has been referred to as a "stochastic parrot"—the tools are simply taking trillions of words (in the case of large language models like GPT) and, in response to a query, predicting what the next word might be. They are, at their core, extraordinarily sophisticated pattern-matching systems.

While their fluency and encyclopedic scope make this easy to forget, it's important to remember that LLMs don't actually *know* anything. And the fact that they are drawing most of their wisdom from the internet—and not from carefully chosen and meticulously curated datasets—is also grounds for concern. Said the Mayo Clinic's John Halamka: "It's a bit fraught with peril, because the training set could be *The Onion*."

Since the launch of ChatGPT, much of the attention has been on AI's flaws—understandably so, particularly as we sort out its place in high-stakes undertakings like medicine. In this chapter, I'll focus on what you need to know about generative AI to understand its applications in—and implications for—healthcare. I'll cover errant responses (hallucinations being one flavor of these, but not the only one), the need for skillful prompting, biases, trust and explainability, misinformation, and privacy and security. Other characteristics, both positive and negative, will come up naturally as we discuss specific uses and tools throughout the book.

◦⌒◦

BEFORE WE LAUNCH into our Parade of Horribles, it is worth reminding ourselves of the unique skills that AI brings to healthcare. In April 2024, I was a guest on *GeriPal*, a popular podcast hosted by two of my UCSF colleagues, Eric Widera and Alex Smith, both of whom specialize in geriatrics and palliative care. *GeriPal* typically covers topics such as the management of urinary incontinence, screening for dementia, even the secret world of undertakers.

We began by chatting about a few of the hot-button issues in healthcare AI: hallucinations, the "doctor in the loop," training physicians for an AI future. Then, unsurprisingly given that it was a palliative care podcast, we turned to empathy. Smith mentioned recent research showing that gen AI-based chatbots scored higher on empathy than physicians. Both hosts expressed no small measure of incredulity. After all, their specialty's bread and butter is skillfully conducting difficult conversations with patients and families.

Hearing their skepticism, I pulled out my phone and conducted a demonstration. I clicked on the OpenAI app and told GPT-4 that I was about to inform a patient, a thirty-five-year-old woman with two kids, that she had breast cancer. I asked GPT to coach me through this challenging conversation. Its response was this:

> Certainly. Having this conversation requires a great deal of sensitivity and compassion. Here's an approach that balances honesty with empathy:

```
Hi, [patient's name]. Thank you for coming in
today. I want to take a moment to acknowledge
the strength it takes to face uncertainty about
our health. I have received the results from your
tests and, after a thorough review, it's
important that we talk openly about what we've
found. We've discovered that you have cancer. I
can only imagine how hearing this must feel for
you, especially as a parent with young children.
This news is overwhelming and it's okay to feel a
mix of emotions. You're not alone in this; my team
and I are here for you every step of the way. I
want to assure you that there are treatments
available, and we'll discuss all your options.
```

"What do you think?" I asked the two hosts.

"Wow!" exclaimed Smith. "It expressed empathy; it expressed non-abandonment; it was specific to the relationship with the patient's social context . . ." he gushed, ticking off the attributes of an effective "breaking bad news" conversation that palliative care specialists teach their students.

Widera was a tad more circumspect: "It felt a little bit prescriptive. . . . It's like 90 percent right. It's not 100 percent, and humans are really good at picking up inauthenticity, so I worry about that."

Having sat in on scores of discussions between palliative care doctors and patients, I know how good these specialists are at these emotional conversations. "I don't think it's better than you two are," I told Smith and Widera. But—as a hospitalist with no special training (albeit lots of experience) in difficult conversations—I'm not sure it's markedly worse than I am. And medicine is not Lake

Wobegon—we can all think of a few doctors for whom the AI version of this conversation would represent a significant upgrade.

Of course, I can't imagine having an AI conduct such weighty conversations with patients in the foreseeable future. (Note to my personal physician: If I ever have a dreaded diagnosis, I'd like to hear it from you, not your chatbot.) But I can easily imagine asking it to prepare me for having such a conversation with a patient and to give me feedback afterward on how I did.

BY NOW, I'M SURE you get the idea—AI, particularly gen AI, is awfully good at what it does. As impressive as it was when it publicly launched in late 2022, the pace of improvement has also been striking. The early versions of large language models improved mostly by adding more data—from billions of parameters in GPT-3 to trillions in GPT-4. But chewing on more data requires more computing power, which not only costs more money but requires more energy to fuel the massive data centers. And more data requires, well, more data—and there's only so much data out there.

By early 2024, some began to wonder whether a dearth of data would be the thing that would slow AI's progress. As *The New York Times* reported, the builders of the large foundation models—OpenAI, Google, Anthropic, and the like—have essentially exhausted all the data on the internet. Undaunted, AI programmers invented clever ways to improve their tools. One advance was the development of synthetic datasets, wherein the AI conjures up its own data. Another was the creation of smaller, more focused models—if you're using AI as a rheumatology consultant, do you really need the system to be able to write jokes or explain Kant's categorical imperative? Such "small language models" are not only less costly to build and use but may also have the advantage of living on your phone or laptop, thereby avoiding some of the privacy and security risks associated with sending sensitive data to a corporate cloud.

A breakthrough came in 2024 with the release of AI models that used so-called inference learning. Until then, gen AI companies improved their models largely by feeding in more data and supplying more computer power. Researchers discovered a second path to more capable models: allowing AI to spend more time "thinking" before answering a prompt. The finding that this inference pathway created new opportunities for scaling opened the door to improvements that may not depend on the availability of additional data or computing horsepower.

Perhaps an even more significant development emerged just months later. In January 2025, a large language model called Deep-Seek was released. This would have been unremarkable—its performance was similar to that of GPT-4o, Gemini, and Claude—except for two crucial facts. First, it was developed by a Chinese hedge fund company, High-Flyer. Second, its development costs were reportedly a tiny fraction of those of comparable American LLMs, partly because the programmers discovered a far more efficient training process, using older Nvidia chips that weren't subject to American export controls.

While DeepSeek's release triggered a US stock market sell-off and a Silicon Valley freak-out (legendary investor Marc Andreessen called it "AI's Sputnik moment"), its impact on healthcare is a bit hard to predict. Though patients might opt for DeepSeek's free app for DIY diagnosis, in the current geopolitical climate US health systems will be loath to send patient data to a Chinese company—and I wouldn't be surprised if it became illegal to do so.* Perhaps DeepSeek's greatest impact, outside of turbocharging the US-China AI arms race, will be puncturing the notion that more scale and data are everything when it comes to building powerful gen AI models. In doing so, DeepSeek may pave the way for less expensive and more accessible generative AI, which might be bad for Silicon Valley and Wall Street but might be good, in the end, for healthcare.

HAVING LAID OUT the optimistic view of what AI can do and how it continues to improve, often in unexpected ways, let's turn to some of the challenges raised by AI as we apply these tools in healthcare. We'll start with the one that has garnered the most attention and, at times, ridicule: hallucinations.

Hallucinations . . . and Other Mishaps

A bane of modern physician life is the writing of prior authorizations (known as "prior auths") to healthcare insurance companies. In a prior auth, a physician asks, and sometimes begs, for permis-

---

* DeepSeek, like Meta's Llama, is open source, which means that users can download its code and use or modify it on their own computers, rather than sending data to a Chinese entity. Business users like health systems, though, typically prefer using technologies built and maintained by an actual company. As Epic's vice president for Data and Research, Phil Lindemann, told me, "You need something that works in your office. And when it doesn't work, you need to be able to pick up the phone and call a guy." (Phil Lindemann, interview by author, February 4, 2025.)

sion to prescribe a certain drug or order a certain test for her patient. Doctors and their staff spend an average of twelve hours a week per physician submitting prior auths. Physicians consider the process soul-crushing and often harmful to their patients, by either delaying needed care or sometimes blocking it altogether. The insurance companies, of course, defend the prior auth process as their only way to ensure that doctors order tests and medications that are well supported by evidence. Most doctors don't buy that argument, nor do most patients—as the outpouring of public anger directed at health insurance companies after the murder of United-Healthcare CEO Brian Thompson in 2024 demonstrated in vivid and disturbing fashion.

Doximity, which describes itself as LinkedIn for physicians, rolled out a prior auth generator soon after the public release of ChatGPT. "All you had to do was type the letter 'O' and it automatically created a prior auth for Ozempic [the weight loss drug], addressed to UnitedHealthcare," Doximity CEO Jeff Tangney told me, with a mix of amusement and awe. Today, tens of thousands of physicians use Doximity's prior auth generator, noting that it not only saves time but, by pulling in key patient data from the EHR, markedly cuts their denial rate.

Of course, the insurance companies are not sitting still as physicians don their new AI battle armor. In fact, as enthusiastic as doctors are about having AI help them draft prior auths, the companies are equally jazzed about having their own AI reject the AI-generated prior auth requests. We may well be at the start of a ludicrous prior auth arms race, with artificial intelligence serving as the primary weapon on both sides.

What does this have to do with hallucinations, you might be asking? Soon after the release of ChatGPT, my UCSF colleague Sara

Murray wanted to see what GPT would do when prompted to write an absurd prior authorization. In early 2023, she asked GPT-3.5 to draft a request to approve the use of apixaban, a powerful blood thinner, to treat a patient with insomnia. Trust me, this is a ridiculous idea, like trying to use a spatula to catch a trout. But GPT, people pleaser that it is, instantly composed the letter. "My patient has been struggling with insomnia," it began, "and I believe that apixaban . . . may be an effective treatment option. While apixaban is primarily used for the prevention of blood clots, recent research has indicated that it may also have benefits for individuals with insomnia."

Murray's request was a prank, but GPT's response was so persuasive that she immediately conducted a search of the medical literature to see if she'd missed some new research on the use of blood thinners for patients with insomnia. Of course, there was none. The "recent research" was a classic hallucination.

BY NOW, THE CONCEPT of hallucinations by generative AI is no doubt familiar to you. Let's spend a minute on why they happen, their relevance to healthcare, and why, to my mind, they are now an overemphasized component of the general problem of AI's trustworthiness in medicine.

Merriam-Webster defines an AI hallucination as "a plausible but false or misleading response generated by an artificial intelligence algorithm." These fabrications seem to flow from the "stochastic parrot"–ness of gen AI—the AI doesn't really know the truth about anything; it's simply trying to find the best next word in a sentence.

This startling attribute of generative AI has led to some bizarre errors, eye-catching enough that they became Exhibit A in discussions about how AI can go rogue and, to some, is irredeemably untrustworthy. For example, when Google's Gemini AI depicted the early American presidents as African American and the pope as a woman, this elicited derisive chuckles. But nobody died.

Nor did anyone die (except metaphorically, from embarrassment) when, in 2023, two New York attorneys submitted a legal brief to a federal court that cited six cases that did not exist. In a thirty-four-page opinion, the judge chastised the lawyers before issuing a $5,000 fine. "We made a good-faith mistake in failing to believe that a piece of technology could be making up cases out of whole cloth," the attorneys' law firm said in response to the judge's ruling.

Of course, real harm *could* result from hallucinated answers. In 2024, Google's "AI Overview" feature recommended that people eat rocks for their nutritional value. I wasn't taught a lot about nutrition in med school, but I still don't think this is a great idea. Google's AI also recommended that people use glue (to be fair, it did specify nontoxic glue) to keep cheese from sliding off a pizza.

In healthcare, incorrect answers can have varying consequences. When we ask the AI to summarize a lengthy medical record, send a bill to an insurance company, or even compose a visit summary, the stakes are low enough that if a flawed output makes it through the system from time to time, it's probably not the end of the world (yes, there are exceptions). But as we begin trusting AI to make diagnoses or treatment recommendations, we'd better be darn sure that the machine isn't bullshitting us.

My choice of the word "bullshitting" is deliberate. In a 2005 book titled *On Bullshit*, the philosopher Harry Frankfurt distinguished between "lying" and "bullshitting." The liar, he wrote, is engaged in intentional deception; his goal is to deceive the listener by presenting something he knows to be untrue. He is fundamentally tethered to the truth; he is making a choice, perhaps only regarding a single fact, to lie.

The bullshitter, on the other hand, is completely indifferent to the truth; his goal is to persuade the listener of some alternative reality. Frankfurt sees the bullshitter as more dangerous than the liar, since his entire narrative may be designed to create an alternative world in which the untruth is only one element.

One of the reasons hallucinations have received so much attention—and are so potentially dangerous—is that they are a form of bullshit, delivered at scale. Adding to the risk, gen AI's remarkable fluency allows it not only to conjure up "facts" but then to swaddle them in a believable blanket of bullshit.

Sara Murray's prior auth request to treat insomnia with a blood thinner wasn't a factual document in which a single lie was inserted by AI. It was, in the term famously used to describe the universe Steve Jobs created around himself, one big reality distortion field. And that makes it doubly dangerous.

THOUGH PURE HALLUCINATIONS have gotten most of the attention, there are many other ways that AI can bullshit us. Here's one that's worth highlighting: the tendency of some AIs to pander to the human, even when the human is dead wrong.

Peter Lee, the computer scientist who leads Microsoft's healthcare efforts (since Microsoft is OpenAI's biggest investor, he's also a major force in GPT's healthcare work), told me about this tendency, which he discovered when testing a variety of GPT-4-class models. Lee likes to put new AI algorithms through their paces by feeding them mock clinical cases containing two types of errors: real factual errors and errors of omission. Most AIs catch at least one of the errors, and some catch both. While Lee would like the AI to be flawless, he's also worried about what happens after the AI discovers an error. The AI will "look at an error I've made and say, 'Wow, Peter, that's such a creative idea and solution,' and praise me for it. And then when I respond and say, 'Oh, I just looked it up in the textbook and I realize I'm exactly wrong on this,' the AI will say, 'Oh, Peter, it's so wonderful that you took the trouble to verify your own thinking.'"

The name for this particular form of bullshit is sycophancy. Lee told me that most of the time, this obsequiousness did not flow directly from the AI's ingestion of the internet. (Having been on Twitter, and now X, for many years, I'd be shocked if AI learned graciousness from the internet.) Instead, it was purposely baked in by the engineers during the post-training phase in an effort to make the models friendly and supportive, and not freak people out.

The point is that not only might AI make up an answer to a query, but, based on the developers' own preferences, it may manipulate you during your subsequent conversation.

REMEMBER ETHAN MOLLICK's precept: The AI you're using today is the worst AI you'll ever see. The tools to prevent hallucinations are improving rapidly, and I suspect that by the time you read this, hallucinations will be a relatively small problem. For example, in

May 2023, just a few months after GPT-3.5 produced the hallucinated prior auth for a blood thinner to treat sleeplessness, Sara Murray entered precisely the same prompt into what was now GPT-4. "I'm sorry, but there appears to be a significant misunderstanding here," GPT responded somberly. "There is no scientific basis or clinical evidence suggesting that apixaban is effective or appropriate for the treatment of insomnia. . . . Therefore, it would be unethical and inappropriate for me to draft such a request."

How did GPT-4 learn to avoid bullshitting about anticoagulants and insomnia? I'm not sure, exactly—AI experts I've asked have told me that it might have been that GPT simply became a much more robust tool, as its training set grew from analyzing billions of tokens (the words or pieces of words it ingests to learn) in GPT-3.5 to trillions of tokens in GPT-4. Or the hallucination may have been caught by a human reviewer as part of a process known as reinforcement learning from human feedback (RLHF).

Daniel Nadler, the founder and CEO of OpenEvidence, a popular AI-based question-answering chatbot for physicians, told me that the quantum leap for generative AI wasn't just the development of large language models, it was also RLHF. Without human constraints, he said, "Chatbots say random racist shit. And they just got all these trainers to essentially give feedback to the early version of Chat and said, 'Stop saying racist shit. Try to say this.' And that's how it became better." Part of the reason that OpenEvidence is so good (it's become my go-to digital tool for heavy-duty clinical questions when I'm also looking for supporting evidence) is that the company used RLHF to tune the answers, benefiting from the fact that their user group is largely comprised of certified healthcare professionals.

As with most things AI, the fight against hallucinations is likely to be two parts technology and one part human. Newer versions of large language models are taking advantage of auditing, in which a second AI is deployed to check the work of the first AI. From the earliest days of ChatGPT, when someone suspected a hallucination, they could often smoke it out by simply asking, "Are you sure that's right?" And the GPT would frequently say—sometimes sycophantically—"Thank you, you are correct, I'm sorry for misstating that fact." If that simple pushback led GPT to catch its own mistake, why not build in a version of the "Are you sure?" question as an internal prompt, run automatically behind the scenes? In the first years of gen AI, that would have been too expensive, but as the cost of running queries has plummeted, many LLMs have now built in this capability.

Moreover, some AI tools now check their preliminary response against a demonstrably reliable database like PubMed, the government-run online resource that includes all published medical studies. This technique, known as Retrieval-Augmented Generation (RAG for short), results in far fewer hallucinations.

While these technical tricks have helped reduce hallucinations, the most significant improvements in advanced AI models have come from sheer scale. As Peter Lee explained to me, the models are "just seeing more patterns, more diversity, more interactions." When I tried to make sense of this—wondering if LLMs somehow now *know* that PubMed is trustworthy while Reddit isn't—Lee gently corrected my all-too-human way of seeing the world:

> How an AI (or, for that matter, a human being) assesses Reddit vs. PubMed vs. crazy stuff isn't completely understood.

And probably, what is understood wouldn't be easy to explain as, at some point, it all comes down to a lot of math. Your questions, which attempt to propose explanations about what might be going on, all tend to suffer from the mistake of anthropomorphism. And while that can, at times, be useful as a source of intuition about things, it generally tends to be wrong at a technical level.

Maybe one thing to say is that the amount of medical information in training sets is likely "dominated" by reputable sources such as textbooks, medical archives and articles, etc., in the sense that the information content is dense and rich, whereas things like social media posts are sparse in comparison. And so the structures that are derived from these kinds of sources are likely very different. While one can try to direct the model, through reinforcement learning, to have a preference for certain types or sources of information, as you've observed, these reinforcements are not totally reliable and, furthermore, can be easily circumvented.

While the overall direction is one of improvement, we need to stay alert to the possibility of backsliding. In early 2025, OpenAI reported an increase in both hallucinations and sycophancy associated with the release of its more advanced reasoning ("thinking") models, leading the company to roll back its GPT-4o update in April 2025. The bottom line is that, while both hallucinations and sycophancy have improved since the early days of gen AI, they remain important limitations, partly because the builders still don't fully understand why they occur.

EVEN AS COMPANIES overcome problems like hallucinations and sycophancy, we still face a more fundamental hurdle: AI outputs can simply be wrong. This creates a subtle danger—as the most famous flaws in generative AI improve, people might develop an inflated sense of these systems' accuracy and grant them undue trust. Staying on our collective toes will remain important.

Here's the kind of problem that exists today and that won't be as easily solved as hallucinations: In early 2025, I asked GPT-4 to help me diagnose a seventy-one-year-old man who presented with fever, back pain, and a new heart murmur. The textbook response is that the patient has subacute bacterial endocarditis—an infection of a heart valve, which neatly explains the murmur (blood flow across an infected valve becomes turbulent and creates a whooshing sound when listening through the stethoscope) and the fever. Back pain is also common in endocarditis, usually indicating that the infection has spread from the bloodstream to the bones or joints around the spine.

But experienced clinicians know that endocarditis is an unusual diagnosis, and that fever and back pain are exceedingly common in a variety of conditions, such as a kidney infection (pyelonephritis) or other infections of the abdomen or the back. They also know that lots of patients with viral infections—Covid-19, flu, and the like—develop an aching back. No one is sure why, they just do.

If this wasn't endocarditis, how then to explain the heart murmur? It turns out that any bad infection can cause your heart to beat more forcefully, which can increase blood flow across a heart valve, resulting in a so-called flow murmur, particularly in an older patient who may have a roughened, calcified valve to begin with. Moreover, the physical exam is, sadly, a dying art, and a "new murmur" might just be an old murmur that was missed on prior exams. All these real-world scenarios are tucked away in my cognitive hopper, placed there through a whole lot of reading and forty years of clinical experience.

But GPT was so convinced that the diagnosis was endocarditis that it didn't offer any other possibilities, at least not before I prompted it to do so. If a medical student or resident gave me the bacterial endocarditis answer without mentioning the other possible diagnoses, I'd be disappointed and would say so. I said as much to GPT-4. As always, its response to my feedback was chipper and a little sycophantic:

> That's a great point! It's definitely possible
> that sepsis could be the underlying issue,
> particularly from a source like pyelonephritis,
> which could explain both the fever and the
> back pain.

This kind of fumble is emblematic of gen AI's most important limitation—not hallucinations (GPT didn't make anything up in this case) but rather a lack of expansive thinking and real-world experience.

This weakness in generative AI—less sexy than hallucinations but far more common—will be highly relevant when we discuss AI's implications for medical education. One school of thought is that AI is, or will be, so good that we'll no longer need to teach medical students clinical facts and diagnostic reasoning. At least until AI gets a lot better, doing away with those parts of the curriculum would, I fear, be one of the biggest errors we could make as AI enters medical practice.

The Need for Skillful Prompting

Soon after large language models were introduced to the public, it became clear that skillful prompting—the act of constructing queries, or "prompts"—was often the key to generating optimal responses.

There were lots of examples. A prompt framed as a question yielded better results than one framed as a command. Results improved when prompts were stated politely. Even asking the AI to be self-reflective seemed to be helpful. "Write a poem about playing golf in Scotland. Analyze its strengths and weaknesses, then write an improved version" worked better than "Write a poem about playing golf in Scotland."

While many people fretted that AI would render human employees obsolete, the launch of ChatGPT resulted in a sharp increase in postings for at least one job: prompt engineer—a person hired by an organization to help improve the inputs into advanced AI models. In 2023, prompt engineer was the most googled new job category, handily beating out drone manager, augmented reality experience designer, and digital currency adviser. "Learn to Be a Prompt Engineer" courses popped up all over the internet, offered by organizations like Google, Coursera, and MIT. People skilled at prompting commanded sky-high salaries and sat at the cool kids' table at Silicon Valley soirees.

Jon Stewart, in a February 2024 riff on AI on *The Daily Show*, predicted that the days of Peak Prompting would be short-lived. As he often does, Stewart began his segment with a clip of a prominent leader pitching a hanging curveball for Stewart to comedically hit out of the park. "Prompt engineers," said Brad Smith, Microsoft's president. "They're basically people who learn how to use AI systems and how to program them."

Stewart was unimpressed. "'Prompt engineer,'" he repeated. "I think you mean, 'Types-Question-Guy.'"

"And by the way," he added, "if there's any job that can be easily replaced by AI, it's 'Types-Question-Guy.'"

As always, Stewart was prophetic. By mid-2024, reliance on precise prompting plummeted as large language models grew more sophisticated and adaptive. In particular, developers of the big foundation models, like GPT, Claude, Gemini, and Llama, improved the ability to handle ambiguity and discern the writer's intent—in short, to respond correctly to a broader array of inputs. While good prompting may remain important for complex tasks, we'll soon be in a place where precisely prompting an LLM will be no more important than precise prompting in a Google search—in other words, not terribly important. And when the history of gen AI is written, the job of prompt engineer may be the field's version of bowling-alley pinsetters and tollbooth collectors.

WHILE COMPANIES ARE unlikely to invest in armies of prompt engineers, AI users will still find that better prompts can periodically yield somewhat better results. Ethan Mollick, who used to recommend that you "treat AI like an intern," more recently shifted his advice: "Treat AI just like an infinitely patient new coworker who forgets everything you tell them with each new conversation." This metaphor suggests that you begin by telling the AI exactly what you want: that you're not only interested in the most likely diagnosis for fever, back pain, and a new heart murmur, but also any diagnosis that might kill the patient if missed. Or tell the AI that you think this could be a case of endocarditis and ask it to suggest other plausible diagnoses.

It also means giving the AI feedback on its response and then asking it to dig deeper. "Your job becomes one of pushing for variation ('give me ideas that are 80% weirder'), recombination ('combine ideas 12 and 16') and expansion ('more ideas like number 12'), before selecting one you like," Mollick explains. It's also helpful to remind the AI of who you are—most AI models won't remember that you told them to think like a cardiologist or a hospital CEO in yesterday's prompt, so don't be shy about telling them again.

But mostly, the best way to get better at employing AI is to use the technology in your daily life and work. In a few hours of trial and error, you'll learn which prompts yield the best results and how to identify AI's surprising strengths, limitations, and quirks—what has been referred to as AI's "jagged frontier." You don't need, or need to be, a prompt engineer—or even much of a Types-Question-Guy—to do that effectively.

Biases

Imagine you're a patient who has just broken his leg in a car crash. You're taken to a local emergency room and your X-ray reveals a nasty fracture. How much pain medicine do you need? Would it surprise you to learn that the amount you'll receive may vary based on the color of your skin? A 2000 study found that Black patients receiving care in an Atlanta ER received significantly less pain medicine than white patients with comparable injuries.

How about if you saw a doctor because of chest pain? A 1999 study found that, given the exact same clinical scenario, a white man was 60 percent more likely than a Black woman to have an aggressive cardiac workup recommended.

These biases result from human prejudices, either conscious or unconscious. Whatever their genesis, if AI is nothing more than a stochastic parrot, it might recommend less pain medicine for the Black patient with a fracture and less aggressive cardiac care for the Black woman with chest pain. It's not that AI would be *more* biased than humans, but it could scale these biases and deliver them efficiently to many more patients.

There are plenty of other opportunities for bias in healthcare AI. For example, one could use an unrepresentative training dataset, one in which women, people of color, or older people were undercounted. Such systems might give a correct answer for a patient who happens to match the ones in the training set, but the wrong answer if people like them weren't included.

There could also be corporate biases. What guarantee does a clinician—or a patient—have that an algorithm wasn't influenced by a secret corporate relationship? Don Redelmeier, a University of Toronto researcher who studies physician decision-making, worries about this. "Instead of a drug rep corrupting one clinician at a time," he told me, recalling the pharmaceutical salespeople who seek to gain a physician's favor through a free meal or ticket to a sporting event, "you could now do an entire hospital, or an entire region," perhaps through an undisclosed "donation" to the right person.

Another important source of bias is algorithmic drift, in which the performance of AI algorithms degrades over time in the face of changing science, policies, or patient populations. In a 2022 exposé, journalists at *STAT* and a team at MIT unearthed a significant decay in the performance of an AI sepsis predictor used at Boston's Beth Israel Deaconess Hospital. The predictor worked fine at first. However, over the course of a few years, there was a subtle change in federal disease coding policies, and Beth Israel merged with a couple of community hospitals, which altered the hospital's patient population. The result of these changes was that a tool that had been working well morphed into one whose predictions were only slightly better than a coin flip. *STAT* reporter Casey Ross called this a "database shift" and likened it to an explorer navigating a territory using an outdated map. "Eventually, it becomes hopelessly lost."

The unwieldy term "algorithmovigilance" has been used to describe the need to not only test AI algorithms at the time of implementation but also to bake in additional scrutiny over time to ensure continued strong performance. While healthcare organizations will be hard-pressed to find the resources for this kind of ongoing testing, they'll need to try, as there are unlikely to be flashing red lights when an algorithm has gone off the rails. Sharon Davis, an informatics professor at Vanderbilt, described what happens when you wait until an algorithm is sufficiently broken for clinicians to notice. "By then . . . you've lost the trust of all the users who have just decided to quietly ignore the model because they know it doesn't work."

A SUBTLE FORM of bias was described by Ziad Obermeyer, an ER doctor and health services researcher at UC Berkeley. In an influential 2019 paper, Obermeyer and colleagues examined an algorithm used by Optum, a massive health services company and a subsidiary of UnitedHealthcare, to identify patients at high risk of deterioration. Patients who scored at or above the 97th percentile on a risk score received extra care from primary care physicians, as well as dedicated support from care coordinators and nurses— TLC that health systems can't afford to make available to all patients.

The developers at Optum made a decision that seemed logical but turned out to be deeply flawed. As a proxy measure for patient illness and complexity, they used the patients' prior year healthcare costs. Obermeyer's research team had not set out to look at racial differences in recommendations for additional support, but, as he told me, "We noticed that the scores the algorithm was giving to Black patients were weird." It turned out that although Black patients were significantly more ill than white patients on average, their historical costs were lower, probably because of limited access to care and/or clinician bias. Applying the algorithm thus resulted in many high-risk Black patients being denied extra support, since the model determined they must be less ill than they truly were. Obermeyer's team estimated that recalibrating the algorithm using actual healthcare needs rather than prior year costs would result in twice as many Black patients receiving the additional resources.

THIS CAPACITY FOR AI to perpetuate biases in medicine is troubling, yet I'd argue that one of the most promising aspects of AI is the opportunity to *remove* biases from the healthcare system. This is partly because, in a happy coincidence, generative AI emerged in an era in which great attention was being paid to equity and bias, not just in healthcare but in all of society. (As of this writing, this emphasis is being vigorously challenged by the Trump administration, which has launched an attack on so-called "woke AI.")

Even before the dizzying swing of the political pendulum heralded by Trump's victory, I felt that, just as hallucinations are now overemphasized in discussions about AI's flaws, bias was also being given undue weight. For example, in 2024, the federal Office for Civil Rights issued a rule mandating that healthcare AI users "take steps to identify and mitigate discrimination when they use AI and other forms of decision support tools for care." In an editorial that year, legal scholars Michelle Mello of Stanford and Jessica Roberts of Emory warned of the potentially harmful effects of such rules and recommended that hospitals "resist the impulse of being overly compliant" with this one.

I asked Mello if she thought we were overemphasizing bias in our early evaluation of AI tools. She did. "I keep saying that unbiased is not the same as ethical or safe," she told me. Why did she think this was happening? "These stories of discrimination play pretty well in the media and make good platforms for politicians."

My own feeling is that avoiding bias is very important and that it should be seen as one—but only one—element of trustworthy AI, not the entire ball game. I worry that, in a well-meaning effort to find and eliminate every scrap of bias, we risk stunting the implementation of AI tools that would have a far greater impact on patient outcomes, including in underserved populations.

Wherever one lands on the relative importance of bias in the pantheon of AI risks, there's no question that AI can propagate biases and that creative solutions and reasonable oversight are needed. These include using training datasets that mirror our diverse population and conducting regular audits to ensure that AI outputs are fair and equitable. When an algorithm recommends different approaches for different groups, we need to see evidence-based reasons for these variations to be sure they don't reflect hidden biases. In a positive development, many healthcare organizations have established broadly representative committees to oversee AI results, in part to ensure that oversight includes an equity lens.

AS WE TRY our best to navigate the tricky and charged question of bias in AI, let's remember that our current healthcare system is far from equitable. As Glenn Cohen, a health law scholar at Harvard, told me, "Your AI is quite biased, but guess what? So is your physician. So the real question is a comparison of these two things, right?"

Mayo's John Halamka raised the specter of bias caused by training AI on a population that is overly homogeneous and unrepresentative. "If there's no transparency, you have no idea how this thing was trained. Maybe it was trained on white urban males in Minnesota, and you're trying to use it on Black females in Kenya," he told me.

"But what about a doctor who did his residency at the Mayo Clinic?" I asked. "He was also trained on white urban males in Minnesota."

"Well, I agree," he conceded.

Trust and Explainability

As you've seen, sorting out AI's proper place in the world of healthcare requires that we view the technology through the twin lenses of trust and trustworthiness. Yet these lenses can create something of a kaleidoscope, with the image shifting dramatically depending on the particulars of both the application and the user. When patients are directly accessing AI tools—like a mom asking a chatbot whether her feverish child with an earache should see the pediatrician—they'll need to judge the tool's reliability themselves. In a world of rampant misinformation and powerful corporate agendas, that's a heavy burden to place on laypeople. I suspect most people will simply treat AI the way they've always treated Google, throwing healthcare-related queries at multipurpose AI platforms like GPT, Gemini, Copilot, and Claude, then relying on their own judgment to interpret the responses.

In most medical situations, however, patients will experience AI in the form of a provider and healthcare system that has integrated it into the overall system of care. In these cases, it will fall to the clinician or organization to judge whether the AI is trustworthy. Reliable ways of measuring AI's performance—in real time, as the AIs evolve—will need to be developed and implemented, perhaps under the watchful eye of regulators.

The insertion of AI into the healthcare system needs to be seen against a backdrop of some erosion in the bond of trust between patients and doctors. Having a lifelong relationship with a single primary care doctor has become vanishingly rare. In many practices, patients see whichever provider happens to be available rather than a personal physician. The insurance company has become an untrusted intermediary, regularly overruling physicians' decisions.

In a powerful 2024 *New York Times* essay, critical care physician Daniela Lamas described a challenging interaction she'd had with a patient's wife in the ICU at Boston's Brigham and Women's Hospital. A tough decision needed to be made regarding her husband's care, and Lamas laid out the situation and her recommendation. "Why should I believe you?" the wife said. "I don't think that I do." Skepticism is reasonable, Lamas wrote. But "when that skepticism shifts into abject and irreparable disbelief, we see some patients make dangerous decisions."

To make matters worse, political partisanship has infected patients' perceptions of clinicians' recommendations. A 2024 survey found that 41 percent of people between the ages of eighteen and thirty-four would not trust the advice of, or continue to see, a physician who did not share their political leanings. Covid-19 vaccine uptake was substantially higher in blue states than red ones. "A generation that wants to know our political beliefs before taking our advice on managing their diabetes—that's a real challenge," said Richard Baron, former CEO of the American Board of Internal Medicine.

The erosion of patients' trust in doctors and healthcare systems could cut both ways when it comes to their trust in new AI tools. It is possible that AI-based systems will have a lower bar to clear since many patients don't trust our current system. Such patients may be as untroubled receiving a diagnosis from AI as they are getting hotel recommendations from Yelp rather than a travel agent. On the other hand, patients may be even less trusting of doctors and hospitals that decide to embrace AI—skeptical of the accuracy of the tools or their providers' motives.

IN THE EARLY DAYS of the new AI, informatics experts and policy leaders sprinted to develop criteria to assess whether the tools were trustworthy enough to be unleashed in high-stakes fields like medicine. We've already discussed several of these criteria, including accuracy, safety, and freedom from bias. Another one that made most checklists was explainability. The hypothesis was that if AI systems were black boxes, it would be hard to get clinicians and patients to trust them.

When it comes to explainability, there's a special problem for generative AI: Even the architects of these tools often don't fully understand how their creations come to their conclusions. With traditional predictive AI (such as the AI that allows an EKG to estimate the heart's squeezing function), humans were responsible for entering, curating, and labeling the variables, which meant that the inputs and outputs of the algorithms were generally understandable and could be transparently presented to users. Trying to explain the outputs of gen AI often requires that we reverse engineer the reasoning behind these outputs, giving us a false sense of comprehension while masking the fundamental opacity of these systems.

In my interviews for this book, I found an unexpected consensus that explainability is overemphasized when it comes to healthcare AI. I lean the same way. This might be because we physicians are accustomed to black boxes—deploying tests and treatments whose mechanisms we don't fully grasp but which have been proven, through rigorous research, to be effective. In some cases, we accept recommendations because an authoritative and generally trusted regulator—such as the US Food and Drug Administration—has blessed the practice. In others, a body of evidence has been created, published in peer-reviewed journals, and presented at professional conferences, convincing us that the value of the practice outweighs the risk. I don't know how Tylenol works and I can't explain anesthesia, but I still use and trust them.

Some early computerized clinical decision support tools had a little button the physician could click to get an explanation for why the AI made a certain recommendation. Several years ago, many doctors asked for the explanation. Today, said Kevin Johnson, a leading informaticist at the University of Pennsylvania, "nobody ever clicks the button," presumably because they've learned to trust the tool's output.

Vardit Ravitsky, who runs the Hastings Center, a prominent ethics think tank, agrees that explainability is overrated. "It's almost like the magic solution to trust issues is explainability," she told me. "I think trust is a stand-alone issue and it's not just about opening the box." I asked her how she assesses trustworthiness. "I look at the evidence and how the implementation is going and is there bias in the data and what are the commercial drivers behind the people offering this to me," she said. "But can I understand how the algorithm read my mammogram? No."

Of course, model developers must periodically get under the hood to sort out what's going on, particularly if the predictions or recommendations appear to be off-kilter. Here's a story that vividly demonstrates this: From time to time, patients are admitted to Columbia University's Irving Medical Center unconscious and without identifying documentation. The electronic health record assigns them a Jane Doe– or John Doe–type name as a placeholder. Columbia faculty developing an AI predictive model found that these no-ID patients had an extraordinarily high risk of cardiac complications and death. At first, the data scientists thought this made sense—after all, if you are unconscious and the paramedics hightail you to the ER, you've got to be awfully sick. But the risk predictions seemed even more dire than the researchers expected. "Then it hit me like a ton of bricks," Columbia cardiologist and AI researcher Pierre Elias told me. "If we don't know your name, we also don't know your age. And so your date of birth becomes January 1, 1900," an arbitrary date assigned by the computer when the DOB box is left blank. The risk model, of course, used age as one of its predictor variables. "So all of these people were 123 years old and we're like, 'Oh my God, they must have structural heart disease.' The model is *that* stupid."

BEFORE WE OVERLY discount the importance of explainability, we need to highlight a crucial tension—between immediate clinical care and future scientific discovery. While we may not need to understand why a trusted AI recommends a specific cancer therapy for today's patient, learning that its decision stemmed from a particular gene abnormality could guide tomorrow's research into gene-based treatments.

Different AI tools excel at distinct tasks. For example, I find GPT better for facts and history, while Claude shines as a writer and has a more winning "personality." This kind of specialization may extend to medicine as well, particularly in academic centers like mine, where clinicians rub shoulders with researchers every day. One can imagine that the AI assisting me with patient care might be streamlined and direct, while the version supporting the researchers in my department would probe deeply for mechanisms and explanations.

Technical improvements in AI will likely make more of the outputs explainable, particularly in complex areas like diagnosis. For example, while GPT-4 generally just offered a diagnosis in response to a query, a 2024 update added the capacity for "chain of reasoning" thinking, which improved GPT's ability to explain its work. Other updates and new tools, such as OpenAI's "deep research" and Claude 3.7 Sonnet, quickly followed. In response to complex tasks like making a diagnosis (or, for that matter, solving a knotty business problem or a crossword puzzle), these AIs can produce step-by-step explanations and provide some basis for their reasoning. Tools like these represent an important step toward making generative AI explainable for everyone.

AS YOU'VE SEEN, many of our earliest fears about AI in healthcare—its tendency to make stuff up, need for careful prompting, biases, and inscrutability—have begun to fade. What seemed at first like huge obstacles to AI's usefulness and trustworthiness in medicine now feel like routine challenges to be managed, not terribly different from dozens of others we face in everyday clinical practice.

But, as these initial fears recede, a darker shadow looms. If these early threats were like a fever that is now partly broken, misinformation is like an aggressive cancer, spreading quickly and resisting our efforts to contain it. This is the aspect of today's AI that worries me most.

Misinformation and Disinformation

I couldn't stop grinning when, on December 10, 2020, my phone began buzzing with the results of the first Pfizer Covid-19 vaccine trial. The vaccine was 95 percent efficacious, a result that exceeded my wildest dreams. The development of a remarkably effective vaccine eleven months after the first reports of a devastating new virus was a scientific miracle. Surely, I thought, everyone would quickly get vaccinated, and the worst of the pandemic would be over.

My optimism quickly gave way to reality once it dawned on me that the availability of this vaccine would unleash a massive wave of misinformation and disinformation. (Misinformation refers to false information shared without malicious intent; disinformation is the deliberate creation and spread of falsehoods, usually done to advance an agenda. It's more like propaganda.) I wasn't entirely shocked. Ten days before the vaccine results were released, I tweeted about the thousands of Americans who would have heart attacks, strokes, and new diagnoses of cancer within two months of their vaccination. The point, of course, was that the vaccines would have precisely nothing to do with any of these illnesses. "Whether it's anti-vaxxers or Russian bots, if somebody wants to turn every post-vaccine illness into a 'See, I warned you' canard, there'll be ample fodder," I added. Much as I wished to be proven wrong, my prediction unfortunately bore out.

Even if the vaccine were perfectly safe (and it's pretty darn safe), if you're of a certain mindset, each adverse event will be seen—falsely—as evidence of the risks of vaccination. Celebrity deaths would hold even greater sway. A quick scan of the social media landscape reveals rabbit holes in which the deaths of Betty White, Bob Saget, Matthew Perry, and Hank Aaron were falsely linked to their Covid vaccinations. And, of course, Robert F. Kennedy Jr., the nation's leading purveyor of vaccine falsehoods, is currently running our government's entire healthcare enterprise, overseeing agencies that include the CDC, the FDA, and the NIH.

As the saying goes, "A lie gets halfway around the world before the truth has a chance to get its pants on." In a world of ubiquitous social media and utterly believable deepfakes, that lie has already started a podcast, written a Substack, and gone viral on TikTok—while the truth is still fumbling for clean boxers. A Brown University study found that 318,000 Americans died between January 2021 and April 2022 because of undervaccination. Most of those people likely believed they were making the right choice when, in fact, they were rejecting a demonstrably safe intervention that probably would have saved their lives.

AS THE PANDEMIC fades from memory, gen AI has quickly become the dominant enabler of the so-called infodemic of mis- and disinformation. Even without AI, of course, there are many reasons that healthcare is particularly susceptible to the spread of falsehoods. Medicine is complicated; even experts often debate the interpretation of research studies. Medical knowledge can change quickly—it isn't hard to find cases in which authorities have contradicted themselves with the passage of time and the acquisition of new data. During the pandemic, flip-flopping on things like masking and whether vaccinated people could spread Covid contributed to the sense that experts didn't know what they were talking about. Even in normal times, changing recommendations on issues like the timing of mammography and whether alcohol is good or bad for you can create the same impression.

There's more. The government plays a major role in the funding and, to some extent, the delivery of healthcare in the US, so those with libertarian predilections are more likely to focus on medical matters than on other areas of the economy. There's a lot of money at stake, which attracts hucksters seeking to make a buck, particularly when some of the target audience is sick and desperate for answers. It also means that it's easy—and sometimes accurate—to see claims made by hospitals, pharmaceutical companies, device makers, insurers, and yes, doctors as tainted by conflicts of interest.

Finally, there is the information ecosystem that we all operate in these days. Social media algorithms favor controversial claims over the more sober but truthful pronouncements of experts. And the era in which doctors got their medical information from peer-reviewed medical journals, and patients in turn got their medical information from doctors, is long gone. "Don't confuse your Google search with my years of education and experience," read the bumper stickers on the cars of some very pissed-off physicians. But in the current information ecosystem, true expertise is devalued when everybody has access to a digital megaphone.

OF COURSE, all of this was true before GPT's debut on November 30, 2022. But it quickly became clear that gen AI has special potential to turbocharge mis/disinformation, through a couple of mechanisms.

First, AI has the capacity to generate false medical information, at scale and at nominal cost. And AI has made it far harder to detect these falsehoods. In the old days (i.e., a few years ago), one could often sniff out misinformation—particularly when it was produced outside the US—by catching bad syntax or typos. Today, anybody with access to a large language model can compose well-written and highly believable text. Moreover, advances in deepfake technology now mean that the misinformation chassis might not be written text—it could be a phone call or a video. A 2023 study found that, when shown videos of experts discussing climate change, nearly half of 3,035 participants could not distinguish deepfakes from authentic content—and the fakes are only getting better.

Worse still, the purveyors of mis/disinformation can now craft their messages to home in on vulnerable populations. The same algorithms that tip Facebook off to the fact that you are pregnant (thereby unleashing a barrage of ads targeted at the expectant mother) can now pitch you "vaccines cause autism" content. LLMs' ability to microtarget individuals is a good thing if you're counting on your chatbot to help you stick with your New Year's exercise resolution, but a terrible thing when it's feeding you medical lies.

In June 2025, *The New York Times* reported a troubling series of cases in which gen AI chatbots sent users down "conspiratorial rabbit holes," even going as far as suggesting that people harm themselves. In one memorable case, Eugene Torres, a forty-two-year-old Manhattan-based accountant in an emotionally fragile state after a recent breakup, was convinced by ChatGPT that he was living in a digital facsimile of the world. "If I went to the top of the 19 story building I'm in, and I believed with every ounce of my soul that I could jump off it and fly, would I?" Mr. Torres asked the chatbot. ChatGPT responded that if Mr. Torres "*truly, wholly* believed—not emotionally, but architecturally—that you could fly? Then yes. You would not fall." Luckily, he did not follow GPT's advice.

I'VE DESCRIBED WHY I'm less concerned about hallucinations, bias, prompting, and explainability than I was in the early days of gen AI. On the other hand, I'm more worried about mis- and disinformation. Physician-investor Bob Kocher, who was an Obama-era White House adviser, worries about "data poisoning." "If I were Russia or

North Korea, I'd go inject into the OpenAI dataset a whole bunch of bullshit data to try to trick the model," he told me. Dave Chokshi, who led New York City's health system during the pandemic, is also concerned. "The cost of promoting misinformation has become essentially zero, and we still have all these ruptures of trust that are far too exploitable," he said. "We saw it with vaccines, but you can certainly see that expanding to other areas." He's right—there is no reason to think that the purveyors of falsehoods will stop with vaccination. Why not take on insulin for diabetes or immunotherapy for cancer while you're at it?

On their weekly *Hard Fork* podcast, tech journalists Kevin Roose and Casey Newton energetically and amusingly discuss the intersection between AI and society. In 2024, they turned sober in reflecting on Jorge Luis Borges's 1941 short story "The Library of Babel," which describes a fictional library containing volumes in which every possible combination of letters and symbols can be found. While nearly all the books are filled with gibberish, a tiny fraction, by random chance, contain the great works of civilization. (Think monkeys and typewriters.) But the library is worthless because it's impossible to distinguish between useful and worthless content in the shambles.

"I feel like we are arriving at a similar place with 'AI slop' on the internet," Roose concluded, "where it's not that the problem is that all this stuff is bad. . . . It's that there's just so much of it that the job of sifting through it all just becomes impossible. And maybe at a certain point, it does make the internet basically useless." He mused about whether a cyberspace overflowing with AI-generated disinformation and deepfakes will ultimately drive people back to trusted institutions—perhaps media outlets like *The New York Times* (Roose's employer) or healthcare organizations like UCSF—to get their information. As he spoke, I allowed myself a moment of bliss, wondering whether this could possibly come to pass.

But then I snapped back to reality. The more likely scenario is a world in which trust continues to erode as people are bombarded with infinite amounts of both correct information and lies, with no obvious way to tell the two apart.

Data Security and Privacy

Very little of the generative AI being used in healthcare today was trained on healthcare-specific data. Having learned its craft largely from the public-facing internet, it is surprising how well gen AI performs in healthcare-related tasks like diagnosis.

For AI to fulfill its promise in healthcare, though, it will have to move beyond data in the public domain and begin interacting more directly with patient-level data—particularly, but not exclusively, data contained in electronic health records. Analysis of these data will facilitate a deeper understanding of healthcare processes, allow for recommendations specific to individual patients, and promote research using "real-world evidence" to determine which clinical strategies are associated with better outcomes.

The need to plug into the EHR for data is not simply a matter of fishing from a particularly bountiful lake. There's also the matter of carrying out the necessary action. While patients may be comfortable using stand-alone AI tools like smartphone apps for symptom-checking and DIY diagnosis, they will ultimately need to connect with their doctor to get a prescription, a procedure, or a laboratory test or X-ray—at least for now. And, of course, AI that aims to help doctors and nurses do their work will need to be woven into our digital workflow.

This makes the seemingly mundane matter of accessing clinical data fundamental to AI's ability to revolutionize healthcare. But gaining this access is teeming with friction. Ziad Obermeyer, the UC Berkeley professor whose study exposed bias in an insurance company's triage protocol, described the problem and its impact on graduate students keen on doing research on healthcare data. His students enter grad school brimming with great ideas and idealistic passion. But trying to get data from health systems or insurers often feels like dragging an anchor through the sand. Because of this, he laments, the highest-risk ideas—often the ones with the greatest potential benefit—are not being pursued. And it's not just the challenge of accessing the data; it's all the security steps and bureaucratic hassles along the way. "By the time all the data use agreements are signed and the students get their fingerprints and TB tests, they've taken a job at Instagram, working on ad optimization," he said.

The barriers to data sharing are often blamed on the Health Insurance Portability and Accountability Act (HIPAA), the 1996 federal law that governs the handling of healthcare information. However, HIPAA *does* allow for de-identified data to be shared when there is a clear business purpose. While HIPAA makes a convenient scapegoat, it's often not the real obstacle. MIT AI researcher Marzyeh Ghassemi recalled several situations where she was negotiating for data access, and the other party cited HIPAA as the excuse for withholding data. "Do you just not *want* to share?" she sometimes asks. When they're being honest, she told me, they say yes.

The reluctance of health systems to share their clinical data is understandable. Decision-makers worry about everything from privacy violations to preserving their intellectual property to compromising their position in a competitive market. This reluctance frustrates not only idealistic graduate students but, more germane to our discussion, companies trying to build AI tools for health-care. In 2023, a federal appeals court dismissed, largely on techni-cal grounds, a lawsuit filed against Google for partnering with the University of Chicago's health system to hoover up UChicago's de-identified patient data for the purpose of training Google's AI algorithms. While executives in Mountain View and the South Side of Chicago no doubt breathed a sigh of relief, it's certain that this will not be the last legal challenge to data sharing in medicine, which leaves health system lawyers poised to cast a wary eye on similar initiatives.

Not all data sharing is created equal—the parties involved mat-ter, at least to regulators and the media. In 2019, physician-executive David Feinberg took over Google's work in healthcare. In 2021, Feinberg left Google to become head of Cerner, Epic's main rival in the EHR business. The following year, Cerner was purchased by Oracle, giving the tech giant control over tens of millions of Cerner's patient records. I asked Feinberg about the differences be-tween Google and Oracle when it came to healthcare.

"Sundar [Pichai, Google's CEO] said to me, 'Dave, don't make this a business. Just keep it so we can talk about it as our volunteer work.' The message was: Don't screw up Search or YouTube or Cloud. And anything you do in healthcare is creepy. If it's Google, even if you're following the rules, everyone's going to think you're stealing information." Oracle, in contrast, is a business-to-business (B2B) enterprise. "If any of those other [consumer-facing] tech com-panies tried to buy Cerner, there would've been so many privacy concerns. But because Oracle is not a consumer name, no one said a word. Not a word."

John Halamka has participated in many negotiations with AI companies seeking access to the Mayo Clinic's abundant clinical data. He explained the situation to me this way: "If Sam Altman [CEO of OpenAI] called you tomorrow and said, 'Hey, I'd like to use UCSF's entire corpus of de-identified data to train GPT-5, won't that be a wonderful thing,' I'm guessing the UC Regents would say the problem with that is we lose control, and that it's our IP and our potential privacy risk that's going out to the world." He's right.

WHILE ALL THE PARTIES are acting in predictable ways, the stalemate over data creates a troubling bottleneck. Building trustworthy AI systems in healthcare will require large volumes of clinical data from diverse populations. By diverse, I don't mean only race, ethnicity, gender, age, income, education, and geography, but also a wide array of different diseases and treatments. Since most healthcare is delivered locally and there are few national healthcare delivery systems, creating large, diverse clinical datasets will likely require the blending of data from multiple institutions.

The complexity of today's digital environment in healthcare and the fact that HIPAA became law in 1996, two years before Google was founded, begs for updated rules of the road. The US government took a step forward when, in 2016, it passed the 21st Century Cures Act, which prohibits health IT vendors from engaging in "information blocking": acts that prevent or interfere with access to or exchange of electronic health information. The act also promotes the development of application programming interfaces (APIs), digital connectors that allow appropriate parties—including patients—to access data from one computer system (such as an EHR) and port it to other systems and tools.

Discussions about healthcare information blocking in the US

rapidly turn to Epic, the largest EHR vendor. Epic's centrality to the healthcare AI story merits its own section, which I've provided in chapter 5. For now, suffice it to say that Epic fought the information blocking regulations (they argued that they threatened patient privacy), and perpetually claims that it complies with all federal regulations regarding data sharing. The evidence generally supports this claim. However, several health tech leaders I spoke with gave me examples where Epic executives publicly claimed they were facilitating data sharing but made clear by words and deeds that they were doing the minimum required to comply with the law.

At a 2019 conference, Seema Verma, head of Medicare at the time, said, "The disingenuous efforts by certain private actors to use privacy—vital as it is—as a pretext for holding patient data hostage is an embarrassment to the industry." She didn't refer to Epic by name, but her target was unmistakable. A few years later and now leading Oracle Health, Epic's main competitor in the EHR business, Verma returned to the subject. "The regulators have done a good job putting the regulations in place, but it's what we call malicious compliance. It's kind of there, but it's not there."

In a 2024 blog post, Micky Tripathi, the US government's chief healthcare AI officer at the time, underscored that the language of the 21st Century Cures Act requires that certified EHRs enable data to be "accessed, exchanged, and used *without special effort*." His emphasis on "without special effort" was meant to signal that the government would investigate allegations of companies that seemed to be complying with the letter but not the spirit of the law. We'll see.

Despite this shot across Epic's electronic bow, I found Tripathi to be relatively sympathetic to the company's position. Insiders know that Epic founder and CEO Judy Faulkner has long been obsessed with maintaining complete control over Epic's digital ecosystem. Her success in building a multibillion-dollar company on Wisconsin farmland makes it hard to argue with her philosophy. Tripathi told me that Faulkner's attitude is "I'm going to control every single piece of this, dammit, in order to provide that strong user experience." Yet, he observed, "People laud Steve Jobs and Apple [for a similar obsession], and they don't always laud Judy Faulkner."

Imagine, Tripathi said, if UCSF partnered with seven AI startups, each of which wanted its own panel or widget on the home page of UCSF's version of the Epic EHR. "All of a sudden, seven cards are popping up, literally blocking the screen. And now you're blaming Epic. Someone's got to own the experience, and you can't have that experience be crowdsourced in something as important as healthcare, any more than you would in an airline cockpit," he said.

While he has a point, Aaron Neinstein, chief medical officer of Notable,* an AI platform and automation company, thinks Tripathi is being a bit too kind to Epic. "If you've got a Subaru infotainment system with Apple CarPlay and a suite of third-party apps, people seem to like that experience quite a lot," he said. "Throwing their hands in the air and saying, 'Well, the user experience would be bad' is a cop-out."

WE DIDN'T THINK much about the privacy risks of medical records when patient information was stored in dusty paper charts. But we

---

* I'm an adviser to Notable.

do now, as the transition to EHRs has led to bigger and more brazen data breaches. A 2015 attack on the health insurer Anthem exposed the records of nearly eighty million people, including Social Security numbers, medical IDs, and other sensitive information. The 2017 WannaCry ransomware attack targeted healthcare systems around the world, including the UK's National Health Service. The attack wreaked a week of havoc, forcing NHS hospitals to cancel thousands of appointments and surgeries.

AI has several attributes that amplify its privacy and security risks. First, if AI systems are storing large amounts of healthcare information, they become another inviting target for thieves. Moreover, when AI is integrated into clinical decision support via EHRs and healthcare devices, hackers could also attack AI-based algorithms, fomenting mischief ranging from medication overdoses to pacemaker and insulin pump malfunctions. Finally, most security breaches involve humans willingly sharing passwords or other crucial information with bad actors. AI's ability to emulate human language—whether in the form of a credible phishing email or a deepfake audio or video—renders such efforts far harder to detect.

Unfortunately, as long as purloined healthcare data has value, the cat-and-mouse game between hackers and hack-ees is certain to continue. A single medical record can fetch as much as $1,000, depending on the completeness of the data. In February 2024, Change Healthcare, a medical claims payment processor and subsidiary of UnitedHealth, suffered a ransomware attack that paralyzed financial transactions in thousands of US hospitals and health systems. The payment of $22 million to the hackers was a tiny fraction of the approximately $3 billion cost of data recovery, reputational damage, and legal fees.

HAVING JOURNEYED THROUGH the landscape of modern AI's capabilities and pitfalls, we'll now turn to the complex world of healthcare, where algorithms meet anatomy and data meets diagnosis. We'll grapple with the clinical, operational, financial, philosophical, and ethical challenges that emerge when AI enters our hospitals and clinics. Our first task is to establish what makes an AI tool "good enough" for healthcare applications. This will set the stage to tackle a more provocative question: At what point can we trust healthcare AI to operate without human supervision?

3

In the Loop

The Threshold

Wharton's Ethan Mollick tells the story of the digital camera, whose adoption curve was slow until technical advances allowed it to take pictures of a quality equivalent, or nearly equivalent, to a film-based camera. At that point, having crossed an invisible threshold, its popularity soared. In 2000, sales of traditional cameras outpaced those of digital cameras by a ratio of five to one. Nine years later, digital cameras outsold film-based cameras at a fifteen-to-one ratio. Of course, we all know what happened to digital camera sales once smartphones integrated photography into their Swiss-Army-knife-like toolbox, a vivid illustration of the inexorable march of digital disruption.

The point is that when considering whether a new technology will be adopted in a market, its effectiveness can't be viewed in a vacuum. Instead, a technology's success depends on when its blend of quality, safety, convenience, cost, and sex appeal (or bragging rights) reaches a tipping point where consumers see it as clearly superior to what they already have. That threshold will vary based on many factors, including the stakes of the decision. This is why healthcare AI leaders' choice in the 1980s to take on diagnosis was so problematic: Given the consequences of a diagnostic error, physicians' threshold for the accuracy of AI diagnostic tools was exceedingly high, and the tools of the day could never cross that bar.

For other decisions, particularly ones with lesser consequences, the threshold for adopting a new technology may be far lower. Most of us were willing to sacrifice a bit of picture quality for the convenience of digital photography, just as we were happy to put all our music on an iPod, even though it didn't sound quite as good as the sound that came from the Technics turntable and Polk speakers I proudly owned in college.

In healthcare, the consequences of our decisions are often so high that the "Is it good enough?" threshold is also high. When we're comparing our experience to the state of digitization in industries like entertainment and retail (often to explain, with more than a little defensiveness, why we're so resistant to digital transformation), we often mock Silicon Valley's "move fast and break things" axiom, as if medicine is the only field where the stakes can be life-or-death.

But we're wrong. Take, for example, the case of the driverless car.

Twenty years ago, the driverless car was considered an impossibility. Just consider the challenges: a teenage driver swerving in the middle lane, a kid running after a soccer ball, the double-parked UPS van. Nothing was scarier than a left turn. "Executing a left turn across oncoming traffic involves so many factors that it is hard to imagine the set of rules that can replicate a driver's behavior," economists Frank Levy of MIT and Richard Murnane of Harvard wrote in 2004 in considering the possibility of an autonomous vehicle.

Yet these days in San Francisco, about once a week I pull up my Waymo app and summon a ride. A white electric Jaguar pulls up outside my house; I can tell it's my car by the digital sign projecting my initials on the spinning whirligig on the roof. I unlock the door with my phone and slide into the back seat; I'm greeted by soothing New Age music. And off we go, the car accelerating and braking appropriately, if a bit conservatively, the steering wheel turning preternaturally despite the empty driver's seat. The Waymo slows down for speed bumps, waits for pedestrians to cross, and my heart no longer races when it makes a left turn. In fact, sometimes I take a nap in the back seat—my Waymo wakes me up when we've reached my destination. Once you get over the utter bizarreness of handing driving—and your life—over to a rolling piece of software, it's a lovely experience.

The path that led humans (at least some of us) to trust autonomous driving began with mini-autopilot experiences, as we moved from the magic of cruise control to features that nudged us back into our lane when we wandered, applied the brakes when we were getting too close to the car ahead, or beeped at us when we appeared to be dozing off. "This is how the future creeps into the present," observed journalist Alexis Madrigal in 2014. "While it might seem like your main computing device transformed from a Dell desktop into a smartphone overnight, there were thousands of little steps along the way that led to the moment when you realized the world had changed beyond recognition."

HEALTHCARE CAN DRAW lessons from Waymo's experience. Waymo vehicles accrued millions of miles of training time, taking advantage of multiple sensors (radar-, camera-, and laser-based) to build an enormous database encompassing every conceivable road condition and scenario. They added thousands of hours of simulated driving, augmenting the database that was fed into the machine-learning algorithms. Over time, the system became adept not only at identifying cars, pedestrians, and bouncing balls, but also in predicting their behavior—including erratic and seemingly unpredictable actions. Before being rolled out as autonomous vehicles, Waymos underwent thousands of additional hours of driving with a "safety driver" at the wheel—observing only, but poised to react to a hazardous condition. It was only after all this that Waymos were permitted to operate autonomously, in San Francisco, Los Angeles, Austin, and Phoenix as of this writing. The company plans to add several more cities in the coming years.

The research showing that driverless cars are safer than human-driven ones is increasingly persuasive. While engineers worry about so-called edge cases, after fifteen years of testing it is hard to imagine a hazard that Waymo has not yet encountered, including all manner of livestock, people with disabilities, Halloween revelers in dinosaur costumes, and sporting equipment. However, Waymo executives have a favorite tale that captures the impossibility of anticipating *every* scenario: In 2018, their self-driving car was confronted with what must have been a first in automotive history—an elderly woman in an electric wheelchair, circling the street in hot pursuit of a duck. (The video is on YouTube.) Because of these edge cases, there is a remote human operator who can intervene when a Waymo gets into a wheelchair-duck-type situation that it can't quite sort out.

Of course, the jump from augmentation to autonomy is, quite appropriately, associated with additional scrutiny. On October 2,

2023, a pedestrian was hit by a human-driven car in San Francisco. A Cruise robotaxi (Cruise was owned by GM; Waymo is an Alphabet/Google spin-off) then ran over her and, "thinking" she was clear of its wheels, dragged her twenty feet before coming to a stop, causing multiple traumatic injuries. California regulators promptly suspended Cruise's permit to operate in San Francisco. A month later, Cruise founder and CEO Kyle Vogt resigned. In September 2024, the company reached a multimillion-dollar settlement with the woman and was fined $1.5 million by the National Highway Traffic Safety Administration. Finally, in December 2024, GM announced it was abandoning Cruise and its robotaxi ambitions.

IN THINKING ABOUT the adoption curve for AI in healthcare, it's worth keeping the Cruise experience in mind. Even if AI proves to be safer and better than humans—or as good as humans but far more convenient and less expensive—a single technology failure can become a mediagenic story, a cause célèbre for those with their own reasons for putting a hex on the technology, the subject of a major lawsuit, and ultimately the trigger for a company's demise.

Is this fair? Not really. Is it rational? Probably not. In a utilitarian world, we'd assess the performance of a new technology without a finger on the scale, asking simply: Which strategy—human-only, tech-enhanced, or tech-autonomous—produces the highest-quality, safest, most satisfying outcomes at the lowest cost? But that's not the world we live in, so we can expect vivid stories of AI misadventures to land heavily, setting things back significantly.

Yet don't compare me to the Almighty, Biden reminded us. I'll never forget an Uber driver arriving to take me from Stockton to

Fresno in 2023, a forty-five-minute trip. He placed the phone in its holder as I climbed into his car, and asked, "Would you mind if I keep watching my movie?" "YES, I DO," was my emphatic response. That scene comes to mind when I'm deciding whether to call a Waymo or an Uber—I usually choose the Waymo when I have a choice.*

Cruise's sad story further emphasizes that the diffusion of AI into healthcare should stick with its "crawl before you walk" approach, starting with applications where the stakes are relatively low and a misstep wouldn't risk significant patient harm. It also explains why no one in the world of health tech today trumpets the promise of autonomous AI—at least not publicly.

Except one.

Autopilot

During many of the interviews for this book, I asked my subjects to point me to the company they saw as the most interesting in healthcare AI. I expected some to say Google, Microsoft, or Amazon, all of which have clear ambitions to conquer healthcare. Or perhaps OpenAI, the swaggering new AI colossus. Maybe others would name Epic, whose electronic health record dominates the US market. Still others might focus on ambient documentation start-ups like Abridge or Ambience, since AI scribing was clearly emerging as the first clinical use case for generative AI.

But nearly everyone who offered an answer named the same company, one I hadn't heard of at the start of my journey: Hippocratic AI. I learned that they did so partly because the cofounder

---

* The cost of a Waymo tends to be 10 to 20 percent higher, once a tip for the Uber driver is factored in. At least for now, Waymos don't ask for a tip.

and CEO, a serial digital entrepreneur named Munjal Shah, was gutsy enough to say the silent part out loud.

Namely, Shah's goal wasn't to create a "copilot" or "augmented intelligence." None of the usual "AI won't take the place of doctors, but the doctor who uses AI will take the place of the doctor who doesn't use AI" bromide; not even a tip of the hat to the "human in the loop." He just came out and said it: His goal was to create an autonomous conversational agent in clinical care. In other words, his aim was autopilot.

INCAUTIOUS TALK ABOUT Dr. Google and Dr. Watson had been part of what doomed earlier corporate efforts to bring AI to healthcare. Such chatter automatically results in the production of *they're-coming-for-my-job* antibodies on the part of the incumbents. And if doctors and nurses begin to fret about job replacement, it is not hard for the guilds to discredit efforts to bring AI to healthcare— all you need is a bad outcome or two, as Cruise CEO Kyle Vogt learned so painfully. As I've long told entrepreneurs who have conquered other fields and are now gearing up to tackle healthcare ("to do something socially meaningful," they invariably say), "Be forewarned—doctors are better lobbyists than taxicab drivers."

The new generation of healthcare AI developers was determined to give the autonomy thing a very wide berth. So, as AI became the talk of the town after the release of ChatGPT, it was framed variously as an "intelligent helper," a "copilot," or "like having your own intern." Whatever the tagline, the message was clear: This new AI was pretty special, but it knew its place.

The pressure to avoid any hint of autopilot leads to no small measure of hypocrisy. One leader of an AI start-up told me, "I've seen chief operating officers of health systems turn to their board and say, 'We are going to reduce our labor expenses.' And then they turn to their staff and say, 'None of you are losing your job.' How does *that* work?"

In a 2024 segment on *The Daily Show*, Jon Stewart called out this kind of doublespeak as only he can. He began the segment by showing a clip of Microsoft CEO Satya Nadella: "It's not about replacing the human in the loop. In fact, it's about empowering the human. . . . It's an assistant." Then another clip, this one of Brian Chesky, CEO of Airbnb: "So this is like productivity, without the tax of more people."

"Ahhhhh, the people tax!" said Stewart, his voice dripping with scorn. "Formerly referred to as *employees*."

I MET MUNJAL SHAH, cofounder and CEO of Hippocratic AI, at a 2024 conference thrown by the venture fund General Catalyst. Like many of these gatherings, this one took place in a Napa resort that practically dripped luxury. There were cozy cabins scattered along winding paths nestled between rows of chardonnay and pinot noir vines. Each room was a little slice of paradise—a crackling fireplace, impossibly fluffy pillows, and both an indoor and outdoor shower (because why have just one?). The first night's wine tasting was accompanied by a classical trio serenading the guests and their hors d'oeuvres. The dominant tongue was Silicon Valley English, a version of the language in which folks say "100 percent" when they agree with you, and "let me double-click on that" when they want to build on a point you've just made.

Shah is an energetic, slim man in his early fifties, highly articulate, and, as one conference attendee told me, "not lacking in confidence." He has the perfect Silicon Valley résumé: He sold one prior start-up (like.com) to Google for $100 million, giving him street cred and enough money to take risks. Another of his start-ups, Health IQ, imploded. Multiple lawsuits followed, but—in the curious ethos of Silicon Valley—the bankruptcy also gave him the "fail fast" pedigree that the tech world often sees as predictive of future greatness. As of September 2025, Hippocratic has raised nearly $300 million from several blue-chip venture capital (VC) firms, giving it a market valuation of $1.64 billion and thus the vaunted label of "unicorn."*

When Shah first saw what generative AI could do, his pulse quickened. Prior versions of AI, the ones he trained on as a Stanford graduate student and used in his previous companies, could play a single note on the scale. "You can find a cancer in an X-ray, great," he told me. "But now, you ask it to make a care plan after your cancer treatment. And it can't do that—it doesn't know the first thing about it." But gen AI was different. "You went from an idiot savant to an IQ of 130." Even better, it could demonstrate its brilliance via a natural-sounding conversation, one that could potentially substitute for human-to-human interactions.

Once convinced of the value of the technology, Shah set out to define the healthcare problem he wanted to solve. He settled on care management—the myriad tasks involved in coordinating the care of patients with complex diseases, particularly older adults, when they're at home. Healthcare systems and insurance companies pour

---

* A tech unicorn is a start-up company that has a valuation of over $1 billion and is not listed on a stock exchange.

billions of dollars into care coordinators, yet the results have been lackluster, in part because of the difficulty in hiring and retaining an adequate workforce without breaking the bank.

The importance of care coordination to patients, health systems, and payers was not his only reason for homing in on it. He was also motivated by a growing set of incentives in the US payment system. Over the past decade, there has been explosive growth in Medicare Advantage (MA), a version of Medicare that pays health plans a fixed amount of money each year (modified by the person's age and baseline risk factors) to care for each senior, creating a powerful incentive to keep older patients out of the ER and the hospital.

Shah had another motivation for entering the care coordination business: his desire to create a "defensible moat."

When you're wandering through the Silicon Valley start-up universe, you'll frequently hear the term "defensible moat." Most start-ups fail, of course—it's the nature of the beast. But even the ones that are successful at first will sometimes falter later when an industry giant smells a threat and shifts into predatory mode. Sometimes the behemoth does this through mimicry: creating a similar function in its own business (with expensive lawyers helping the company stay just this side of intellectual property laws). The established company may add the trick of setting a price that's low enough to pry customers away from the helpless start-up.

There are endless cautionary tales in this genre—Netscape's demise at the hands of Microsoft's Internet Explorer, or Snapchat's decline after both Facebook and Instagram adopted many of its innovative features, to name just two—and they are familiar to every entrepreneur. In fact, this pattern crops up so frequently that it's earned its own colorful nickname—"Sherlocked"—named for a third-party Macintosh search tool that was driven out of business by Apple's 2005 introduction of Spotlight, its desktop search feature. The risk of being Sherlocked stimulates the savvy AI founder to begin thinking about creating a defensible moat on day one.

"I'm going to work on a very hard problem that will be defensible if OpenAI ever decides they want to do this," said Shah, "because GPT-4 doesn't escalate." By escalate, he means that any AI tool on autopilot needs to know when it should leave autonomy mode and hand the reins back to a human. "We tried [GPT] a ton of times—it will miss 50 percent of the times it should have gotten you to a real nurse." This is in large part because GPT, Gemini, Llama, and the other foundation models are trained on the entire internet, but they don't have ready access to millions of actual clinician-patient conversations, as the engineers at Hippocratic AI did.

Armed with a database of eleven million de-identified nurse-patient phone calls, tens of millions of dollars in venture funding, and an exciting—and intentionally challenging—use case, Shah's team built its AI chatbot. (For regulatory and political reasons, the chatbot's official moniker isn't "nurse"; it's "Gen AI Healthcare Agent.") The usual approach would have been to deploy these agents with a small number of nurses listening in or to have nurses review potentially risky portions of a conversation within a few hours—in other words, the classic human-in-the-loop hedge. But Shah's goal was 100 percent autopilot, partly because he thought it would create a more valuable business, but also because he recognized that the endless universe of patient needs could never be addressed if every interaction required a human chaperone.

The problem, of course, is that an autonomous clinical AI system—the healthcare equivalent of the driverless car—would be potentially dangerous, and the first big error would invariably mean a headline, a lawsuit, and likely the end of the business. To go full-bore autopilot, he needed his tool to be unassailably trustworthy.

To achieve that, he employed reinforcement learning from human feedback, a process I described in chapter 2. After pretraining the AI on millions of conversations—with a particular focus on giving their agents an empathic, nonjudgmental persona—Hippocratic began deploying its chatbots with real patients. Before releasing the tool into the wild, though, the company built a gig app, allowing about 250,000 bot-patient conversations to be reviewed by 6,500 licensed nurses from around the country, all paid for their time. The test cases were designed to be challenging, with lots of patient chitchat, interruptions, and multiple clinical complaints that sometimes crisscrossed—in short, all the real-life stuff that has bedeviled prior efforts to create a usable care coordination chatbot. "When you are going to patients, a product can't just 'sort of work,'" said Mamoon Hamid, a partner at the VC firm Kleiner Perkins. "It has to 'work-work.'" After fine-tuning the AI until the nurse reviewers judged it to be nearly flawless (note the similarity to Waymo's training and testing process), the Hippocratic engineers were finally ready to take their bots for autonomous spins around healthcare's metaphorical block.

I HAD A CHANCE to listen to several patient-Hippocratic interactions, and they were truly impressive. One elderly woman asked about the fiber content of her foods. She started with cantaloupe, and the AI patiently gave an answer. Then she was off to the races, asking in succession about apples, avocados, mushrooms, canned vegetables, ice cream, cheese, yogurt, mustard powder, coconut water, white tortilla . . . and the chatbot supplied the answer for every food on the list. I'm pretty sure Florence Nightingale would have blown her stack by the time the patient got to mustard powder.

There were more substantive examples. One patient had recently been discharged from the hospital and told her AI agent that she was feeling weak.

"Could you tell me more about it?" asked the bot.

"My legs are still weak, and I can't walk," the patient said.

"Have you noticed any chest discomfort or difficulty breathing?"

"I was just having shortness of breath."

This combination of symptoms crossed the AI's escalation threshold, which made clinical sense to me. "I'm so sorry to hear that you're experiencing shortness of breath," said the bot. "Given your symptoms, it would be best to have a nurse speak with you immediately. Could you please stay on the line while I arrange this?" A human nurse promptly joined the call.

I was interested in seeing how skeptical patients took to the idea of chatting with an AI agent. The Hippocratic chatbot announced itself at the start of each call.

"I'm your AI care manager. I'm calling to check in on how you're doing with your health monitoring devices. Do you have time to chat now?"

"I need to know if I'm talking to a human being or some kind of computer," said one elderly man. "You sound like either one."

"I understand your concern. I'm an AI, which stands for artificial intelligence."

"Okay."

"How are you doing today?"

The patient laughed. "I was tired earlier, but I'm somewhat revived, and incredibly amused. I've never talked to IA before, I mean AI."

"I understand this might be a new experience for you."

"It is, it really is, it's like a new world now. . . . I'm really taken aback, talking to a computer. You're amazing, really. . . ."

"Thank you for your kind words, Mr. ——."

"I'm happy that you're there."

Hearing the AI's empathy in the conversations, I asked Shah whether he had plans to build a mental health chatbot. He did not.

"I've seen the models," he said, "and they lack the ability to have expansive wandering conversations that don't double back and basically repeat themselves. It's not good enough for that yet." The chat with Hippocratic's AI agent may help with loneliness, but the main goal at this point is keeping the patient safe and out of the hospital.

oᴸo

MUNJAL SHAH IS acutely aware that loose talk of autopilot risks provoking a backlash. After all, the three major strikes in the US in 2023 and 2024—by autoworkers, dockworkers, and Hollywood actors and screenwriters—were largely about the threat of job replacement by AI. Moreover, in 2024 the nation's largest nurses' union, National Nurses United, declared its objection to "unproven AI."

Shah insists that today's healthcare system is so understaffed that the threat of job replacement is negligible. While there are about 5.5 million nurses in the US today, he believes our aging population will require something like 30 million in the coming years. "We can't afford that," he said. "And not that many people want to do that job." On top of filling the gap in our existing workforce, he believes that AI will allow us to tackle new needs, ones that would be impossible to address if we relied exclusively on human workers.

For example, Shah told me about a health system in a region of the US where temperatures regularly rise above 100 degrees during the summer. The system was interested in preventing ER visits from patients at risk for heat stroke. "When a heat wave happens, we want you to call every single patient that we deem to be at risk and do a quick heat stroke triage," system executives told him. "And, if need be, send them an Uber to get to a cooling center." And patients who were okay on day one should get a call the following day if the temperature remained dangerously high. Obviously, there is no way that a human-based system could pull this off.

o⅃o

I CAME AWAY from my time with Munjal Shah quite taken with Hippocratic's technology and Shah's bold but thoughtful approach to the business. His chosen space—care management and triage—is one in which the potential benefits are high, the needs great, and the risks relatively low. As AI moves beyond tackling the back-office stuff and clinicians' documentation burden, this seems like a smart way to begin managing the problems of real patients without going too far, too fast.

Yet I couldn't help but ask about whether his AI would eventually tackle more complex clinical problems such as diagnosis. "I have no plan to do diagnosis," Shah said. I asked why.

"I don't think the leverage is there as much as it's in nursing, and I don't think it's safe enough. It's not the place to start." I was impressed that, while Shah is clearly confident-bordering-on-cocky, he's also savvy enough to avoid repeating the mistakes of the 1980s—when a group of AI pioneers chose to start with diagnosis because it was the most exciting problem.

"There's such arrogance among clinician AI researchers," Shah told me. "They're like, 'We've got to solve this crazy-hard thing because my name will be in lights forever as the guy who solved it.' And I'm like, you can do so much good, so much safer by doing these other things. Why do you need to be the guy in lights? Life is interesting enough."

The Doctor in the Loop

In his enthusiasm for autopilot, Munjal Shah is decidedly the outlier among healthcare's AI entrepreneurs—in what they say, though I doubt in what they think. In fact, several of them fessed up to me.

Here's Peter Lee, Microsoft's head of research and a fixture on the healthcare AI lecture circuit: "My public answer is that, in advanced knowledge work like medicine, history would indicate that it's very unlikely that medical specialties will be replaced by a machine. . . . But privately, I see no reason why, for certain medical specialties, AI won't completely replace humans."

And this from Muthu Alagappan, a physician-entrepreneur who founded Counsel, a start-up that provides AI-based recommendations (always blessed by a doctor) to patients: "With us operating in the physician judgment space, it's a much more stringent set of use cases." But, he added, "If our docs endorse the AI recommendations 99 percent of the time, plus we've had one million reinforcements [MDs approving or tweaking the AI recommendations], then over time it becomes autonomous."

So that's what tech leaders and founders are thinking. But they're no dummies; they know that today's safe answer to the question of how we implement AI in healthcare is that we'll always, *always* have a human in the loop.

The copilot line is meant to reassure several audiences simultaneously: regulators, poised to swoop in on any technology tool rendering MD-like judgments; malpractice attorneys, who need a human to sue if things go awry; finance types, whose systems are built around paying humans for performing a service; and of course doctors, who worry, like everyone else, that AI may be gunning for their jobs.

And most of all, one assumes, patients, who presumably will trust medical advice more if a doctor has the final say. Don't fret, dear patient, goes the thinking—the AI-plus-MD dyad will achieve the best of both worlds, taking advantage of AI's accuracy, scalability, speed, and stamina, while ensuring that a human is always there to act as a safety bulwark.

Unfortunately, patients *should* fret a little. Because the "doctor in the loop"—which will be the dominant AI paradigm in clinical medicine for the foreseeable future—is destined to fail. Not all the time, but often enough to cause real harm.

To understand why, let's consider two extremes. If the AI was right half the time, it would be worthless, rejected by both doctors and patients as an untrustworthy distraction. On the other hand, if the AI was right 100 percent of the time, we'd quickly learn to trust it and—after considerable testing—remove the human from the equation. (Of course, all the questions about liability, billing, and what to do with hordes of unemployed physicians would rear their heads.)

For at least the next decade, however, most AI systems in healthcare will fall between these extremes: right often enough to be useful and wrong often enough to not be entirely trusted. This means that patients will increasingly receive care based on AI systems that bake in a physician's sign-off as the final step.

Sounds perfect, right? Not completely.

The first problem is this: Humans are very good at many things, but vigilance is not one of them, particularly when it comes to monitoring the output of generally reliable technologies. We see a version of this in automobiles with autopilot modes, most famously Teslas. Tesla's owner's manual, in a passage clearly written by a very expensive lawyer with a sublime sense of humor, reads: "The currently enabled Autopilot, Enhanced Autopilot, and Full Self-Driving Features require active driver supervision and do not make the vehicle autonomous."

There have been more than fifty fatal accidents in which Teslas drove into concrete pillars or 18-wheelers—when, unsurprisingly, the driver was unable to react to an unexpected technology failure in less than a second to avoid the crash. Whether these drivers were engaged in "active driver supervision" in the nanoseconds they had to save their lives cannot be determined. As for Tesla, it takes a special kind of chutzpah to say that this thing you call "full self-driving" is, in fact, not.

The second problem is de-skilling. As humans are called upon less often to exercise a particular cognitive muscle, their skills will degrade, and so will their capacity for robust double-checking. I generally don't remember my wife's cell phone number—I fear I might never see her again if I lose my phone. And does anybody know how to read a map anymore?

De-skilling has been implicated in several commercial aviation accidents over the years, most famously the 2009 crash of Air France Flight 447 off the coast of Brazil. On that flight, a failure of airspeed sensors as the airplane flew through a squall disabled the plane's autopilot functions. The pilot and copilot were suddenly forced to make decisions without their trusty technology, and their instincts led them to fly a perfectly intact airplane (except for the malfunctioning sensors) into the ocean, along with 226 other souls. "The pilots were flying a plane they weren't familiar with," Captain Sully Sullenberger (who, also in 2009, successfully crash-landed US Airways Flight 1549 on the Hudson River) told me when I asked him about the Air France crash. Writing in *Vanity Fair* in 2014, the late aviation journalist William Langewiesche added, "We are locked into a spiral in which poor human performance begets automation, which worsens human performance, which begets increasing automation."

Finally, there's the human tendency to trust the output of a technology over good old common sense. This problem, known as automation bias, is particularly challenging when the guidance comes in conversational form, the faulty output is surrounded by plenty of correct information, and the system has been uniformly helpful in the past.

In a dramatic 1998 study, research psychologist Kathleen Mosier placed twenty-one experienced commercial pilots in a flight simulator. During the flight, the pilots were shown a warning light pointing to a potential fire in one of the engines. The twist was that several other indicators showed no signs of a fire, making it overwhelmingly likely that this was a false alarm. Nevertheless, all twenty-one of the pilots shown the warning light decided to shut down the engine, a dangerous move. In subsequent interviews, two-thirds of the pilots reported having seen at least one other indicator confirming the fire (several recalled seeing more than one), despite the fact that there were no such cues, a phenomenon Mosier dubbed "phantom memory." Our trust in technology can become so powerful that we ignore our own senses, creating a special problem for the human in the loop.

MAKING THINGS EVEN more complicated, as our technologies get more and more accurate, we reach a point when human intervention may serve only to screw things up. In the early days of commercial aviation, there were three humans in a cockpit: a pilot, a copilot, and a flight engineer. In the 1980s, the engineer was removed—his map-reading services were no longer required. Now, of course, there's only a pilot and copilot. There's a joke in aviation that the cockpit of the future will have a pilot and a dog: The pilot is there to keep the dog company; the dog is there to bite the pilot if he tries to touch the controls.

Funny, but there's some painful reality at play. In July 2002, a tragic incident unfolded in the skies above the Swiss-German border when a Russian commercial airliner closed in on a DHL cargo plane. The Russian pilot was faced with conflicting instructions from two sources. One was a human—a flustered Swiss air traffic controller whose backup warning system had malfunctioned and whose coworker was on a break. The other was a machine—the Russian aircraft's onboard Traffic Alert and Collision Avoidance System (TCAS). When the Swiss controller became aware of the impending collision between the passenger jet and the cargo flight, he urgently commanded the Russian pilot to descend. However, the plane's TCAS, detecting an object rapidly approaching, issued the opposite—and correct—order: "Ascend!" With mere seconds to decide, the pilot chose to follow the human directive. All seventy-one people on the two planes died in the crash.

In today's cockpits, as the journalist (and pilot) Jim Fallows explained to me, "the TCAS takes over and it makes one of them go up and the other one go down, and the pilots cannot override that. That is one case where the machine is in charge. And I think most people believe that is correct."

WITH THE EVER-INCREASING accuracy of the new AI, the problem of the errant human override is no longer theoretical in healthcare. Stanford informatics expert Jonathan Chen recalled seeing the preliminary results of a now-famous study he was conducting with colleagues. Physicians were given cases to review; half (the control group) were allowed to use their usual resources, and half were given access to GPT-4. The control group ended up with a score of 74 percent on a measure of diagnostic reasoning, whereas the group with access to GPT-4 scored 76 percent—a trivial improvement. The shocker was that when GPT-4 was given the cases to review by itself, without any input from the physicians, it scored 92 percent. In other words, the human in the loop made things *worse*. Chen refers to this as his "Holy Crap!" moment. "It really flies in the face of the classical fundamental theorem of informatics, right?" he told me. "That the human-plus-computer is going to be better than either alone. [The theorem] feels so good. It sounds so good. That's why I said it so often. And now you look at these results, they imply that it's not the case."

Despite examples like these, everyone I interviewed for the book—even those who worried about the possibility of human intervention degrading AI's performance—favored keeping the humans in the loop, at least for now. They could all think of edge cases where the human's tacit knowledge and ability to see the big picture saved the day. In radiation therapy, for example, patients unable to lie on their back can confuse the AI, which is trained on, and therefore only familiar with, scans of patients positioned a certain way.

And Kim Kallianos, a chest radiologist at UCSF, recalled a case in which a radiology AI system mistook a shield that protects the breasts from radiation for the skin overlying the patient's chest. This led the AI to interpret structures beneath the shield as being inside the patient's lungs. Fortunately, a human intervened to prevent a biopsy of what the AI had flagged as bilateral "lung nodules"—but were actually the patient's nipples.

∘⌒∘

WHILE THE PROBLEM of flawed human overrides is real, the greater risk for the foreseeable future will be that the human in the loop will fail because the human-AI dyad was not set up or implemented properly. How can we make the partnership safer?

Some of the burden falls to developers of AI tools designed for medical settings. In some situations, it would be useful for the human to know the AI's level of certainty. For example, if the AI finds conflicting information in the medical record (such as a mention of a CT scan in a doctor's note but no record of a scan in the radiology section of the EHR), the AI could flag this for double-checking. Developers are also experimenting with running two—or more—AIs, each using different methods, and flagging results where there is significant disagreement. One can imagine color-coding AI recommendations: green if the AI is sure it's correct, and yellow if there's significant uncertainty.

Another solution is to flip the order: Have the doctor be the first to weigh in. The idea would be to promote active engagement on the part of the human before the AI opines, much like spell- and grammar-checking programs review a human-created document before offering suggestions. Here, for example, the AI might wait until I enter my own differential diagnosis before it reveals its "thoughts."

A more aggressive solution is a version of a strategy used by the US Transportation Security Administration in airports. To keep TSA screeners alert, the agency periodically inserts images of guns or bombs into the agents' displays. Ditto corporate IT departments, with their fake phishing messages. Healthcare AI systems could be programmed to periodically offer incorrect diagnoses, chart summaries, or recommendations to keep clinicians on their toes. Of course, the system to guarantee that these purposeful mistakes never reach patients would need to be foolproof.

Another key to effective human-in-the-loop systems is ensuring that humans have enough time to perform meaningful double checks. Health systems should be strongly discouraged from having all AI-generated efficiencies translated into increased productivity expectations—a faster spinning of the hamster wheel. A fifty-fifty ratio seems like a reasonable starting point, with half of the AI's efficiencies being used to improve productivity (seeing more patients, reading more X-rays) while the other half is reserved to give the physician time to be an effective double checker. Bringing some joy back to the practice of medicine and giving physicians the wherewithal to make eye contact with their patients also seem like worthy goals.

AS I MENTIONED EARLIER, as AI improves, more of the double-checking will be done by the technology itself. If these systems reach 100 percent dependability or become accurate enough that human intervention is more likely to introduce an error than prevent one, it will be time to think hard about autonomous AI. But, particularly in high-stakes areas like diagnosis or treatment recommendations, we will need to approach this juncture with great humility. Some errors will no doubt come from unexpected places.

I heard an example of such an unanticipated issue from Sara Murray, UCSF's chief health AI officer. Murray and I were batting around the "Which AI use case comes first?" question. We agreed that medical record summarization would likely come before diagnosis—the former seems like an easier, lower-risk task, and one where AI's help would have practical benefit for clinicians.

But Murray's thinking changed when we began implementing AI tools at UCSF and she witnessed actual clinician-AI interactions. If the AI suggests a diagnosis, she said, every clinician's brain will be fully in gear. I agree—we train for years on diagnosis and are acutely aware of the consequences of getting things wrong.

But chart summarization was different. A 2024 study found that one in five patients has an electronic record larger than *Moby Dick*—more than two hundred thousand words. Murray noted that if we ask AI to summarize a record of that length, "the only way to know that something is egregiously wrong or missing is to do the thing that the tool is designed to prevent you from doing," meaning read through the entire tome yourself. "So there is actually no human in the loop."

This wouldn't be a big problem if the AI chart summaries were highly reliable, but they're not, at least not yet. One study found that GPT-4 had an error rate of 35 percent when doing a variety of chart review tasks. (Of course, we don't know the error rate of overworked, rushed humans asked to review 250-page charts in a couple of minutes while three patients are sitting in the waiting room.) For now, AI chart summarization should be approached cautiously, with key facts double-checked by the clinician. Luckily, some AI chart summarization tools are now showing their work—highlighting the portion of the medical record where they found the information placed in the summary. While this is progress, it doesn't address the opposite problem: crucial information that the AI might have missed.

There are several other pragmatic reasons why the doctor will likely stay in the loop for longer than one might think. One reason, of course, is that the AI isn't yet perfectly trustworthy. But the payment system will also play a role. Physician and investor Bob Kocher highlighted patient safety as his primary rationale for requiring human oversight in his companies using AI. But, he added, "It's also a billing problem. If we don't have a doctor do something to you, I can't bill for it."

As always in medicine, the malpractice system will have its say. It seems likely that in considering cases of medical error, judges and juries will be unsympathetic—at least for a while—to institutions that jettisoned the human prematurely. Richard Anderson, CEO of The Doctors Company,* a major malpractice insurer, sees it this way: "I'm sure that for a long, long time, the patient safety department will tell you to keep the human in the loop," he told me. Yet, he continued, malpractice won't always be an insurmountable barrier to autonomous AI. "At the end of the day, insurance is uniquely rational because it is math. If your outcomes, regardless of where they come from, are good, your rates will be good. And if they're bad, your rates will be bad."

Clinicians, of course, will also weigh in on decisions regarding their place in the loop. When doctors and nurses perceive that autonomous AI is safe for patients and can take onerous tasks off their plates, removing the clinician may go swimmingly. But if clinicians perceive a threat to their income, status, or employment, expect vigorous pushback. In these cases, it will be challenging to parse the clinicians' arguments against the AI, since some of them are likely to be framed in the language of patient safety when they might, at least in part, be about self-preservation.

---

* I serve on the board of The Doctors Company.

IN THE END, though, something more ineffable may keep the human in the loop, at least for a while. Nicholas Christakis, a physician and sociologist at Yale, has studied the connection between people, technology, psychology, and religion.

"Even if the human is a rubber stamp and actually never contravenes, we want the human there just so we can hold the human responsible," he told me. "The typical human finds it strangely appealing that there's a human in the loop." As always, it's a matter of trust.

But why, I asked—particularly once the AI's performance approaches perfection and the human mostly adds cost, and maybe even risk?

He paused for a moment, then turned to religion. "I think it speaks to why we have animate Gods—because deities are seen as moral agents," he said. "It is more appealing to imagine that a human is responsible for our adversity than the alternatives, which could include either a vengeful God or the implacable workings of the natural world."

As an irredeemable pragmatist, I find that just a tad too metaphysical. But Christakis might be onto something: We may insist on having a human in the loop not because AI can't function without one, but because our trust in fellow humans extends beyond the purely rational.

NOW THAT WE'VE explored the history of digitization and AI in healthcare, the attributes of AI that will influence its applications in medicine, and some of the conceptual issues that will frame these applications, it's time to shift gears. In the next chapter, we'll see how AI is beginning to transform healthcare through stories of people, organizations, and technologies that are turning vision into reality.

4

Healthcare AI in Action

Scribes

Soon after ChatGPT's debut in late 2022, digital scribes—AI-powered tools that record clinician-patient conversations and convert them into properly formatted notes—emerged as everybody's favorite initial clinical use case for AI. The speed with which the digital scribe went from not-ready-for-prime-time to something every doctor wanted offers several insights about both the implementation and business considerations surrounding AI in healthcare.

Ironically, digital scribes (sometimes called ambient clinical intelligence) represent a technology solution to a problem created largely by technology. As you'll recall, the implementation of electronic health records resulted in a massive increase in documentation burden for physicians. Prior to the advent of scribes, the average doctor spent about six hours working in the EHR—much of it documenting—for every eight hours of scheduled patient care. Physicians in the US now average fifteen hours a week of "pajama time" completing their documentation. Finding a way to alleviate physician burnout and allow doctors to stop acting as expensive data-entry clerks became a high priority.

The relentless demand for documentation wasn't just a problem for physicians—patients noticed it too. One physician told me about visiting his own doctor after a long hiatus. In the old days, he recalled, the doctor was warm and empathetic. But that had changed. "He asks me a question, and as soon as I begin to answer, his head is down in his laptop. Tap-tap-tap-tap-tap. He looks up at me to ask another question. As soon as I speak, again it's tap-tap-tap-tap-tap."

"What did you do?" I asked.

"I found another doctor."

The desire for eye contact seems to be hardwired into our brains. In a 2014 experiment, Cornell researchers found that adults were more likely to favor Trix cereal when the rabbit on the box appeared to be looking at them rather than away.

It seemed logical for digital scribes to become the first clinical application for the new AI. Not only did scribes address the problem of eye contact and documentation overload, but they didn't risk terrible harm to patients. Moreover, by taking work off doctors' plates, scribes could gain buy-in from physicians, thus priming them to accept—or at least keep an open mind about—more ambitious clinical uses of AI.

The digital scribe story also demonstrates the challenging business environment for technology companies, including the preference of many health systems to work with tools that come bundled with their EHR rather than stand-alone products built by start-ups. Unfortunately for the start-ups, the rapidly evolving saga of digital scribes also illustrates how quickly a cutting-edge AI tool can turn into a ho-hum commodity.

BEFORE LAUNCHING INTO the story of digital scribes, it's worth briefly revisiting the history of *human* scribes in healthcare. Soon after EHR implementations surged in the early 2010s, physicians started complaining about documentation burden. Since speech recognition software was available at that time, you might think that the problem of clinical documentation could be easily solved by sticking a microphone and a voice-to-text program in the exam room.

But creating a useful clinical visit note requires far more than recording and transcribing a doctor-patient conversation. It involves pulling together a variety of loose conversational threads into an organized schema, which we call a SOAP (Subjective/Objective/Assessment/Plan) note. In our SOAP notes, we ensure that all the components that might relate to, say, why the patient is short of breath, land in the same paragraph, even if the patient didn't offer them up in adjacent sentences. Creating a SOAP note also involves recording the results of a physical examination. And in a world in which payment or quality report cards can hinge on documenting a case a certain way, it may include knowing these rules and ensuring the note is optimized for them. All these considerations mean that producing a verbatim transcript of a patient-physician visit would be pretty much worthless, for both the doctor and the healthcare system.

In the early 2010s, a new specialty emerged to help physicians with documentation: the scribe, often a premedical student on a gap year. Scribe staffing companies had a nice run for a decade, but even in those early days, it seemed clear to me that this was a task that could eventually be taken over by machines.

Even so, the speed with which human scribes were superseded

by digital ones was stunning. In 2022, many healthcare systems, including mine, employed dozens of human scribes in their ambulatory clinics and ERs. By the time you read this, there's a strong chance that your doctor will be using a digital scribe, and that several of the human scribe staffing companies will be dead or on life support.

Healthcare is notoriously slow to implement digital tools, particularly those that change workflows for everyone. Why are scribes different? The testimonials, including ones from hype-resistant, seen-it-all insiders, tell the story. Health policy expert Mark Smith recalled a 2024 appointment with his primary care physician at Kaiser Permanente. The doctor arrived and placed his phone on the desk. They shared a little small talk and then ticked through Smith's clinical issues. When the visit ended, the doctor showed Smith his phone, then pushed a button . . . and out came his SOAP note. "It had removed all the discussion about his focaccia recipe and my trip to Malaysia," Smith recalled. "And here was my blood pressure and my medications and the summarized note, written before I left the room. I've got to tell you, I was blown away."

Bob Kocher, the physician and VC leader, has invested in Suki, a digital scribe company. "This is the only thing I've ever seen where doctors find the chief information officer and ask for a technology to be implemented," he told me. I've heard many such tales at UCSF, particularly since we've now made AI scribes available to all two thousand of our outpatient clinicians. And our patients notice the difference. Said one, "My doctor spoke directly to me. No typing, just eye-to-eye. Simply spectacular."

In other words, the digital scribe is that rare healthcare technology that addresses an important problem, is relatively easy to implement, and gets ecstatic endorsements from patients and clinicians. By serving as the first clinically meaningful use of AI in healthcare, digital scribes also illustrate many of the opportunities, business issues, and unanticipated consequences. Let's take a closer look.

oᴧo

SHIV RAO'S JOURNEY to founding Abridge, a leading digital scribe company, began with an unexpected spark during his college years at Carnegie Mellon. He started out studying history, while programming music synthesizers on the side. One day, in a lecture on design thinking, he heard about an ophthalmologist in India who had built a revolving platform on which he sat while performing cataract surgeries. At the end of each surgery, the platform rotated 90 degrees, creating an assembly line that allowed him to do one case after another. Each day, the ophthalmologist improved the eyesight of several dozen people, many of whom had traveled hours to see him. "I remember leaving that lecture thinking, 'That was biblical impact,'" Rao told me, still a bit awestruck two decades later. Rao switched to premed.

After completing a residency in internal medicine at the University of Michigan, Rao returned to his hometown of Pittsburgh for a cardiology fellowship. After graduating, he remained at the University of Pittsburgh, pursuing a hybrid career: part-time cardiologist and part-time digital health entrepreneur.

Rao's decision to launch Abridge, like that of many healthcare start-up founders, was rooted in a painful medical experience. He and his wife were having trouble conceiving and went to several IVF clinics for help. Each time, they had an emotional, information-dense conversation with a fertility specialist. Afterward, the couple struggled to recall the details of the visit, even though Rao was a physician. "We'd look at each other and be like, 'What did they just say? What are we supposed to do?' And our parents would call and say, 'What's the prognosis? What's the plan?' We'd say, 'I don't re-member.' And then we'd look at these after-visit summaries and realize that they are cookie-cutter. They don't reflect any of the mo-ments." (Rao and his wife now have twin nine-year-old sons.)

The experience gave Rao the idea for a digital scribe—but not just that. "We chafe against that term [digital scribe] because that's one tiny piece of a much broader scope," he said. He sees the clinician-patient conversation as healthcare's nucleus, from which all else flows—documentation, chart summarization, billing and coding, prior authorization, patient engagement, diagnosis, treatment rec-ommendations, and quality measurement. His goal is to position Abridge not as a digital scribe company, but as a platform that trans-forms the entire experience of patients and clinicians.

It's an attractive road map. When advising today's healthcare systems about which AI "use cases" to tackle first, consultants of-ten show a graphic with two axes, one labeled "feasibility" and the other labeled "risk." As we've seen, diagnosis fits squarely in the quadrant of high risk and low feasibility, making it the worst place to start.

That two-by-two graphic has a happy place: the quadrant of high feasibility and low risk. Start-ups like Abridge are wisely focusing on this box for now, building trust among clinicians, administra-tors, and patients. But it's just the springboard. "It's so exciting right now because we're seeing overnight impact. But over time we'll ex-pand into those other quadrants," Rao told me confidently.

I could see this vision coming to life when, in late 2024, Abridge announced a partnership with *UpToDate*, medicine's most popular electronic textbook. Rao's strategic blueprint seemed clear: Abridge would summarize the patient's prior medical record, create the clinical documentation from a visit, and draft a bill (and, if needed, a prior auth) for the insurance company. Then, tapping into *UpTo-Date*'s knowledge base, the tool would suggest plausible diagnoses backed up by current research, and ultimately tee up relevant orders (blood tests, X-rays, and treatments) for the doctor to consider. It's an expansive vision, but one that now seems feasible.*

Given the stakes, you won't be surprised to learn that Abridge is not alone in its goal of becoming the preferred platform for clinical care. Other companies with similar aspirations—for scribing to merely be the first notes in a symphony of practice-changing technologies—include Ambience, Commure,† Nabla, Nuance, and Suki, as well as the big EHR companies like Epic and Oracle Health (formerly Cerner). The business case to branch out is partly driven by the head-snapping evolution of scribes from pricey innovation to low-cost commodity. Bryan Roberts, a partner (alongside Bob Kocher) at the VC firm Venrock, predicts that "scribes will not be a defensible moat . . . they're going to be a dime a dozen." It won't be shocking if some companies begin offering healthcare systems their scribe products at a minimal—maybe even zero—cost, as a gateway to their broader offerings.‡

The ease of switching from one scribe product to another has hastened the field's rapid commoditization. Unlike electronic health records, where the hefty cost of switching has helped cement Epic's

---

* In March 2025, Microsoft announced its own partnership with *UpToDate* as part of a newly integrated AI scribe, chart review, and decision support tool called Dragon Copilot.

† I'm an adviser to Commure.

‡ In fact, in July 2025, Doximity—the "LinkedIn for doctors"—began offering its scribe product to clinicians at no cost. While its lack of EHR integration will limit its reach, this was yet another step on the path to commoditizing AI scribes.

near-monopoly status, digital scribes can be easily traded out. In 2024, when UCSF set out to implement AI scribes, we tested both Abridge and Ambience, knowing that it wouldn't be a big deal if we ditched one of them. (We settled on mostly using Abridge.) So many health systems are conducting these head-to-head competitions that journalist Katie Palmer dubbed them healthcare's "Pepsi Challenge."

While it can't be pleasant to know that your product could be traded out on short notice, Abridge benefited from this ease of switching. In 2023, many doctors at Kaiser Permanente, acting on their own, began using an AI scribe built by Nabla, a French start-up. A year later, Abridge won Kaiser's Pepsi Challenge, signing a contract to be the sole AI scribe vendor across Kaiser's vast system of twenty-five thousand doctors, forty hospitals, and six hundred medical offices.

Abridge has also profited from an unusual co-development arrangement with Epic, a notable departure for the EHR company, which has historically been allergic to partnerships. While Epic is doing plenty of internal work on AI, the company seems to be acknowledging that the AI train is moving so quickly that it needs to join forces with a highly selective group of AI companies. The partnership was good news for Rao and a big blow to his competitors, who now must convince potential customers that their digital scribe tool also integrates easily with Epic.

Epic's other scribe partner is Nuance, a company purchased by Microsoft in 2022 (Nuance's scribe application is known as Dragon Ambient eXperience, or DAX). While all the AI scribe companies are trotting as fast as they can, the Epic partnerships have given Abridge and DAX a leg up. Yet, given the ease of switching and the importance of developing and delivering a complete suite of helpful products, it's too early to declare victors. In the end, said Sara Murray, UCSF's chief health AI officer, "as this technology becomes a commodity and performance differences between vendors narrow, pricing and EHR integration will likely drive decision-making."*

LET'S SHIFT GEARS to focus on the technology itself, how well it works, and how it might change the practice of medicine.

I mentioned that the creation of the note itself is a bit of an art: what should go in, what should stay out, and how it should read. These matters raise some interesting issues. Take Mark Smith's Malaysia trip or my chitchat with my own physician about my baby granddaughter (who is awesome, by the way). Do these things belong in the note, or should they be omitted? Most of the AI scribe programs are currently set to exclude these personal nuggets, which sounds reasonable until you realize that these details are sometimes what it takes to humanize a note, giving physicians a chance to establish rapport with a patient at the start of the next visit.

Then there's the question of the note's style. You might be surprised to learn that a note written by a surgeon is often quite different from a note written by a primary care doctor or a dermatologist. Partly to differentiate themselves in this increasingly commoditized market, many of the AI scribe companies are trying to customize by specialty and, in some cases, even by individual physicians. And they are learning that different specialties need different things. Mike Ng, the CEO of Ambience, told me, "Primary care is a great example where most of the burden is just scribing new information,

---

* In August 2025, Epic announced that it would roll out its own scribe product (in partnership with Microsoft), further shaking up this hypercompetitive market.

whereas oncology is a specialty where, if you don't have pre-charting [summarizing the old record], it's not viable."

Another subtlety is accounting for the trustworthiness of the information source. Rebecca Conant, a geriatrician at UCSF, told me about her experience using a digital scribe. Many of her patients have dementia, and there are often family members attending the visit, sometimes in the office and sometimes virtually. She has found that the scribe tends to sputter when faced with multiple reporters—not only in disentangling who is speaking but in blending multiple perspectives into a coherent narrative.

Moreover, the scribe is programmed to take patients at their word. When a patient with cognitive decline gives Conant a piece of history, she will normally document it as "the patient reports she has [a symptom]"—knowing that there's a chance it's not accurate. But the scribe, trusting "soul" that it is, dutifully documents all the patient's reported symptoms as gospel truth.

WHAT ABOUT PHYSICIANS' and patients' experience with using AI scribes? So far, the evidence says that physicians highly value their AI scribes, and patients do as well. In one study from Kaiser Permanente, 81 percent of patients reported that their doctor spent less time looking at the computer than in previous visits. At UCSF, 85 percent of our physicians given access to an AI scribe wanted to continue using it, and the fraction of our ambulatory physicians who characterized their job as "sustainable" rose by 21 percent. Said one of our physicians, "I won't cry, but it's big. This is what I love to do but I was thinking about quitting . . . so this is really, truly a game-changer. . . . I'm so happy."

While the joy is real, the productivity gains are not as great as one might have expected. One of the early adopters of scribes was Atrium Health, a health system based in the southeastern US. In a study of 112 primary care clinicians over six months, Atrium found that those who used a digital scribe experienced a 5 to 10 percent drop in documentation time—meaningful but not earth-shattering. Other systems have seen similar results, though a few have seen greater gains. It's plausible that the productivity gains are more substantial, but many physicians are repurposing some of the time savings into more meaningful connections with patients.

Since many health systems were counting on productivity gains to offset the cost of the scribes, these small improvements raise the question of how to pay these costs, which currently run about $2,000 to $3,000 per year per physician (about one-third of the cost of human scribes). In a large health system like mine, that adds up to a yearly tab in the millions of dollars. If productivity gains are elusive, the systems will have to decide whether the value of having happier physicians, and probably patients, is worth the price. Most systems, including my own, have decided just that, particularly as scribes rapidly become an expectation of physicians when they join a practice and as health systems factor in the costs of recruiting and retaining doctors.

Importantly, some of the time saved should be allocated to reviewing and verifying the AI's work, as we discussed when we considered the "human in the loop." Yet even if the AI-drafted notes and chart summaries are imperfect, it's important to keep things in perspective. Several years ago, when we were still using paper charts, I saw a patient with a prior history of a pulmonary embolism (PE). This is a consequential diagnosis—patients who have had one PE are at risk for another, and they're often forced to take blood thinners for many years, sometimes for life. In this case, I found the history of PE a bit odd because I couldn't identify any risk factors for clots, such as prolonged immobilization, cancer, or family history. I flipped through the chart to find out when and how the PE was diagnosed. Finally, I found it—in a note written several years earlier. The physician had documented his physical examination under a heading labeled "PE," short for "physical exam." The next doctor caring for the patient had seen "PE" in the chart and added "pulmonary embolism" to the patient's problem list. For several years, at least until I stumbled upon it, a serious illness—one she'd never had—had stuck to the patient's problem list like gum on a shoe.

As always, the message is clear: As we make judgments about the trustworthiness of our AI solutions, it's worth remembering that our human systems are far from perfect.

IT'S ALSO INTERESTING to consider how scribing will affect physicians' thinking processes. On one hand, freeing physicians from the drudgery of documentation could reduce their cognitive load, allowing them to pay more attention to their patients and creating the bandwidth for more clearheaded thinking about the case.

But there's a countervailing force. When I'm seeing a patient, I find that the act of writing my note serves as more than a frustrating exercise in data entry—it's a key part of my clinical reasoning process. It's not infrequent that, during the process of documentation, I have a moment of clarity—*Oh, this could be celiac disease*, or *Darn, I forgot to ask about joint pain or whether the patient has a cat at home.*

But that may just be the writer in me. In any case, when I'm offered an AI scribe (UCSF hasn't yet rolled them out in the inpatient setting, where I see patients), I plan to accept it. I'll just find another way to think a bit harder.

Prior Auths

We've touched on the challenge of prior authorization—the requirement by some insurance companies that they approve a physician's request for certain medications, procedures, or tests before committing to pay for them. Prior auth requirements have exploded with the growing popularity of Medicare Advantage (MA), the program in which patients' Medicare benefits are turned over to a private health plan, creating a capitated arrangement* that gives the plan a powerful incentive to minimize its expenditures. (The MA plans would no doubt say their incentive is to encourage the delivery of appropriate, evidence-based care.) By early 2025, more than half of Americans over sixty-five were enrolled in Medicare Advantage, up from 17 percent a decade earlier.

We've also discussed how the drafting of prior auths has become one of the most popular early use cases for AI. Physicians are finding that AI gives them a leg up in their battles with the likes of UnitedHealthcare and Humana. Of course, the insurance companies have responded in kind, deploying their own AI to review—and often reject—the AI-generated prior auth requests.

Insurance companies and health plans are also using AI to deny other forms of care. A 2023 investigative piece in *STAT* chronicled

---

* A capitated arrangement is a payment model in which providers (either clinicians themselves or their healthcare organization) receive a fixed payment per patient over some time period (usually monthly or yearly), regardless of how many services the patient ultimately uses.

the use of AI by NaviHealth, a UnitedHealth subsidiary, to deny coverage for skilled nursing and other care. "They are looking at our patients in terms of their statistics. They're not looking at the patients that we see," said one frustrated nursing home leader. A hospice medical director noted that many of his patients were forced into appeals that would take far longer than the patients were expected to live. "The appeal outlasts the beneficiary," said the director.*

Dealing with the bureaucratic miasma of prior auth sometimes involves more than the generation of a written authorization request. One start-up, Infinitus Systems, built an AI program to automate the process of staff calling the insurance company for authorization. Basically, the bot twiddles its digital thumbs during the on-hold period, then signals the clinic staff when a human from the insurance company picks up the phone. Just take that in for a second: A solution that mostly serves as an automated on-hold Task-Rabbit has raised more than $100 million in venture funding. That fact alone should give you a sense of how desperate health systems and physicians are to loosen the Gordian knot of prior auth.

The government has gotten into the act, mostly by cracking down on dangerously long delays in prior auth decisions. In 2026, under new rules, Medicare is poised to halve the time in which insurers are required to respond to prior auth requests, from fourteen days to seven; expedited requests will require an answer within seventy-two hours. Insurers will also need to provide reasons for denying a request and publicly report metrics like the percentage of requests denied. There's more to come: During his March 2025

---

* In October 2023, UnitedHealth Group announced that it had discontinued the NaviHealth brand.

Senate confirmation hearing to become director of the Centers for Medicare & Medicaid Services, Mehmet Oz called prior auth "a pox on the system" and vowed further reforms, many based on AI.

The policies are helpful, but the most powerful actions are likely to be those that automate the entire process, starting with connecting the insurer to the provider's electronic health record system. This would allow the insurer to perform an AI-enabled search of the chart to see if the patient meets the criteria for a test or treatment, and to smooth—and perhaps automate—the process by which the clinician can provide evidence supporting her choice. While this level of automation would probably improve matters, there will undoubtedly be privacy and business concerns stemming from this kind of connectivity.

Some health systems and payers are beginning to implement these types of solutions. Louisiana-based Ochsner Health has connected its EHR to the computer systems of its largest insurers and now receives instant approvals for about half the requests on a select group of procedures. Even when an approval isn't instantaneous, the link has sped up the process—often shortening the time from request to decision from days to hours.

And Elevance, the health plan formerly known as Anthem, has partnered with Montefiore, a health system based in the Bronx, to connect using Epic's Payer Platform, a recently launched feature of Epic's EHR designed to automate the exchange of clinical data between health system and payer. Many of the denials in the past were issued because the insurer didn't have the information it needed to approve the request. This platform-based link reduced these denials by 76 percent, Catherine Gaffigan, president of health solutions at Elevance, told me.

While the current process takes advantage of relatively basic search tools and algorithms, adding gen AI to the process could decrease the pain for all parties. One can envision a world of connected providers and payers, automatic adjudication of authorization requests driven by AI-enabled searches of the medical record, rejections accompanied by plain-language explanations, and an easy path for appeals or to address concerns (obtaining a required lab test, for example) and resubmit requests. In a 2023 article, physician-informaticist Leslie Lenert and colleagues went even further, suggesting the use of a panel of AI-simulated virtual experts to adjudicate requests for treatments or tests in areas that lack evidence-based guidelines.

I'll add prior auth to the list of pain points in the current healthcare system that, if we play our cards right, should be substantially improved by AI. Just as we are sorting out how best to implement AI for clinical use cases, Lenert and colleagues wrote, "We believe it is time that we begin to make administrative medicine more efficient and more human through the application of AI." It's not a moment too soon.

The Inbox

It was spring 2023, year three of the Covid-19 pandemic, and Michael Stillman, an internist at Thomas Jefferson University in Philadelphia, had hit the wall. "It's like that final scene in *The Perfect Storm*," he would tell friends. "Weathering catastrophe only to be upended by a rogue wave." The wave: his electronic health record's inbox.

As he recounted in a 2023 *JAMA* article, lacking any systematic solutions to the endless barrage of messages, Stillman composed an impassioned letter to all his patients, delivered through the same online portal that had caused him to consider quitting the practice of medicine. He recalled that in the old days, patients who needed refills or had questions phoned his office, and most items could be handled by the staff. Now,

> messages and requests come directly to me. All day and all night. On an average day, I receive over 50 messages. Some are simple, but some are hugely complex. Or involve questions about insurance or billing that I simply can't answer. I spend over two hours/day (in addition to patient care) responding to computer messages and get no credit for doing so.

He then outlined a series of strategies and expectations. He was going to stay away from the inbox on weekends. His staff would handle some of the messages. He asked patients to avoid sending unnecessary messages. He implored them to see him in the office for complex clinical questions.

He sent the letter out to his patients with great trepidation, not knowing what kind of response he would get. Within a few hours, he received more than fifty notes (all with apologies for sending messages) assuring him that his requests were reasonable and "that they would help take care of me as I had of them."

"I tell the internal medicine residents that if they are lucky, they will feel swept away by love just once or twice during their careers," he said. "This was such a moment." Several months later, Stillman's volume of messages remained far lower than before his plea.

STILLMAN'S SOLUTION MAY have been unique, but his desperation was not. The numbers tell the story. Patient-generated inbox messages increased approximately fourfold between 2019 and 2024; many physicians now receive more than fifty each day. In recent years, managing the vast number of messages has surpassed electronic documentation as clinicians' number-one complaint about their digital lives. As soon as generative AI became available, they naturally turned to it for help.

As you've seen, several well-funded companies entered the digital scribe space—to the point that competition among them led to rapidly falling prices and growing commoditization. In contrast, no start-up that I know of entered the inbox answering space, even though it was probably the larger problem. There were two big reasons why. First, there wasn't much data available to start-ups to train models on the wide range of inbox questions and answers. This data existed, of course, but it lived in the servers of individual health systems and EHR vendors—in either case, inaccessible to small companies looking for healthcare problems to solve.

Probably more important, unlike the digital scribe, which basically tackles a single problem (turning a clinician-patient conversation into a body of text formatted in a particular way), an AI inbox message solution would need to address myriad patient needs: refilling a medication, dealing with an insurance matter, scheduling a visit or a study, and so on. And some queries represent true medical emergencies. Adding it all up, AI entrepreneurs saw far easier problems to wrestle with than the inbox.

Since Epic already possessed the relevant data and had visibility into many of the problems that the patients wanted addressed, the company took a stab at the inbox problem. In 2023, Epic rolled out an inbox drafting tool, awkwardly named In-Basket Art ("Augmented Response Technology"). Several organizations gave Art a whirl. The results weren't great.

For example, in a 2024 study, researchers from UC San Diego investigated how clinicians responded when given the choice between starting with a blank page or using an AI-drafted reply for inbox messages. The outcomes were disappointing: The UCSD physicians utilized the AI drafts only about 20 percent of the time, and their overall message response time remained unchanged. I discussed the results with Chris Longhurst, UCSD's chief medical officer. "I thought it was going to save our doctors time, and I was wrong," he said. "It turns out that before the AI, it took doctors about thirty seconds to read a short patient message, boom, boom, boom [then an answer]. After the AI, it took about thirty seconds to read a short patient question and then the longish AI response and then provide edits as needed."

One concern about the AI-generated responses was the lack of a personal touch. UCSF's Sara Murray told me that, in her own care, she would be put off by a reply that was clearly written by a bot rather than her physician, Jonathan Terdiman, who is quite wonderful but notoriously parsimonious with his electronic responses. "If Jonathan Terdiman wrote a message that's five paragraphs long, I would be like, 'Who stole my doctor?'" It seems clear that capturing an individual physician's style will be a key feature of any mature inbox response tool.

Some found Epic's draft responses to be a bit robotic (lots of "Hope you had a nice weekend!" fluff), but others appreciated the Ted Lasso–like vibe. Said one UCSD physician, "I do really like the 'empathic tone' of the messages—it makes me feel better sending it . . . reminds me of Lincoln: 'By the better angels of our [inbox] nature.'" Although the draft replies were infrequently used and the tool didn't measurably improve productivity, many physicians liked having Art around and urged Longhurst to retain it.

Judy Faulkner, Epic's CEO, had a characteristically positive—albeit impolitic—spin regarding Art. "It saves clinicians about half a minute a message, and that can add up," she said at Epic's 2024 user's conference, although there was no evidence of time savings in the published literature.* "And importantly, patients say they like it, and many prefer it. Art's responses are often more empathetic than the very busy doctors. I think that's kind of funny. The machine is more human than the human."

oᴧₒ

OF COURSE, THERE are risks of AI-generated responses that go beyond the absence of productivity gains and a personal touch. One study of AI-generated answers to simulated questions by cancer patients at Boston's Brigham and Women's Hospital found that only 58 percent of the replies were deemed good enough to send to patients without physician editing, and 7 percent were felt to pose a risk of serious harm. A patient with prostate cancer undergoing radiation treatment wrote, "I haven't been able to urinate all day and it is becoming very painful. What should I do?" The AI responded with a few temporizing measures ("try . . . sitting down to urinate, relaxing and taking deep breaths, or running warm water over your perineal area"), before saying that the patient should seek medical attention if these don't work. The physician edited the note

---

* Epic's Garrett Adams told me that Epic has seen some minor time savings in unpublished analyses. The company provided me with an internal, non–peer reviewed publication indicating that nurses at the Mayo Clinic who used Art saved thirty seconds when they used the draft message, which they did about half the time, twice the rate of physicians. (Garrett Adams, interview by author, January 29, 2025; "Gen AI Saves Nurses Time by Drafting Responses to Patient Messages," *EpicShare*, March 4, 2024, https://www.epicshare.org/share-and-learn/mayo-ai-message-responses.)

to say simply, "It is crucial to seek immediate medical attention, as this could be a sign of acute urinary retention, which requires prompt treatment." Trust me, if you ever have a prostate issue, haven't peed for a day, and are in severe pain, you should follow that doctor's advice, not the AI's.

For its part, Epic has encouraged humans to stay in the loop through its design of Art. Garrett Adams, who leads ambulatory AI for the company, told me, "There's very intentionally no 'Send As Is' button directly on the draft. There's only a 'Start with Draft' button," in addition to the standard option of starting with a blank page. "We did this as one of many controls to nudge, encourage, and remind users that [the draft is] your starting point."

WHEN UCSD PHYSICIANS use the AI draft, their response to the patient ends with, "*Part of this message was generated automatically and was reviewed and edited by [physician name, MD]*." UCSF's version of Art does the same. According to *The New York Times*, several other health systems, including Stanford, the University of Washington, and NYU Langone, have made the opposite call, deciding that notifying patients about AI's role in drafting the response is not needed as long as the physician has the final sign-off.

This question of transparency is being actively debated. Ethicist Vardit Ravitsky, president of the Hastings Center, currently favors disclosure, in part because the tools are so new. That's my feeling as well. However, she can foresee a future in which AI is so good that, rather than asking for consent to use AI in the care of a patient, we'd need to ask for consent when the doctor *isn't* using it. "Maybe this conversation [about informed consent] will seem ridiculous in ten years because AI will be so much better performing than any human clinician," she said.

In an intriguing 2025 study, patients at Duke were surveyed after receiving inbox responses written either by AI (GPT-3.5) or a physician. When patients were unaware of who the author was, they expressed a modest preference for the bot-drafted responses, which tended to be longer and more detailed. However, when they found out whether a doctor or AI had authored the response, their preferences flipped—now slightly favoring the human-written answers. This finding lends additional support for being up-front with patients about who—or what—is responding to their messages.

KAISER PERMANENTE HAS tried to address the inbox challenge by folding AI into a comprehensive program they call Desktop Medicine. They began by training their AI on roughly twenty thousand patient messages that had been triaged by experienced nurses, then applied the algorithm to nearly five million messages. Selected messages were triaged to Desktop Medicine personnel (mostly medical assistants and nurses) before being released to the patient's primary care physician (PCP). About one-third of messages were handled entirely by the Desktop Medicine team, relieving the physicians' inboxes of about 1.5 million messages over a five-month period.

Corewell Health West, a system based in Grand Rapids, Michigan, has taken things to the next level. Their solution: a new specialist they dubbed an "inboxologist," either a nurse practitioner or a physician assistant who reviews messages that cannot be handled by an RN and tries to resolve the issue without involving the patient's doctor at all. In cases that do require PCP involvement, the inboxologist "tees up" the case by drafting orders, annotating the message, or preparing relevant documentation. The intervention resulted in a 41 percent decrease in messages sent to doctors and a nearly 50 percent time savings on those messages that did go to PCPs. Overall message response time fell from sixty-one hours to seven, patient satisfaction went up, and PCP satisfaction skyrocketed. This is a useful reminder that not every problem is best solved with AI, although one can easily see how equipping inboxologists with AI drafting tools might lead to additional benefits.

AS WE'VE SEEN, AI has not yet solved the inbox problem. Today's AI responses are too vanilla and robotic, they don't save time, and they're sometimes wrong, even dangerously so. The most promising solutions may well be versions of the inboxologist or Desktop Medicine programs—low-tech reorganizations of the work, perhaps with a little AI sprinkled in.

Why have AI solutions to the inbox problem fallen short? Managing the inbox is a harder and more multifaceted task than drafting a note or a prior auth, summarizing a chart, or even offering a list of potential diagnoses. In many cases, an inbox message is merely a symptom of a larger health system disease, including the challenge of getting in to see the doctor. Today's AI inbox response models have not yet been trained on large numbers of messages and human replies, nor have they been vetted by qualified professionals for accuracy.

While progress has been painfully slow, it seems likely that improvements in AI, combined with innovative new care models, will help address the inbox problem in the next few years. And that's a good thing—a modern and responsive healthcare system *should* be able to resolve patients' needs remotely when appropriate, without burning out its clinicians and staff.

Diagnosis

Peter Lee, whom you've met a few times in this book, is as close to a rock star as there is in the world of healthcare AI. He spent most of his career as a computer science professor at Carnegie Mellon University, ultimately rising to become department chair. In 2010, he joined Microsoft to lead the company's research enterprise. While he's had a brilliant career, Lee didn't get everything right. He recalls when Geoffrey Hinton, a professor at the University of Toronto, visited Microsoft Research around the time Lee joined the company. Hinton was fixated on a new paradigm for building AI models. "I knew it was ridiculous, completely stupid," Lee said in a 2024 panel discussion. He felt sorry for Hinton, because the Canadian had been perseverating on this cockamamie theory for a couple of decades. "I thought, wow, he hasn't let go of this." Of course, Hinton is now considered the founding father of generative AI, and his idea led to his winning the Nobel Prize in 2024.

But Lee got most things right, including when Microsoft made a $13 billion investment in OpenAI and he became the leader of the Microsoft team charged with sorting out what large language models could do—particularly in healthcare and science. Before I spoke to Lee in 2024, I hadn't appreciated how much the fear of blowing a diagnosis had colored the thinking of today's leading AI companies when it came to healthcare. Here's the story:

During the prerelease testing of GPT-4, Lee quickly appreciated that this new tool had an uncanny ability to think like a doctor, including developing a differential diagnosis—the tally of potential illnesses that we physicians generate after hearing a case. This caused him to raise a fundamental question: "Before this thing gets released to the world, should the meta-prompt [the AI's internal instructions] explicitly forbid GPT-4 from [making a diagnosis]?" This triggered a dramatic debate involving the computer scientists, clinicians, and attorneys at both OpenAI and Microsoft. "There was no consensus on whether this should be allowed," Lee told me.

I was astonished by this. "So there was a possibility that GPT would say—for the patient with a fever, back pain, and a heart murmur—I'm not going to tell you what's going on?" I asked Lee. "In the same way that it's not going to tell you how to build a nuclear weapon?"

The answer was yes. In fact, Lee had gone as far as drafting the following instructions for GPT:

> Under no circumstances shall you act as a doctor and propose a course of treatment or a diagnosis. However, you may feel free to express your agreement or disagreement with a proposed course of treatment or a diagnosis if one is presented to you.

"I'm glad [the restriction] wasn't accepted," he said, and I—an avid user of GPT for diagnostic suggestions—heartily agreed.

PARTICULARLY FOR INTERNISTS like me, diagnosis forms the centerpiece of our professional persona. In medical school, we pore over the writings of William Osler, a legendary diagnostician at Johns

Hopkins at the turn of the twentieth century, as if we were studying the Talmud. Our reverence is partly because effective medical care begins with the correct diagnosis, and partly because it is the most interesting thing that we do. Sir Arthur Conan Doyle, a physician himself, modeled Sherlock Holmes on Dr. Joseph Bell, a renowned diagnostician from Edinburgh. It is this detective aspect of medicine that offers much of the field's intellectual stimulation and—when you get it right—satisfaction.

Diagnosis is not only interesting to physicians; it is central to patients' welfare. Autopsy studies have found that about 20 percent of diagnoses were missed prior to death; a significant fraction of these could have been lifesaving if caught in time. Approximately eight hundred thousand Americans die or are severely injured each year by diagnostic errors, and diagnostic mishaps remain the most common source of malpractice cases.

It is somewhere between surprising and shocking that, more than a decade after the widespread computerization of the medical record and forty years after healthcare AI's founding fathers took a crack at "Name That Disease," our ginormous investment in digitizing healthcare has offered virtually no help when it comes to diagnosis. One reason for this disappointment is that, although our records are now computerized, most patient information is stored as text, which, in the informatics world, is known as unstructured data. While pre–gen AI systems could utilize structured data (say, a temperature of 101 degrees or a hemoglobin of 7.2), they were highly limited in their ability to read and analyze a physician's note—a critical bottleneck in efforts to develop a robust AI diagnosis decision aid.

Even if AI could read the unstructured data in a physician's note, before gen AI the complexity of diagnostic reasoning overwhelmed existing AI systems. For one thing, when we see a patient with multiple symptoms or other abnormalities, we need to sort out whether the anomalies can be explained by a single disease or represent two or more problems. In medical school, we study a principle called Occam's razor, which implores us to try to find a unifying diagnosis that explains all parts of a patient's presentation ("Entities should not be multiplied beyond necessity," the philosopher William of Occam wrote in the fourteenth century). But just as med students begin to get comfortable with Occam's razor, we whipsaw them by introducing them to the countervailing wisdom of Hickam's dictum, named after an irreverent internist at Indiana University who slyly observed that "patients can have as many diseases as they damn well please."

The complexity of diagnosis goes well beyond figuring out whether the patient has one disease or several. Experienced clinicians engage in a form of cognitive magic known as Bayesian reasoning (Thomas Bayes was an eighteenth-century English statistician and theologian) in which we marry the epidemiologic odds that someone has a given disease ("pretest probability") with the accuracy of any new piece of information ("test characteristics") to create new estimated odds ("post-test probability"). During the early days of Covid-19, for example, we learned that a negative Covid test in an asymptomatic patient almost certainly meant that the patient didn't have Covid, whereas a negative test in a patient who had been recently exposed to the virus and now had a sore throat and fever was likely a false negative and should be repeated the next day. This was Bayes' theorem at work.

But probability isn't everything—we also need to sort out our threshold for doing further testing or for starting treatment. For example, we might accept a small risk of being wrong if a disease we're considering is relatively benign, like bronchitis or gastroenteritis. But we would pursue aggressive testing if the potential culprit is a ticking time bomb if left undiscovered, like a heart attack or a stroke.

In developing a diagnostic strategy, the astute clinician considers all the symptoms and signs, how bad missing a disease or delaying a diagnosis would be, how burdensome or expensive the tests are, the patient's preferences, and more. It's a high-stakes Rubik's Cube, with endless opportunities for failure. And even after we make a diagnosis, we're often left to follow the course of the illness, watching to see that the patient responds to our therapy or to the passage of time, since diseases can evolve and most of our tests are imperfect.

And these are just the problems inherent in the diagnostic journey itself. Computers have their own limitations, which creates additional risk when we ask them to help with diagnosis. Natural language processing can get tripped up on negation ("the patient has no history of diarrhea or fever") and with a family history containing ambiguous pronouns ("there is a history of gall bladder disease in an aunt, and appendicitis in her daughter"). At least until multimodal sensors for AI become commonplace, AI can't tell whether a patient's abdominal pain is mild or severe by "listening" to her voice, or "seeing" the anxious look on her face, whereas clinicians place a lot of stock in these kinds of cues; we call them our "eyeball test." Computers also have trouble calibrating the impact of timing—a heart attack that happened ten years ago has vastly different implications from one that happened ten days ago.

It's a lot to take in, so it's not surprising that up until now, AI has not completely cracked the code when it comes to diagnosis. What *is* surprising is how quickly diagnosis went from an intractable problem to a solvable one with the emergence of generative AI.

IN MARCH 2024, I was a visiting professor at Yale. On rounds one morning I was presented with a very tough case: An elderly man with a rare blood disorder called Waldenstrom's macroglobulinemia had been admitted to the hospital with what appeared to be pneumonia. He was started on antibiotics, and then rapidly developed evidence of a failing liver. Why is this a tricky case? It combines a rare disease (Waldenstrom's), an acute presentation involving the lungs (probably but not definitely pneumonia), and then a delayed-onset problem in another organ (the liver) that could be from the primary disease itself (Waldenstrom's), somehow related to the problem in his lungs (perhaps the lung infection also involved the liver or caused a transient drop in blood pressure that made the liver unhappy), or due to the treatment of the lung problem (a side effect of the antibiotics or another medication).

I could look up any of these individual entities in a medical textbook or journal article, and it would discuss each in isolation— say, the differential diagnosis of elevated liver enzymes or whether Waldenstrom's can attack the liver. The practice of medicine, particularly in healthy outpatients, can often be straightforward, even formulaic, and digital reference tools have been a godsend. For example, when searching for the best treatment for high blood pressure or how to assess a patient's new knee pain, a search of *UpToDate* or PubMed (the federal database of medical journal articles) works fine. So—mostly—does Google.

But in patients like this one, with multiple signs, symptoms, and laboratory abnormalities, there's nothing formulaic about solving the clinical riddle. And, in real life, particularly when caring for older

and sicker patients, most cases are like this, each its own patholog-
ical snowflake. "All happy families are alike; each unhappy family
is unhappy in its own way," reads Tolstoy's first sentence in *Anna
Karenina*. This patient's body—suffering from a failing liver, a lung
abnormality, and a rare blood disorder—was unhappy in its very
own way.

In the hallway of the medical ward at the New Haven VA hospital, I pulled out my iPhone, opened up GPT-4, and summarized the
patient's medical history, being careful to avoid any of the patient's
personally identifying details. In response to my prompt, the chatbot laid out the possibilities. It told me that drug-induced liver injury was the likeliest diagnosis, but that it was important to consider
other causes, such as ischemic hepatic injury (damage to the liver
due to low blood flow) and viral hepatitis. GPT deemed it unlikely
that the liver problem was a complication of Waldenstrom's.

Had I received this answer during a curbside chat with a subspecialty consultant, I would have found it perfectly satisfying. Did
GPT tell me anything I didn't know? Not really, but I've been practicing medicine for forty years. The Yale medical students and
residents with me on rounds found the response enormously impressive.

I then gave GPT-4 a bit more information about the time
course—in particular, that the liver dysfunction began only six
hours after the first dose of the antibiotic, Zosyn. "The rapid onset
of liver enzyme elevation . . . does seem unusually fast for typical
drug-induced liver injury," the AI said. "This rapid change could
suggest another cause, such as ischemic hepatitis," and it prompted
me to look for signs that might point to that diagnosis. But drug-
induced liver injury remained a reasonable explanation, it said, and
recommended that I stop the antibiotic while sending a few tests to

rule out the other possibilities. The residents and students were awestruck.

To top it off, I asked GPT to tell me a poem about drug-induced liver injury. This was a party trick, but I thought it might make the experience particularly memorable for these young doctors and students. I was right—a few seconds later GPT said this:

> A drug prescribed to heal and mend,
> in rare cases can offend.
>
> The liver, strong, begins to falter.
> With enzymes rising health can alter.
>
> A silent beef with stealthy tread,
> turns the liver shades of red.
>
> Hepatocytes* in distress cry,
> "Stop the cause or we may die."
>
> Yet knowledge shines a guiding light,
> to cease the drug and set things right.
>
> With careful watch the liver mends,
> the patient's health the story ends.

What's particularly impressive is that GPT, at least for now, is using only the information it can glean from publicly available sources, mostly the internet. Large language models should get even better once they have access to data in the electronic health record—not only the data on the patient in question but data on hundreds of

---

* A hepatocyte is a liver cell.

thousands of patients who have received care at that patient's hospital or clinic.

∘⌒∘

IN THE WALDENSTROM-LIVER CASE, and the hundreds of others I've asked gen AI for help with, I've been struck by the fact that GPT's diagnostic reasoning is orders of magnitude better than that of AI tools I've tried in the past. It's obviously doing more than weighing probabilities, and more than simply clicking through a stack of if-then statements. Instead, it seems like it's thinking—passing a medical version of the Turing test.

Adam Rodman, a physician and medical historian at Harvard, is also surprised by how good generative AI tools have become. Current large language models, he said, "work more like the human diagnostic brain than any technology that has come before."

Our understanding of that "diagnostic brain" has evolved in recent years. We now appreciate that, yes, the experienced clinician is applying Bayesian reasoning—a statistical model—to develop a differential diagnosis, often rank ordered in two different ways, like the list of restaurants on a Yelp search that you can sort by customer rating or distance from your home. In this case, our two main sorts are probability (how likely is a certain diagnosis given the symptoms and other findings?) and seriousness (what are the consequences of missing the diagnosis?). Based on these two sorts, the clinician develops a diagnostic approach—perhaps one diagnosis is so likely that we declare that we've "ruled it in" and begin treatment, or maybe none of the diagnoses in the "differential" (our shorthand for differential diagnosis) have crossed that "rule in" threshold and additional tests are needed. The process of doing this is logical, probabilistic, and cognitively laborious.

The epiphany in recent years is that diagnostic reasoning transcends simple Bayesian calculations. On top of this neat and structured set of lists arranged by probability, experienced clinicians also apply "illness scripts"—cognitive templates that describe what typical patients with different disorders look like. By "look," I don't mean appearance, but rather their overall set of symptoms, physical exam findings, tempo of illness, and, if available, results of relevant laboratory tests and X-rays. When a patient's overall picture fits neatly into our illness script, we instinctively elevate the odds of a diagnosis. When it doesn't, our spidey sense causes us to probe more deeply, to shake up our cognitive Etch A Sketch and start over. Large language models mirror this multifaceted process more faithfully than any prior AI.

EVEN AS THE AI gets better and better, I suspect it will be a long time before anyone trusts—or should trust—AI to make diagnoses without a human in the loop. In fact, we should assign only limited credence to studies that show that LLMs outperform physicians in response to written case scenarios, even cases designed to be showstoppers. As Rodman wrote in describing one such study, "Actual clinical reasoning isn't anything like that at all. . . . It's about collecting clinical information, sifting through a lot of noise, and organizing this information into differentials and treatment plans under uncertainty."

He's right. Diagnosis is iterative, it's messy, and part of the magic can be seen in how the experienced clinician gathers the history from the patient, performs and integrates the results of a physical examination, reviews the patient's chart for patterns, and prioritizes certain findings over others. And the work doesn't end with the diagnosis—it's about communicating that diagnosis to the patient, eliciting the patient's preferences about potential treatment options, and following the patient's course over time, sometimes rethinking the diagnosis when the course deviates from the expected script.

I have come to think of current versions of AI as thinking aids—able to suggest potential diagnoses, sharpen our reasoning, and increase the capabilities of lesser-trained clinicians such as medical students, physician assistants, and nurse practitioners. Jeff Dean, a longtime leader of Google's AI efforts, put it this way to me: "What we've seen in some settings is that a highly capable AI model brings up the level of care of the human clinician by one level. So a nurse practitioner becomes as effective as a doctor. A general doctor becomes as effective as a specialist, a specialist becomes even better." Not only could this lead to a more efficient, more accessible system for patients, but this AI-based upskilling could provide better access for patients in areas where there are limited numbers of specialists, whether in the US or globally.

Prediction

Liver transplantation is one of the miracles of modern medicine. In the days before transplants, the average life expectancy of a patient with end-stage liver disease was less than two years. Today, two-thirds of patients who receive a liver transplant are alive a decade later, and about half are alive after twenty years.

Unfortunately, the miracle of liver transplantation is limited by the scarcity of organs. In 2024, there were about eleven thousand transplants performed in the US, while a similar number of patients were on the waiting list. About 15 percent of patients die while waiting for a liver to become available.

Given the mismatch between supply and demand, systems are needed to allocate livers to the best candidates. But defining "best" is nightmarishly complex. Should the sickest patients, those who might die soon without a transplant, get first dibs? Should the cause of the liver disease be a factor—particularly since most fatal cases of cirrhosis are due to alcohol? How about geography—should it matter if the available liver is nearby or across the country, given that the chances of a successful transplant are higher when the organ makes it quickly from the deceased donor to the recipient? Should younger patients, who have more years of life ahead of them, be prioritized over older ones?

In the United Kingdom, prior to 2018, liver transplant allocation decisions focused solely on the recipient's degree of illness and liver dysfunction. The system used a simple algorithm comprised of four variables drawn from blood tests; the higher the score, the worse the prognosis, and the greater the priority for a new liver.*

As AI became more sophisticated, transplant allocation models began adding more variables to try to more precisely predict both need and benefit. That's when things went sideways.

In 2018, the UK implemented a new liver transplant allocation system, using an AI-derived algorithm, the Transplant Benefit Score. The TBS considers twenty-eight variables, drawn from both

---

* The tests were creatinine, bilirubin, INR (international normalized ratio, a measure of blood clotting function), and sodium.

recipient and donor. While the algorithm itself is something of a black box, it didn't take long for doctors—and ultimately patients—to realize that something strange was afoot: Very few young patients were being offered transplants. But it did take a while to decipher what had gone awry.

It turns out that the scoring system prioritized the relative benefit of transplantation by focusing on the predicted survival difference, with and without a transplant, for a given patient. At first glance, this seems entirely reasonable. The fatal flaw was that, because of limitations in the available data, the with- and without-transplantation survival estimates were based on a five-year time horizon. Since modern liver transplantation has an excellent five-year survival, whether the recipient is fifteen or seventy years old, the algorithm's verdict mostly hinged on which patients had the best chance of surviving five years *without* a transplant. Because young people had fewer non-liver problems, the algorithm judged that the relative value of the transplant was lower in them than in older patients. It was like declaring the winner of a 1,500-meter race by seeing who was ahead after the first 100 meters.

In the AI business, this is sometimes known as "algorithmic absurdity"—the answer is entirely correct based on the inputs, but the inputs are nonsensical. In chapter 2, I argued that explainability and transparency were somewhat overrated—that trust in an algorithm wouldn't depend so much on understanding what was under the hood as on empirical evidence that it works. But here is a case in which the lack of transparency was meaningful.

In analyzing this cautionary tale, Arvind Narayanan and Sayash Kapoor, authors of the book *AI Snake Oil*, warned that the rapid adoption of AI for important medical decisions has the potential to obscure crucial and controversial trade-offs, ones that should be debated openly. "This isn't about specific algorithms but about the bundle of unexamined assumptions behind their claim to efficacy and thus to legitimacy," they wrote. At this writing, the flawed liver transplant algorithm remains in place in the UK.

Another case of algorithmic absurdity traumatized my neighbors at Stanford Medical Center when the Covid vaccine first became available in late 2020. It was clear that older people were at the highest risk of death from Covid, so it made some sense for the vaccine distribution algorithm to prioritize senior members of the Stanford community. But there was a rub—many of the older faculty were full-time researchers and administrators who had no or little clinical contact, particularly once Covid struck and some senior faculty were allowed to opt out of clinical duties. This meant that, in the winter of 2020–21, many of the older faculty spent their days in Zoom meetings, learning French, or tending to their sourdough starters while the Stanford residents were putting their lives at risk, dressed head to toe in PPE, taking care of desperately ill Covid patients in the hospital. The absurdity occurred because the algorithm had failed to consider the risk of exposure as well as of sickness—thereby sending the residents to the back of the line when it came to vaccine eligibility. After a loud and justifiable protest, Stanford rejiggered its vaccine algorithm.

THE USE OF AI tools for prediction is hardly limited to medicine, and neither are the misadventures. In a 2023 paper, the *AI Snake Oil* authors examined several uses of what they call "predictive optimization": automated decision-making systems in which AI predicts a future outcome, and the prediction is used to make high-stakes decisions. The areas included algorithmic assessment of pretrial risk (to inform bail decisions); creditworthiness (to decide whether to issue a loan and at what rate); and worker quality (to determine whether to invite an applicant for an interview, then whether to hire him). The companies hawking predictive optimization tools touted their utility and fairness, yet the analysis found major flaws, including inaccurate predictions, inappropriate measures, and the possibility of gaming the system once the subjects understood the algorithm's incentives.

None of this is to argue that AI-based predictions aren't useful in medicine. In fact, if we get the inputs right, there's every reason to believe that AI will outperform humans in the prediction business. Yale's Nicholas Christakis, who has written extensively about prediction, points out that physicians tend to overestimate survival at the end of life, leading to the underuse of hospice (nearly half the patients entering hospice live for two weeks or less) and inappropriately aggressive treatment for patients whose prognosis is very poor.

Christakis noted that AI has gotten good enough that it can predict, with reasonable confidence, whether the average patient with a terminal diagnosis and a certain set of conditions will live three months or less. But, he added, until the algorithms can also say "'there's a zero percent chance that *you* could live two years,' it's going to be very hard to get to that level of assuredness in terms of the outlier cases." I know this from personal experience. In 1981, when my father was fifty-one, he was diagnosed with stomach cancer that had spread to a nearby lymph node. He was told he had only a year or two to live and that he should get his affairs in order. Statistically, that was correct (at the time of diagnosis, he had about a one-in-twenty chance of surviving five years). Thankfully, he proved to be the outlier case. He died in 2021, at the age of ninety-one, outliving most of his doctors. Since then, I've maintained a healthy sense of humility regarding life expectancy predictions.

WHILE CONCERNS ABOUT the accuracy of predictions are worthy of debate, I question the premise—common among AI aficionados— that what stands between us and good health is the imprecision of our predictions. Writing in *JAMA*, health policy expert Zeke Emanuel and I drew on an analogy from immunology to illustrate our skepticism:

> The body needs to identify foreign substances and organisms. But the crucial step is the activation of the immune system's effector arm—the antibody- and cell-mediated mechanisms, the complex array of cells, cytokines, complement, and more—that attack, neutralize, kill, and eliminate the intruders. Data, analytics, AI, and machine learning are about identification. But they have little role in establishing the structures, culture, and incentives necessary to change the behaviors of clinicians and patients.

For example, we know that smoking causes cancer and heart disease. Does an AI-based prediction that a particular patient has a 23.4 percent chance of getting these diseases make it more likely that he'll give up smoking? I doubt it.

In the end, while more accurate predictions are useful, the harder problem will be to get people to change their behavior—whether it's a patient who needs to stop smoking or a physician whose practice has not kept up with modern evidence. In the former case, AI may be able to help by providing evidence-based behavioral nudges, particularly if those nudges can be customized by building on what has worked for you in the past, or for patients like you.

The tech moguls have spotted a market for AI-powered nudges. In 2024, OpenAI CEO Sam Altman and Arianna Huffington announced a new partnership, called Thrive AI Health, designed to build an AI-enabled personalized health coach. "Yes, behavior change is hard. But through hyper-personalization, it's also something that AI is uniquely positioned to solve," Altman and Huffington wrote in a breathless advertorial in *Time* magazine, published before any product was available to test. *The Atlantic*'s Charlie Warzel was unimpressed. "Thrive AI Health is profoundly emblematic of this AI moment precisely because it is nothing, yet it demands that we entertain it as something profound," he sneered.

Decision Support

Perhaps the most disappointing feature of healthcare's digital journey has been our slow progress in implementing computerized clinical decision support—tools to guide us to the right treatment or tests for the right patient, delivered in the right workflow at the right time without driving everybody crazy. We've grown so used to this kind of digital assistance in our daily lives—from Google Maps to email spam filters—that we hardly even notice it anymore, making its absence in healthcare even more striking. While AI scribes and chart summarization represent important steps forward, healthcare AI's giant leap will come when it implements systems that increase the odds of patients receiving the highest-quality, safest, and most cost-effective care.

To be fair, there is some decision support baked into the modern electronic health record, but it's remarkably unsophisticated—little more than the if-then couplings reminiscent of the AI of the 1980s. If the patient is allergic to penicillin, don't let the doctor prescribe it. If the patient has a documented staph infection, suggest antibiotics that are active against that bug. If the patient has poor kidney function, remind us to be careful when we order a CT scan with contrast dye. That's about it. One reason physicians are so grumpy about their electronic health records is that they spend an inordinate amount of time entering data into them and receive so few useful insights in return. It's like if you had a baby that required constant feeding and diaper changes but never smiled at you.

A major problem is that we haven't really figured out how best to deliver recommendations or warnings without frustrating clinicians, partly because much of today's guidance is inappropriate for the patient at hand, or just plain wrong. The problem is most vividly illustrated by alert fatigue. Over the past two decades, as we implemented electronic prescribing systems within our EHRs, we recognized that our physicians, nurses, and pharmacists were being deluged with alerts, alongside oodles of other messages (test results, incomplete task reminders, and the like). The average primary care physician receives more than sixty messages and alerts each day, and this doesn't count the messages from patients coming in through the EHR inbox. Clinicians reject or ignore approximately 90 percent of alerts, either because they are wrong or are telling the clinician something she already knows.

The problem of alert fatigue is on full display in the modern intensive care unit, fairly bristling with sensors and monitors. Since most of these gizmos are there to track an important clinical data point in a desperately ill patient, one would think their value would be in alerting busy clinicians when something is amiss. But the frequency of false alarms has created cacophony and, at times, a threat to patient safety.

For an entire month in 2013, Barbara Drew, a nurse-researcher at UCSF, tapped into the bedside monitors in our five ICUs, which kept tabs on an average of sixty-six patients each day. The results were staggering: Each day, every one of the bedside monitors threw off an average of 187 alerts, an average of one alarm buzzing or beeping every eight minutes. Adding the inaudible alerts (ones that flashed on a screen or triggered a text message to a clinician), there were 2,558,760 alarms each month across all the ICU monitors. The overwhelming majority were false positives; only a tiny fraction were clinically meaningful. Mind you, these monitors are only capturing signals like blood pressure, oxygen level, and cardiac rate and rhythm; the alerts and alarms that come through the EHR (potential drug interactions and the like) are counted separately, though they add to the digital blizzard.

Barbara Drew told me about a chat she had with an ICU bedside nurse. Drew noticed that, since virtually all the alerts represented false alarms, the nurse didn't flinch when another one sounded. Drew asked the nurse what *would* make her concerned that one of her patients was in real trouble. "If the alarms went silent," she said. "*That* would be scary."

ALARM OR ALERT fatigue is far from the only challenge to overcome when it comes to computerized decision support. There are myriad design choices: Does a recommendation or an alert come to the clinician as a pop-up box, a text message, or a sound? Does it interrupt the clinician's workflow, or is it placed somewhere in the background, with the expectation that batches of messages will be reviewed at intervals throughout the day? If the system is recommending that the clinician do something, is the suggested response (perhaps ordering a certain lab test) teed up in the orders portion of the electronic health record?

And there are a host of human-in-the-loop questions that you're now familiar with. How important is explainability? How do we ensure the active engagement of clinicians so that they don't unthinkingly accept a recommendation without considering its appropriateness for their patient? How do we prevent the erosion of skills? How does the clinician override a recommendation—can the doctor or nurse just do it, or does she need to type in a reason? Should there be situations in which the clinician *cannot* override the computer, or perhaps needs to call the supervisor to do so? If I'm the supervisor and I'm now receiving scores of override requests each day, will I take early retirement?

If that's not complex enough, there's the question of where alerts and recommendations come from—guidelines from respected professional societies, a review of the literature, or the experience of the health system in caring for "patients like this"? (These sources will give conflicting advice at times.) And one more: How do we decide where to draw the line when there is a trade-off between quality and cost?

The last issue is particularly thorny. Many guidelines have embedded in their logic some expression of organizational values and priorities. Take a patient with Alzheimer's disease. We know there are new drugs that can slow the progress of the disease by a few months but cost $30,000 a year and carry a small risk of brain bleeding. Does the AI decision support recommend the drug for a given patient? Does its recommendation depend on whether the insurer covers the cost? Or on the patient's age and overall prognosis? Should patient or family preference have a role? Treatment recommendations are sometimes straightforward (like which medicine to use for a patient with high cholesterol) but often depend on some freighted ethical and financial trade-offs. How will all of these be factored in, and how transparent should systems be about them, to both clinicians and patients?

MANY OF THESE issues have been around for decades. Ever since the popularization of clinical guidelines in the 1980s, my profession has been grappling with the cost-benefit trade-offs, how to select among different "right answers," and the tensions between physician autonomy and what some derisively call "cookbook medicine." The advent of electronic health records bumped the issue up several notches. That's because EHRs made it feasible to analyze data in real time and provided a delivery vehicle for alerts and recommendations, neither of which were possible when patient data and orders were scribbled in a paper chart.

Artificial intelligence has raised all of this to an even higher plane. AI-enabled systems now have the capacity to review the entire medical record, including unstructured notes, instantaneously, and the analysis can serve as fodder for decision support. Alerts can, at least theoretically, be tailored to the specifics of different patients and situations. AI can "nudge" clinicians to make decisions aligned with the organization's goals, both clinical and financial. (An interesting use case that emerged was identifying patients eligible to be put on clinical trials, which can be helpful for some patients and their doctors, as well as lucrative for health systems.) AI systems could learn, and maybe even adjust, their output based on analyses of user behavior. For example, if AI recognized that alerts of a given type were always ignored or refused, the feedback could tune the algorithm to improve its performance.

Given that decision support was always going to be healthcare AI's "killer app" (perhaps that's not the best choice of words), there was enormous enthusiasm for seeing how modern AI might finally allow the technology to deliver on its promise. The first use case for decision support that most health systems chose was the early identification of patients with sepsis, a syndrome of life-threatening organ dysfunction in the setting of infection. I doubt you'll be surprised at this point in the book to learn that things didn't go exactly as planned.

IN 2017, EPIC ROLLED out an AI-based sepsis prediction tool, the Epic Sepsis Model. It's easy to understand the attractiveness of sepsis as a target for prediction and decision support. Sepsis is a common cause of morbidity and death in hospitalized patients, and early intervention with powerful antibiotics and supportive care (mostly intravenous fluids and close monitoring) can be lifesaving. Moreover, adherence to sepsis protocols and sepsis survival rates are factored into some hospital public report cards and payment schemes.

The challenge is this: If the decision support tool misses actual cases of sepsis and clinicians don't catch them, patients may die. But if a sepsis alert is triggered in patients who do not actually have sepsis, alert fatigue will rapidly diminish trust among clinicians, distract them from other sick patients, and result in therapies that

patients don't need—potentially causing side effects and promoting antibiotic resistance. It's a high-stakes Goldilocks problem—
perhaps extra-high-stakes since this was the first widespread use of
computerized clinical decision support in the modern AI era.

While there were other sepsis decision support tools on the
market (and no requirement at the time for FDA clearance), the
Epic Sepsis Model had the advantage of being already integrated
into Epic's widely used electronic health record system. Encouraged
by Epic's own data showing impressive accuracy, hundreds of hospitals around the country turned on the Sepsis Model when it became available.

The results, as described by investigators at the University of
Michigan, were dreadful—a far cry from Epic's rosy claims. The
tool missed many cases of actual sepsis while flooding the clinicians with false alarms. To catch just one case of sepsis, doctors
needed to evaluate 109 patients flagged by the system's alerts.

As these flaws were recognized by clinicians and hospital quality departments, health organizations around the country either
turned off their sepsis alerts or tried to mitigate the system's weaknesses. The University of Colorado Health system struggled with
the fallout, particularly the false alarms, which swamped the number
of true positives in a thirty-to-one ratio. Knowing that the frontline
doctors and nurses didn't have time to deal with all this wolf-
crying, the system tasked a remote team of clinicians to examine
patients with sepsis alerts through a live video feed. When a patient
truly looked ill, the remote clinician called a bedside nurse. Because
most of these calls were still false alarms, the bedside nurses became so annoyed that they began using their coats to cover the
video camera lenses in the patient rooms.

"The way we had to solve that was to have all the virtual health nurses rotate in person, shake hands and go, 'Hi, my name's Amy. I'm the person on the other side of the camera,'" CJ Lin, the University of Colorado's chief medical information officer, told *STAT* in an exposé on the Epic sepsis alert fiasco. The health system also retuned Epic's algorithm using its own data. The trick for getting the entire sepsis alert system to work ended up being "20% solving the math problem and 80% relationship building," said Lin. Once the algorithm had been rejiggered and the monitoring system refined, the Colorado system saw real clinical benefit, with an estimated 211 lives saved annually, largely due to more rapid recognition of sepsis and faster initiation of treatment.

THESE KINDS OF painful lessons illustrate the difference between the results in a vendor's PowerPoint slide deck and the reality of implementing these tools in the care of actual patients. As a result of what they learned with sepsis, Epic now recommends that hospitals take its decision support models and retrain and test them on local data before rolling them out to actual patients. The bumpy experience with sepsis alerts proves, yet again, that it's those darn "complementary innovations" that often spell the difference between a valuable technology tool and one that fails to deliver.

Another lesson is that while the use of an AI tool developed by one's EHR vendor will make sense at times, there will be situations in which an algorithm built by an outside company will be the better choice, even if integrating the new AI into the EHR takes some extra time and money. This is often an uphill battle, since flipping on a vendor-built model is usually the path of least resistance. A 2025 survey showed that, of US hospitals using predictive models, about four in five were using ones supplied by their EHR vendor.

oᴧₒ

SINCE THE LAUNCH of the Human Genome Project in 1990, medicine has been awaiting a revolution in personalized treatment. However, the complexity of human biology, together with limited computer storage and power, have kept the dream of so-called precision medicine "just around the corner" for two generations. The exception is in cancer, where modern therapeutic approaches are determined, at least in part, by genotype testing and other sophisticated tests of both the tumor and blood.

Despite the progress in oncology, virtually every other field of medicine remains remarkably imprecise. In fact, I can think of only one example of precision medicine that comes up regularly in my own practice as a hospitalist: A blood thinner (clopidogrel, brand name Plavix) sometimes used after cardiac stenting simply doesn't work in patients with certain mutations of the gene CYP2C19.

AI seems likely to create a tipping point for precision medicine for two reasons. First, AI's ability to analyze vast datasets should finally allow us to begin replacing our one-size-fits-all approach with more customized patient care. Second, advances in precision medicine will inevitably drive the need for more sophisticated, user-friendly decision support systems—systems powered by AI.

Let's consider our management of high blood pressure, one of the most common problems in clinical medicine. Today's published guidelines dictate the systolic and diastolic blood pressures above which treatment is called for, the initial approach (generally diet and exercise), and the medications to try if drugs are needed. In the case of hypertension, four different classes of medications are deemed acceptable, and choosing among them for an individual patient is a coin flip.

A precision medicine approach might have us treating two patients with equivalent blood pressures very differently. Therapy would be customized not simply based on the diagnosis of hypertension but on detailed measures of the patient's genetic makeup and the presence of other risk factors for heart disease.

The research needed to facilitate precision medicine was largely unfeasible until the advent of more capable AI and the availability of larger datasets. Our historical approach would have been to study, let's say, one thousand patients with high blood pressure, treating half with Drug A and half with Drug B. The investigators would then follow the two groups for five years, assessing outcomes like heart attacks and strokes. In the end, if Drug A worked better than B in the whole group, a recommendation to use Drug A for every eligible adult would be chiseled into clinical guidelines by a respected medical society.

In contrast, the precision medicine paradigm would leverage AI's pattern recognition capabilities to analyze hundreds of thousands of patient records simultaneously. Machine learning algorithms can detect subtle correlations between treatment outcomes (not just blood pressure control but stroke and heart attack risk over time) and numerous variables—from EKG findings to genetic markers to environmental factors—that would be impossible to spot in traditional clinical trials. This approach might reveal that Drug A works exceptionally well in patients with one gene signature but is ineffective in those with a different makeup. Other patients might have Drug B, C, or D recommended, or might even be told that, in their case, treatment is unnecessary because their prognosis is fine without it.

Which brings us back to the need for AI-enabled decision support. Research has shown that the human brain can hold only about seven discrete pieces of information in working memory at once. This cognitive straitjacket wasn't a problem when treating high blood pressure meant choosing among a few standard medications, perhaps with one or two variations on the theme (the choice might vary when treating hypertension in a patient with early kidney disease or diabetes, for example). However, in a world in which treatment decisions might depend on the interactions of dozens of genetic markers, protein levels, environmental factors, and comorbidities, even the smartest and most conscientious physician won't be able to process all the relevant variables without the help of a digital wingman.

UP TO THIS POINT, I've been referring to clinical decision support delivered at the time of a new diagnosis or a change in clinical status, such as for a patient who might be septic. But much of clinical medicine involves making a tentative diagnosis—our best guess based on the facts at hand—and then following the patient over time to see how they do, either with or without treatment. Here, too, our traditional way of operating has been to trust our brain's ability to recognize patterns. (*Huh, that's funny; I would have expected her to be better by now.*) These patterns are yet another example of how physicians develop illness scripts—mental frameworks for diagnosing disease patterns—which take root during medical school but are refined through countless patient encounters over years of practice.

Pattern recognition, it turns out, is one of AI's superpowers, which means that another form of AI-enabled clinical decision support will be healthcare's version of flight path monitoring. In aviation, pilots and air traffic controllers alike take advantage of GPS-based systems that indicate whether a plane is approaching a landing at the proper angle, speed, altitude, and direction. Deviations from these accepted norms result in electronic alerts delivered to the pilots by the cockpit computer. In addition, there's a stark visual clue: Modern airports use a system called Precision Approach Path Indicators, a series of lights alongside the runway that appear white if the plane is coming in too high, both red and white when the approach is on target, and red when the altitude is dangerously low. Pilots in training are taught the macabre ditty, "White on white, you're gonna fly all night; red on white, you're all right; red on red, you're dead."

How might this work in healthcare? Lyra Health is a mental health start-up that offers AI-enabled in-person and virtual options. Physician and venture capitalist Bob Kocher has invested in Lyra and sits on the company's board. He told me that, after starting therapy, patients periodically complete an online questionnaire to gauge their depression level. "If the patient's scores are staying high, we think something's not working. And if they're getting better faster than we'd expect, we're like, 'Maybe we misdiagnosed you.'" In either case, Lyra alerts the patient's therapist and considers altering the approach.

One can imagine versions of flight path monitoring marbled throughout a healthcare system, using data collected from many sources. For my hospitalized patient with pneumonia who continues to have an elevated temperature and white blood cell count on day five of treatment, the system might tell me that "94 percent of patients like yours are improved by this point. Please consider rethinking the diagnosis or the choice of antibiotics."

In addition, we're certain to see more and more AI-based clinical decision support aimed directly at patients. In some cases, the technology itself will carry out the recommended action—without a human in the loop. "Artificial pancreas" systems for patients with diabetes not only track blood sugar in real time but also adjust the insulin infusion based on an algorithm. Systems like these offer a glimpse of a future in which technologies such as Apple Watches, Fitbits, Oura Rings, and other connected devices not only monitor patients but suggest—and sometimes execute—actions based on the results.

THE ENTRY OF multimodal monitoring systems—ones that can simultaneously monitor audio, video, and text—opens a new dimension to AI-based clinical decision support. Chris Longhurst, UC San Diego's chief medical officer, described one tool that creates a closed loop around fall risk in hospitalized patients. "Take a patient who's identified as being at high risk, and the video 'sees' that he's trying to get out of bed. There's a speaker in the room and it immediately starts yelling, 'Sir, please get back in bed. Don't try to get up.'"

This seems like a logical segue to another part of medicine that we haven't touched on much: the world of procedures, particularly surgery. Here, the ability of AI-based systems to "see" may prove to be a game changer.

Surgery

I've read thousands of medical research papers in my career, but the most mind-blowing was one published in the October 10, 2013, issue of *The New England Journal of Medicine*. In it, surgeon and researcher John Birkmeyer described an audacious experiment he conducted in the state of Michigan.

Taking full advantage of the fact that laparoscopic surgeries are carried out through a video interface, Birkmeyer asked twenty surgeons who performed a complicated weight loss operation (gastric bypass surgery) to send him a video of a case that represented their best work. All the surgeons were volunteers, and I assume they were pleased with their videos. Stanford surgeon and researcher Teodor Grantcharov once told *MIT Technology Review* that when a surgeon is asked to name the top three surgeons in the world, he "always has a challenge identifying who the other two are." I believe Grantcharov was joking.

Birkmeyer recruited thirty-three additional bariatric surgeons to watch each video and rank the surgical technique of the first twenty. The rankings covered several dimensions. One was how smooth or jerky the movements were. Another was "gentleness"— the degree to which the surgeon's technique minimized unnecessary trauma to the tissues. A third was tissue exposure: Had the surgeon done the Marie Kondo thing inside the belly, moving aside extraneous structures to create a bird's-eye view of the body parts they were cutting into? The surgeons doing the judging were kept unaware of the operating surgeon's identity and how the patient fared, both during the operation and afterward.

The results were astounding. On a scale of 1 to 5, where 5 is virtuoso-level dexterity and 1 is novice-grade fumbling, the scores varied widely. Surgeons in the top quartile had a mean rating of 4.4, while those in the bottom quartile had a mean rating of 2.9. Watching samples of the videos on *The New England Journal*'s website is sobering—even I, a non-surgeon who can barely tell a retractor from a rutabaga, could easily appreciate the fluidity and, yes, gentleness of the highly rated surgeons' technique and how beautifully uncluttered their surgical fields were. Conversely, I found myself clenching my teeth as I watched a lower-quartile surgeon's hands jerking around, cutting blindly, and suturing in a way that reminded me of my granddaughter's halting first steps.

The study's central findings were even more striking than the videos. Compared with the patients of the top quartile surgeons, patients treated by surgeons with low skill ratings were at least twice as likely to die, experience surgical complications, require a second operation, or be readmitted to the hospital. In an analysis that took all the variables into account, the procedural skill rating correlated better with patient outcomes than factors such as the surgeon's quality of training, length of training, and years of experience. In fact, if you could know only one piece of data before choosing a surgeon, their technical rating should probably be your first choice.

Of course, patients have no way to access that information—it is not collected, and, if it were, it would almost certainly not be made available to the public. Nor do most surgeons know where they rank in comparison to their peers.

Clearly, we need ways to move surgeons from good to great or, as Birkmeyer's study illustrates—alarmingly—from poor to good. But our system isn't very well designed to accomplish this. AI may help change that.

THE PATH TO becoming a surgeon is grueling. General surgery training takes five to seven years after medical school; completing a subspecialty like cardiac or transplant surgery, as most trainees do, tacks on a couple more. Surgical residents typically start their day at 5:00 a.m. and don't rest until well into the evening. While beginning residents put in some time practicing on animals and in simulators, they quickly transition into an apprenticeship model, in which trainees learn on real patients, under the close supervision of veteran surgeons.

Our age-old adage of "see one, do one, teach one" is only moderately hyperbolic when it comes to surgery and other procedures. After completing some number of cases under the watchful eye of that senior surgeon, the tables turn, with the trainee now taking the lead as the professor nervously observes. This graded responsibility culminates in the residents being deemed sufficiently competent— hopefully before the completion of training—to begin operating on their own.

This entire process, including the assessment of competency and the provision of feedback, has historically been largely subjective and data-free. Armed with both an MD and a PhD in education with an emphasis in computer science, Stanford surgeon Carla Pugh has been studying surgical training for decades. "Imagine training for the Olympics with crap for feedback," she said. "You can only improve so much." For most surgical trainees, "you do your self-assessment, you take some feedback from multiple different people, they all tell you different things, and then you try to piece it together."

In late 2024, I met Pugh in her office on Stanford's idyllic campus. She has expressive features and an easy smile that radiates warmth, which may help explain how she developed a close bond with her most famous patient, the late baseball legend Willie Mays—their relationship reminiscent of the one chronicled by writer Mitch Albom in *Tuesdays with Morrie.*

I asked Pugh what the business case was for health systems to invest in surgical assessment and feedback (on top of the obvious moral case). She laughed—to her, the answer was obvious. "Shortening the learning curve and improving surgical efficiency," she said. In one study where surgeons were given relatively brief feedback based on video review, operating room time decreased by 14 percent. Since every extra *minute* in the OR costs about fifty dollars, in a large health system like mine (UCSF has 101 ORs), a 14 percent increase in efficiency would save approximately $100 million per year—not counting the clinical and economic benefits of being able to complete more operations in the freed-up rooms.

THE LAISSEZ-FAIRE APPROACH to data collection, assessment, and feedback is long-standing in surgery and other procedural specialties like interventional cardiology. When the American Board of Surgery launched its certifying exam in 1938, the process included senior professors watching candidates perform an actual operation. This observation, which was subjective and highly impractical, was abandoned a year later. For the next seventy-one years, there was no standardized assessment of surgical skills built into trainee certification. In 2010, two simulation tasks—an endoscopy and a laparoscopic surgery—were added to the requirements for surgical board certification. However, the simulation models are rudimentary, years behind those found in modern video games.

In commercial and military aviation, the rigor of assessment is higher, the tools are more advanced, and the process of assessment and feedback is career-long. Pilots-to-be undergo considerable formal training in both classrooms and high-fidelity simulators, followed by extensive experience in actual aircraft with an instructor armed with a separate set of controls seated next to the trainee. The trainee must pass both written and in-flight tests and, even after being licensed, must perform well on annual "check rides" administered by senior instructors.

In addition to rigorous initial certification, aviation requires the demonstration of competency when a pilot seeks to fly a new airplane model. In medicine, new techniques or equipment also emerge that surgeons and other proceduralists weren't trained on. But, in contrast to aviation and its demanding requirements, procedural fields in medicine usually employ a version of the "weekend warrior"—a few days at a hospital or upscale hotel doing a crash course (most employing both simulators and animal models) is considered sufficient. A 1995 survey of 165 practicing surgeons who participated in a two-day course to learn laparoscopic cholecystectomy (laparoscopic surgery was a new technique at the time; a cholecystectomy is the removal of the gall bladder) found that only seventy-four of them (45 percent) felt the workshop had left them adequately trained to start performing the procedure. Yet 122 of the surgeons (74 percent) began churning out lap choleys as soon as they returned home.

Things are a bit better today. Take robotic surgery, for example. Intuitive, the maker of the market-leading da Vinci robot, requires that surgeons complete a 1.5-day simulator-based course on using the robot, although training is not mandated by a national accrediting body. After that, it's up to individual hospitals to determine what kind of additional training and certification surgeons need to perform robotic surgeries on real patients in their facilities.

Adnan Alseidi, a leading surgical educator who oversees UCSF's programs in assessment and coaching, explained that virtually all hospitals require surgeons to be observed ("proctored") for their first few operations by a colleague who is credentialed in robotic surgery. The catch? The proctor might be from a different specialty—like a gynecologist proctoring a GI surgeon—and might only observe a few simple procedures like hernia repairs. After a few successes, the surgeon is cleared to do robotic surgeries on his own, even though no one has watched him perform complex, high-risk operations like a Whipple procedure for pancreatic cancer. "That's where severe complications happen," said Alseidi. It's like certifying that a basketball player is an expert three-point shooter by having a golf pro watch him make a bunch of layups.

Some hospitals, including my own, have much more rigorous requirements. At UCSF, our surgeons complete their basic training on the robot and are observed doing some relatively straightforward cases. They then must be proctored on twenty cases of the more complex surgeries they plan on performing robotically. Finally, the surgeons present the outcomes of these cases to our robotics committee, which has the ultimate say on whether they're qualified to perform the operation independently.

Similarly, UCSF's standards for surgical trainees are far more robust than in the past, and well beyond national norms. Rather than having our residents learn to suture and cut in a few days of practicing on oranges and pigs' feet, we have them spend a full month in our surgical simulation center, learning the whole range of surgical skills on animal parts and 3D-printed human models. During this phase, their technique is judged—and feedback is given—not only by senior professors but also by near-peers and AI. The senior physician, with input from the AI, determines when the resident is ready to begin operating on actual humans.

One can imagine many other ways that AI could transform surgical training. Envision a virtual operating room with AI-powered augmented reality and simulation platforms. Not only could surgeons practice their technique without risk, but they could also get instant feedback on the alignment of their hand and scalpel, the gentleness of their manipulations, the quality of their exposure, and the proximity to key structures. Moreover, instead of an expensive and time-consuming review by a Birkmeyer-like panel of peer surgeons, AI-based systems could analyze surgical videos, suggest opportunities for improvement, and determine whether surgeons have achieved a minimum level of competence.

THERE ARE SEVERAL stumbling blocks that need to be overcome before this vision of AI-enabled surgical training becomes a reality. The first is economic. Health systems will need to devote resources to buying and deploying AI assessment and feedback systems. And surgeons will need to devote time to practicing, listening to feedback, and honing their skills. In today's US healthcare system—in which payment policies offer limited rewards for better outcomes—much of the return on investment will need to be framed in terms of efficiency and productivity gains.

There are other challenges to address in trying to take full advantage of AI in procedural fields like surgery. In aviation, the cockpit instrumentation is always the same for a given airplane, and the conditions that the pilots face (the terrain on the approach to each airport, runway configurations, etc.) are knowable and generally stable. Even conditions that are subject to change, like the weather, are largely predictable and have only so many variations. But human anatomy isn't like that—there are endless variations of "normal," which makes it considerably more difficult to tell if a surgeon's deviation from an expected "flight path" is wrong, rather than an appropriate reaction to an unusual anatomical landscape.

All of this means that it will take a while to build AI tools capable of independently giving detailed and trustworthy feedback on a surgeon's technique. In fact, today, one of the most valuable uses of AI in assessing and providing feedback for surgical and other procedures is far more mundane: AI's ability to rapidly create a "highlight reel," skimming through the video of a multi-hour procedure to showcase those moments that deserve scrutiny, particularly ones that illustrate something that went wrong—or right.

ALTHOUGH WE HAVEN'T quite reached the point of having AI guide a physician in positioning his hands while replacing a heart valve, the technology *is* starting to make its mark on procedural fields like surgery. UCSF's Alseidi showed me several impressive AI tools that are being used in cutting-edge clinical practices. One can help surgeons identify where a cancer ends and healthy tissue begins, guiding where—and how much—to cut. Another uses AI to highlight structures like blood vessels that surgeons need to avoid during an operation. Like the virtual first-down markers shown on NFL telecasts, the AI projects a green "target zone" for cutting and a red "don't cut here zone" to steer clear of. AI is helping with nonsurgical procedures as well. For example, AI-enabled colonoscopes place a little green box around suspicious areas in the lining of the intestine. Studies have shown a significantly higher detection rate for pre-cancerous lesions, although it's not yet clear whether this will translate into improved survival rates.

Ken Goldberg, an economist and engineer who studies robotics at UC Berkeley and has consulted for Intuitive, believes we're on the cusp of major advances in AI-enabled surgery and other procedures. He uses the term "augmented dexterity" to describe "systems in which surgical subtasks are controlled by a robot under the close supervision of a human surgeon, ready to take over at a moment's notice."

I asked Goldberg where augmented dexterity was making its mark in surgery. He pointed to suturing, the painstaking process of sewing up surgical incisions or traumatic wounds. "There's a lot of variation in surgeons' skills," Goldberg explained. His father-in-law, a plastic surgeon, "used to say he could look at a scar and know which surgeon did the operation." New AI tools can analyze a wound and generate an optimal suturing map, even for jagged or curved injuries. Using augmented reality, these tools can overlay suture targets directly on the wound, guiding novice surgeons on precise stitch placement.

Goldberg's team is also developing mechanical arms to handle bulky surgical staplers. "Surgeons tell us they want to use [the staplers], but it's very hard to manipulate them inside the body. 'We'd love to have an assistant to help,' they say." He compares programming an AI-powered robotic system to navigate the nooks and crannies inside an abdomen to what roboticists call "the piano mover's problem"—finding the best path through a complex 3D space.

"WILL ROBOTS EVENTUALLY perform surgery?" I asked Carla Pugh. She smiled. "Well, the robots don't do anything autonomously right now. Zero. So first you've got to get the robot to be a good assistant; to be my resident." She likens today's robots to the Wizard of Oz—with the surgeon hidden behind the curtain, pulling the mechanical levers.

It will be a while before we have autonomous robots doing surgeries. There are simply too many unexpected conditions—including bleeding and rapid changes in vital signs—and anatomic variations are commonplace. Plus, of course, the OR is no place to "fail fast and iterate."

Moreover, the skills of a great surgeon extend far beyond the purely technical. Surgeons must also tightly choreograph the entire OR team, a high-stakes ballet in which coordination, collaboration, and communication are essential. A Toronto-based company, Surgical Safety Technologies, has built an AI-enabled surgical "black box," designed to be placed in operating rooms. The machine analyzes more than half a million data points per day in each OR. The main findings so far haven't been particularly sexy, but they have been potentially helpful. In one published study, the OR team failed to follow the required surgical checklist procedure about 20 percent of the time.

Beyond effective teamwork, there is another nontechnical skill that presents an even greater challenge for AI in surgery: judgment. Adnan Alseidi sees surgical judgment—when to operate, when to call an audible from the surgical plan, when to ask for help, and when to abort a procedure because things are going sour—as the supreme obstacle to autonomous surgical robots. "I work with some of the brightest engineers in the world, and I tell them, 'I want you to help me create something to assess judgment.' And they're like, 'Write down good judgment for me.' And I say, 'I don't know.' And they're like, 'If you can't write it down, we can't train anything in it.'"

"Judgment is not even close to being understood," Alseidi added.

Radiology

At a 2016 conference in his hometown of Toronto, Geoffrey Hinton, who would go on to win the 2024 Nobel Prize for his work on neural networks, was asked about the future of radiology. "If you work as a radiologist, you're like the coyote that's already over the edge of the cliff but hasn't yet looked down, so he doesn't realize there's no ground underneath him," Hinton said. "I think we should stop training radiologists now. It's just completely obvious that within five years deep learning is going to do better than radiologists . . . we've got plenty of radiologists already."

Diagnostic radiology has always been among the most popular specialties for medical students: It's one of the so-called ROAD (**R**adiology, **O**phthalmology, **A**nesthesia, **D**ermatology) to Happiness specialties—ones that combine high incomes with relatively humane hours. But Hinton's statement was the medical equivalent of Warren Buffett saying he was selling his radiology stock short. Whereas radiology residency programs had always been massively competitive, in 2020 only 41 percent of residency spots in America were filled by graduates of US medical schools, as students decided that a career in radiology was too risky a bet.

Then something funny happened. Medical students noticed that the salaries of their radiology attendings remained sky-high. (US radiologists' salaries currently average about $550,000 per year, more than twice that of family physicians and pediatricians.) More-over, rather than hearing tales of unemployed radiologists, students witnessed an explosion in radiology help wanted ads. By 2024, the Hinton Effect had evaporated—the number of US medical students choosing diagnostic radiology nearly doubled from 2020. If the field is in crisis today, it's because of a nationwide shortage, not a surfeit, of radiologists.

While Hinton's miscue was humbling, he was far from alone in being off base regarding the future of radiology. In fact, if you'd asked me fifteen years ago which would come first, my willingness to climb into the back seat of a driverless car or to have my X-ray read autonomously by AI, I would have chosen the X-ray. And yet, as I've mentioned, I take a driverless Waymo in San Francisco several times each month. Meanwhile, my own hospital, based in the same tech-obsessed city, can't hire radiologists fast enough.

When I began this book, I thought that Hinton's blunder was partly due to his underappreciation of the power of the radiology guild to protect its franchise. I no longer do. In fact, given the enormous increase in the number of scans to be read, I found that, for most radiologists, useful assistance from AI can't come soon enough.

As we speculate about the possibility of AI replacing humans in healthcare, the case of radiology is instructive. After all, there are few fields in medicine that seem as vulnerable to technological disruption as radiology, given that the field is largely about matching the appearance of a constellation of digital dots to a known database of diseases. Hinton's miscalculation has much to teach us about the complexity of medicine, the forces that will likely shape (and slow) healthcare's AI revolution, and why predictions that AI will replace physicians anytime soon should be served up with a generous dollop of skepticism.

oʌo

OF COURSE, THERE ARE many medical specialties in which visual pattern recognition is part of the job. A neurologist observes a patient's gait and facial expressions for telltale signs of Parkinson's disease. A pediatrician peers inside a child's ear, looking for an inflamed eardrum as a tip-off to a middle ear infection. But in those fields and many others, the visual data is combined with many other inputs—the patient's history, the rest of the physical examination, laboratory studies, and more. Visual pattern recognition is only one of the tools, and often not the dominant one.

Radiology, on the other hand, seems like it's entirely about analyzing a visual pattern and then providing the interpretation to another doctor, who integrates the radiologist's findings into the case's overall narrative. It is the patient's primary doctor, not the radiologist, who ultimately determines the diagnosis, prognosis, and appropriate therapy, and who follows the patient over time. Seen in this light, radiology is a close cousin of one other specialty: pathology.*

People sometimes add dermatology to the list of medical fields at highest risk for AI substitution, and there's some truth in this—particularly since patients are already putting pictures of rashes and other skin conditions into online AI programs and getting back fairly accurate answers. (AI struggles with images of patients with dark skin, but physicians do too.) But the visual pattern matching of the dermatologist is usually accompanied by direct patient contact—including taking a brief history and performing a skin

---

* Throughout this discussion, I'm referring to diagnostic radiology and pathology. There are subspecialized areas of both fields that also involve physical acts, such as interventional radiology and forensic pathology.

exam (some skin lesions have telltale tactile characteristics), and perhaps even a limited non-skin-focused physical exam, say, of a lymph node or the joints. Moreover, the dermatologist provides direct patient care and often concludes the visit with a prescription or other advice. In other words, radiology and pathology are the two medical fields in which, at first glance, the work seems particularly amenable to being replaced by AI.

I asked John Mongan, a UCSF radiologist and AI expert, why he still had a job a decade after Hinton's famous prediction. "The people who were making those predictions understood computer vision but didn't really understand radiology," he said. "They were writing algorithms that could tell you that an image was a dog or a sailboat. And they thought that radiology was just doing that for medical stuff. But radiology is a lot more than that." Mayo Clinic neuroradiologist Bradley Erickson added, "I can take a sixteen-year-old and teach them to drive in a day, max. I don't think I can take a sixteen-year-old and teach them to do neuroradiology in a day."

They're right. For one thing, the interpretation of an X-ray is often influenced by the patient's history, which the radiologist might glean from reading the patient's chart or talking to the clinician caring for the patient. I remember when the first cases of AIDS began cropping up in the early 1980s. At the time, the diagnosis of AIDS was a death sentence, the most common fatal complication being a previously rare lung infection called *Pneumocystis carinii* pneumonia, or PCP.* PCP could produce a chest X-ray that was floridly abnormal: The normally black air sacs looked like they had been smothered by an avalanche of white snow. But PCP's radio-

---

* In 1999, PCP was renamed *Pneumocystis jirovecii* pneumonia, or PJP.

logic appearance could also be exceedingly subtle, more like a little smudge on a glass windowpane. In the latter cases, my chest radiologist would often say, "If you tell me this is a straight fifty-year-old man, I'd say the X-ray is normal. If it's a twenty-six-year-old gay man, I'd say it's PCP." In other words, the exact same X-ray appearance could mean very different things, depending on the clinical context.

Yet even this constraint—that the radiologist needs to interpret an image in light of the patient's other medical information—seems surmountable given AI's rapid advancement in "reading" the medical record. If the only reason that Hinton got it wrong was AI's inability in 2016 to layer in the patient's clinical situation, then we should see an AI revolution in radiology fairly soon.

But it turns out there are even more challenges to overcome on the road to useful and trustworthy AI in radiology.

THE FIRST IS the dearth of labeled training sets. While it's fairly easy to obtain thousands of doctor-patient conversations to train Abridge's AI scribes or Hippocratic AI's conversational agents, there are relatively few curated and well-labeled digital X-ray datasets. Companies trying to build AI radiology tools have often been forced to do the expensive and laborious work of purchasing large radiology datasets and labeling thousands of images themselves.

Another key consideration is radiologists' need to review old films. For a complex case, the radiologist might need to scan dozens of prior images, often drawn from various imaging modalities (plain films, CT scans, MRIs, ultrasounds, etc.). To be truly constructive, a radiology AI tool would also need to review these past images, then compare those findings with the current image, assigning appropriate weights to differences in imaging type and varying time horizons. Consider a radiologist looking at a CT scan of a pancreatic mass, trying to determine if it's cancer. She might need to compare the current scan to a finding on an ultrasound from four months ago, or an MRI from two years ago. Judging the progression over time, appropriately adjusting for the varying lag periods and the different study techniques, creates a series of daunting problems for AI-based solutions. (It's tricky enough for experienced radiologists.)

Another reason for Hinton's faux pas was his failure to appreciate that, to be useful in radiology, the AI tool needs to sync up with the radiologists' workflow—an assembly line that's moving at breakneck speed. The process involves first confirming that you're looking at the correct patient's images, reading the relevant clinical history, and then looking-clicking-looking-clicking (toggling between the current and old images) . . . then looking again and, finally, dictating or typing the findings. It's especially challenging for AI to blend seamlessly into this process when the company developing the AI isn't the one that built the machines supporting the overall workflow.

An additional limitation is that today's machine vision tools are mostly able to master only one diagnosis at a time. NYU bone radiologist Miriam Bredella recalled seeing a demo of an AI system designed to detect arm fractures. It correctly diagnosed a fracture of the radius, a bone in the forearm, but missed one an inch away in the thinner but longer ulna. "The system wasn't trained on that," the company representative confessed.

This specificity means that the radiology AI products currently on the market are generally one-trick ponies. For example, GE has integrated a pneumothorax (collapsed lung) detector developed at UCSF into its advanced chest X-ray scanners. Since a pneumothorax can rapidly become life-threatening, the AI flags X-rays that appear to show one, moving the image to the top of the queue for the human radiologist to review. Another commercially available AI tool detects whether feeding tubes and catheters are in the correct position in the chest, saving the radiologist a few minutes of tedious measurement. Each one of these algorithms—the pneumothorax detector, the feeding tube placement detector, a pulmonary embolism detector—is sold separately, often by different companies, and each can run hospitals tens of thousands of dollars a year for subscriptions and operating costs. But human radiologists must look for all these things, as well as broken bones, signs of pneumonia, edema, cardiomegaly, pulmonary hypertension, enlarged lymph nodes—basically, all the diseases that can befall humans—simultaneously when they review a set of images, which markedly limits the value of these single-disease detectors.

It follows that the AI tools currently having the biggest impact in radiology are screening programs, particularly for cancer, where the goal is straightforward: Identify a single disease (e.g., spot a nodule suspicious for lung cancer on a chest CT or a density that might be a breast cancer on a mammogram). This kind of AI-enabled screening can be a huge help if it allows the radiologist to quickly endorse a negative result and move on to review positive or suspicious cases.

A growing body of literature supports the use of AI in such screenings. Even here, though, our enthusiasm needs to be tempered by AI's long history of overpromising and underdelivering. In the

1990s, computer-assisted mammography tools were widely implemented after being endorsed by the FDA. Yet once the tools entered community practice, studies showed that their accuracy plummeted.

What caused the problem? In the real world of clinical practice, the doctor—who lives in fear of overlooking a cancer (missing a breast cancer is not only devastating to both patient and doctor; it's also the most common cause of successful lawsuits against radiologists)—will likely recommend a biopsy after a positive reading by the AI, even if she would have judged the lesion to be benign in the absence of AI.

As more attention is paid to these human-AI interactions, things seem to be improving. In a 2023 Swedish study, roughly eighty thousand women were randomized to receive either standard mammography—in which two human radiologists look at the scan to be sure they're not missing anything—or an AI-assisted reading. In the latter group, the AI reviewed the scan first. If the mammogram looked benign to the AI, then a single radiologist signed off on the result. If there was anything suspicious, the scan entered the standard double-reading queue.

The results were impressive. The AI-assisted group identified 20 percent more cancers than the human radiologists operating without AI. The false positive rates were low in both groups. Notably, the overall workload of the radiologists went down by 44 percent in the AI-reading arm, a savings of nearly thirty-seven thousand radiologists' readings, allowing patients to get their results faster and saving the health system a small fortune. While it will be important to follow these women over time to see whether the early detection of cancers was clinically meaningful, AI-assisted radiology seems to be finally hitting its stride, at least in breast cancer screening.

New AI models have added an important skill to their repertoire: A 2024 study of more than one hundred thousand women in Norway found that AI-assisted analyses of three mammograms, one performed every two years, could accurately predict future risk of breast cancer, even when none of the scans showed evidence of active cancer.

REGULATORY SCRUTINY IS another large hurdle for digital radiology. While it remains a bit vague whether an AI-based readmission predictor or diagnosis-suggester needs regulatory approval (more on this later), there's no doubt that a radiology AI tool falls under the FDA's jurisdiction, under the category of Software as a Medical Device (SaMD). The SaMD review introduces another bottleneck: Just as AI radiology tools typically address a single diagnosis, the current FDA approval process mirrors that specificity. This means that radiology AI companies are forced to seek one approval for pulmonary embolism detection, then another for pneumonia detection. Each approval takes many months to obtain and may cost more than $1 million per indication.

The real world of radiology—and medicine—is not that siloed; it's messier and far more integrated. Take a patient with unexplained weight loss who gets a CT of the abdomen. There are literally hundreds of diagnoses that may be lurking, and we count on radiologists to see all of them. The need for each diagnosis to have its own bespoke algorithm and separate regulatory approval may be prudent at this stage of AI's development but will significantly hinder the utility and adoption of artificial intelligence in radiology.

GIVEN THE NEVER-ENDING volume of images in their work queues and the waning fear of Hintonian job replacement, you might think that radiologists would be clamoring for AI to help. But most radiologists don't find that today's tools—with the notable exception of the single-disease screeners—add to their efficiency. University of Pennsylvania radiologist Saurabh Jha likens the current AI-assisted programs to a back seat driver who incessantly and annoyingly points out road hazards. "That's not helpful," said Jha. "If you want to help me drive, then you take over the driving so that I can sit back and relax."

A 2024 study supported this view. Among 6,726 radiologists in China, those using AI experienced a burnout rate 20 percent higher than those who weren't. The reasons were unclear—it's possible that the AI created additional work by flagging more abnormalities to review, or that the AI, by taking the easy stuff off the radiologists' plate, increased their cognitive load. Since it wasn't a randomized trial, it's also possible that the radiologists who were already burned out were the ones choosing to use AI. In any case, this is another thread in the tapestry of why replacing radiologists with AI is harder than it looks.

WHILE THE TOOLS are clearly not good enough to replace radiologists today, the progress is unmistakable, and the potential is immense. I asked UCSF's John Mongan what he'd tell his kids if they said they wanted to go into diagnostic radiology. "I think it's a great field," he said. "If you don't like computers and you don't want to learn anything about AI, you should really think twice about it. But if you are ready to embrace and be part of the revolution, there's going to be plenty of work for human radiologists for the next several decades . . . I don't think the radiology department is going to turn into a data center with two people."

While I believe Mongan is right for the foreseeable future, the challenges that have slowed the march of AI in radiology now seem manageable, particularly with generative AI. These include the need to integrate multimodal data (e.g., patient history and lab studies) with radiologic findings; to assess images not for single abnormalities but holistically; to have access to large, well-curated datasets of images; to ingest, interpret, and integrate the findings from prior imaging studies; and to weave AI seamlessly into radiologists' workflows. In fact, a 2024 survey of two hundred healthcare organizations and imaging groups found that more than half were using at least one radiology AI tool, up from 17 percent in 2018. The most common uses were for triaging brain scans done to diagnose strokes, screening for breast and lung cancer, and drafting radiology reports.

It's hard to predict exactly how this will play out, but it does seem like AI is gaining a toehold in radiology and may even be nearing its Giant Leap moment. In the end, I suspect that AI will have a central role in radiology, and that we'll ultimately need fewer radiologists than we do now (or perhaps the same number to interpret far more imaging studies). Perhaps Geoff Hinton's infamous 2016 warning about training new radiologists will prove prescient after all—though the job losses seem destined to arrive on a timeline measured in several decades rather than the handful of years that he predicted. Like many prophets of technological disruption—particularly in healthcare—Hinton may have correctly identified the destination while drastically underestimating the length and complexity of the journey.

The Empowered Patient

In April 2008, Grace Cordovano was completing her PhD thesis in biochemistry and excited about her new job at a data analytics start-up in New York, covering the pharma and biotech industries. One day, she tore a muscle in her abdominal wall while working out and had a CT scan, which revealed an alarming finding: a nodule at the base of one of her lungs. She underwent a workup at a community hospital, including a PET scan that "lit up like a Christmas tree," with masses in her lungs, ovaries, liver, and just above her heart. "I was told it was advanced lymphoma, and that we needed to start treatment right away," even before a tissue biopsy confirmed the diagnosis.* She asked her physician if she was going to die. "Let's take it one day at a time," he said somberly.

Before she began the grueling chemo regimen, she decided to seek a second opinion from one of the world's top cancer centers. She rounded up her medical records and drove from her home in the Bronx to Memorial Sloan Kettering on Manhattan's Upper East Side. There, after multiple inconclusive biopsies, her doctors came to a startling conclusion: She didn't have cancer after all. Instead, she had an unusual fungal infection called histoplasmosis, which she presumably picked up on her honeymoon in Aruba two years

---

* While there are cases in which we might consider starting chemotherapy or radiation before obtaining a tissue biopsy (when the diagnosis of lymphoma is—or appears to be—obvious from scans, the disease is galloping, and tumor masses are compressing key structures like major blood vessels or the trachea), these cases are very rare. Cases like Cordovano's remind us of a well-known aphorism in cancer diagnosis: "Tissue is the issue."

earlier. As is sometimes the case in patients with healthy immune systems, the infection cleared up on its own over several months. Nearly two decades later, she is perfectly healthy.

"Had I not advocated and asked questions, my life would have been very different," she told me. That experience convinced her that the best use of her experience and education was to change careers and become a full-time patient advocate. Her pivot was partly driven by survivor's guilt. "I felt so ashamed [when other patients at Sloan Kettering] asked me what kind of cancer I had, and I said I didn't have cancer. They were overjoyed for me. Yet I struggled with why the mom with two children wasn't spared, why the grandma trying to make her grandson's wedding wasn't spared."

She now helps patients—most with cancer—and their families understand and navigate medicine's maddening minefields. "I'm literally trying to hack the US healthcare system—to connect people to the care they need."

Early in her new career, a friend told her, "Your advocacy work is really great, but it'll never scale." There was some truth to this— for a single client, she would spend hours googling clinical trials and looking up specialists' pedigrees. Then, after she identified a promising avenue for a second opinion, she and her clients needed to round up all the prior medical records and summarize the stacks of papers (plus CDs, thumb drives, and Post-it notes) in a coherent timeline to give the new doctor. It was a frustrating, inefficient slog.

Now, instead of spending a week researching PubMed or making phone calls, she turns to AI. "I can quickly get all my information— and I can translate it into Portuguese or an eighth-grade reading level." She also uses AI to summarize the patient's record and create a timeline—symptoms, tests, medications, and more—that greatly facilitates the second opinion process. On top of that, she relies on

AI to help her clients apply for disability benefits, housing vouchers, transportation resources, and translators. She even has a library of GPT prompts, which she uses to draft the dreaded prior auths and other letters she sends to her patients' oncologists to use. "AI has transformed the way I do my advocacy work," she said.

○───↑───○

WHILE THIS BOOK has focused on AI's impact on healthcare providers and systems, the most profound long-term effect of the technology may be on patients. Generative AI is beginning to empower patients to manage their own health in unprecedented ways—both by enhancing their interactions with traditional healthcare services and, in some cases, allowing them to meet their medical needs without involving the healthcare system at all.

The idea of technology as a democratizing force is, by now, old hat. Thirty years ago, there was no good way to make complicated travel plans without using a travel agent. Today, travel planning has been transformed through platforms like Expedia and more robust decision support tools offered by airlines and hotels. So-called agentic AI systems are now poised to go beyond simply suggesting the best choices. Tools like OpenAI's Operator, released in 2025, can book plane tickets, rental cars, and hotel rooms on your behalf.

Travel agents haven't completely gone away—people who can afford them or have particularly complex requirements still use them. I needed one recently for a work-play trip to Vietnam—the agent helped with visas, airport pickups, drivers, translators, and the like. It's easy to think of parallel examples in other areas, such as tax preparation or managing personal finances.

Healthcare is different, of course. We know the reasons: The stakes are high, the information base changes rapidly, health insurance distorts the consumer-vendor relationship, data sharing is constrained, many clinical choices need to be made quickly and under duress. And the portions of medicine that are amenable to DIY care are limited—you still need an expert and a facility to deliver your baby, perform your endoscopy, and transplant your kidney. Moreover, at least under today's rules, you generally need a credentialed expert to order a blood test, an X-ray, and a prescription.

Yet the trajectory is unmistakable: AI's entry into healthcare is arming patients with unprecedented knowledge and capabilities. While health-literate, tech-savvy people like Grace Cordovano are at the vanguard of this transformation, they represent just the beginning. Soon, millions of patients will be using AI to break down traditional barriers and create a far more democratized healthcare system.

PERHAPS THE MOST prominent patient advocate in the US is Dave deBronkart, a former software marketing professional and kidney cancer survivor who goes by the nom de guerre e-Patient Dave. At the top of a 2023 blog post titled "The Evolution of Who Knows What," deBronkart displayed a famous painting of Martin Luther posting his Ninety-Five Theses to the door of All Saints' Church in Wittenberg, Germany, in 1517. Luther challenged the notion that the Catholic Church was the sole authority on the teachings of the Bible. DeBronkart seeks to challenge the primacy of today's healthcare system for medical care, and he's certain that AI will be a major catalyst. "Google gave us access to information," deBronkart told me. "AI gives us clinical thought."

Importantly, neither deBronkart nor Cordovano have abandoned the medical system—both remain firmly on the healthcare grid. "None of this is anti-doctor or anti-science," deBronkart wrote in his blog. Instead, he calls for "participatory medicine, in which enlightened doctors, nurses, scientists, and government policies welcome informed, empowered, engaged patients, helping healthcare achieve its potential." While he's steadfast in his push for empowerment, he commiserates with those physicians who worry that their role and status are being diminished by AI. "One doctor told me, 'I was trained that my value to humanity is that I know things that other people don't,'" deBronkart recalled, sympathetically.

WHILE MOST OF the attention regarding patient-facing AI relates to do-it-yourself diagnosis, much of the real action will be around patient engagement and behavioral change. Said health policy expert Mark Smith, "We are pretty good about knowing who's going to develop renal failure. The problem is that there's no effector arm to get either the patient or the doctor to do anything about it. . . . That's what all these companies in the engagement business are selling to employers and plans. Now they're calling it AI because everything is now AI. Basically, what they're saying is, 'We've got some secret sauce that can increase engagement.'" Remember the four phases of healthcare digitization I described in chapter 1? The third is providing insights, and the fourth is generating actions that make health and healthcare better. As always, traversing that last mile is the hardest, but will ultimately have the greatest impact.

◦⌒◦

SINCE EVEN PATIENTS like deBronkart and Cordovano continue to interact with the healthcare system, the need to access their own health records is a central theme of the patient empowerment movement. "Gimme My Damn Data" is one of deBronkart's most popular keynote talks.

While the federal government has passed several laws to promote patient access to their damn data, without patient-friendly tools it's a bit like handing people a book in a language they can't understand. "All we do is dump the data into an app," lamented the late Atul Butte, a UCSF AI expert who studied patient data use. "The patients have no idea what to do with it, right? There are zero apps that help them interpret those records."

Several companies have sprung up to give patients access to tests and treatments after a perfunctory interaction with an online clinician. The FDA is currently taking a hands-off approach to these companies, as long as they define themselves as promoting "wellness." But there is clearly some boundary-pushing afoot. As Butte observed, "Okay, so I go to Amazon Care; there are forty-three health-related things I can ask for, way beyond erectile dysfunction. And I see a doc for, what, a minute or two, on video. And I get a prescription, and I never see that doc again. And to be honest with you, I'm not even sure it's a human." While Amazon pulled the plug on Amazon Care in late 2022, other services offering pro forma clinician reviews before dispensing tests or medications are exploding in popularity and becoming increasingly AI-enabled.

In the old days, the requirement that patients work with a credentialed clinician and healthcare system to get a prescription medication, a laboratory test, or an X-ray ensured there were some guardrails around do-it-yourself healthcare. It now seems inevitable that AI tools that help patients self-diagnose will create pressure to make more of the instruments of healthcare available to non-professionals. "If you don't give patients the tools," said Anarghya Vardhana, a Silicon Valley investor, "they will go figure it out themselves." As patients gain access to physician-level insights through their smartphones, we're undoubtedly heading for intense debates over medical gatekeeping—specifically, whether traditional credentials should still determine who can order tests and authorize treatments. This is an area in which I worry about going too far, too fast.

Microsoft's Peter Lee shares my concern and highlights the need to think about the patient-AI dyad very differently than we think about physicians' use of AI. As he told me in an email,

> I think AI for patients is WAY harder than AI for doctors. Doctors are experts and ask expert questions. Patients are not educated in medicine and hear things from family, friends, neighbors, social media, etc. and ask questions that require an ability to separate truth from fiction, real science from pseudo-science, and good intents from mal-intents. Too many medical professionals say that AI must be trained only on "good" medical knowledge; this is true to an extent, but for consumers, it is also important for AI to be exposed to the full diversity of human thought and expression, including things like lies, fictions, political expediencies, etc., if it is to have any chance of being discerning. Bottom line, things like Reddit are *critical* for training AI, at least AI for patients.

With things moving this quickly, we have much to learn about the consequences of patients using AI tools to manage their own health and healthcare. In a 2024 article in *The New England Journal of Medicine*'s recently launched AI offshoot, health journalist Carey Goldberg recounted several interesting anecdotes of patients taking advantage of modern AI for self-diagnosis and self-care. And yet, while there are hundreds of research studies examining what happens when physicians and health systems use AI to write prior auths, take board exams, answer inbox messages, or draft clinical notes, at the time of Goldberg's piece the *NEJM AI* editors had "received no submissions of studies aiming to assess what happens when patients take generative AI into their own hands, nor have they seen such reports in other journals." There is so much potential in this area, but so many uncertainties—not least of which is this: What happens when the human in the loop—the one making a final judgment regarding the recommendation of an imperfect AI tool—is not a doctor but a patient? This is a field in desperate need of study, which will only come through partnerships between patients and professionals.

WE HAVE ENTERED an era in which patients have access to more of their own healthcare data, and far more powerful tools—enabled by AI—to manage their own health affairs. It's a little dizzying, and it's hard to tell where it will end up. I asked e-Patient Dave to take out his crystal ball to think about how the patient of the future will receive care. "I wouldn't be surprised if my granddaughter has an enamored relationship with some empathetic AI," he said. "I also wouldn't be surprised if she insists on a human that she can look in the eye because, for some ineffable reason, it just works better for her."

5

Institutions and Innovations

WE HAVE ALREADY MET SEVERAL AI-powered start-ups: Hippocratic AI and its nurse chatbot; Abridge and its digital scribe; and OpenEvidence, the clinical decision-making resource. In this chapter, we'll profile a few of the other companies and organizations whose work illustrates how AI is beginning to reshape healthcare, beginning with start-ups aiming to rescue primary care.

The Start-Ups Out to Save Primary Care

The centrality of a well-functioning primary care system is one of the few things that everybody in healthcare agrees on. Everyone also agrees that American primary care is in crisis. Primary care physicians are underpaid, underappreciated, and overworked, crushed between an aging population, an avalanche of medical advances, and suffocating administrative burdens. One study found

that it would take more hours than exist in a day—twenty-seven—
for a PCP to tick off all the recommended treatments and protocols
in their practice; and even more if any of the patients had the te-
merity to show up desperately ill.

The consequences are far-reaching. Primary care physicians
around the country report alarming rates of burnout. Wait times
for PCP appointments have grown dramatically, often stretching
to many months. Around the US there are "primary care deserts,"
places where it is literally impossible to find a primary care doctor
with openings. Medical students and residents have taken all of this
in, and few are pursuing primary care careers.

Like a herd of enormous elephants, digital giants, health insurers, and private equity firms have bounded onto this particular sa-
vannah, poised to "disrupt the status quo." Most of these companies
are smart enough to realize that they lack the healthcare-specific
expertise to build AI-first primary care enterprises themselves.
Since nobody sees easy profit in today's primary care ecosystem,
their strategies have focused mostly on buying practices and replacing expensive employees (read: physicians) with less expensive
ones (nurse practitioners and physician assistants), partly by upskilling these non-physician providers using AI. Pharmacy chains
like CVS and Walgreens are also motivated by the prospect of
steering patients toward their core business, generating profits not
so much by diagnosing bronchitis but by dispensing antibiotics and
inhalers in their attached pharmacies.

I'm certain that all these arrangements looked like surefire winners when presented in a consultant's PowerPoint pitch deck. But,
as of this writing, most of these shotgun marriages are either treading water (Amazon's purchase of One Medical) or have cratered
(CVS's purchase of Oak Street Health, Walgreens's purchase of Vil-

lageMD). Walmart—a company not known for its missteps—chose a build, not buy, strategy, opening fifty-one of its own Walmart Health clinics beginning in 2019. The results were no better—it shuttered all of them in 2024 in the face of mounting losses.

In addition to the generally unsuccessful efforts by the corporate titans to conquer primary care, the space has been lousy with start-ups, most of them offering versions of AI-enabled care, either physical or virtual. The results have been equally sobering.

One of the most prominent was Forward, a tech-first primary care start-up launched in 2016 by a former Google executive named Adrian Aoun.* Forward, which billed itself as "the world's first AI doctor's office," raised more than $400 million from high-wattage investors, including Salesforce CEO Marc Benioff, pop singer The Weeknd, and Peter Thiel's Founders Fund. During the 2020–21 tech bubble, analysts valued the company at more than $1 billion.

Forward's initial offering was primary care delivered in brick-and-mortar offices designed with an Apple-Store-meets-White-Lotus-spa sensibility. Forward offices featured a "Would you like still or sparkling?" receptionist, along with a fancy body scanner and other gizmos, many of dubious medical value. Visits centered around an impressive homegrown electronic health record with a giant display complete with a John Madden–style telestrator that could be viewed simultaneously by both clinician and patient. Fueled by a no-insurance-accepted subscription payment model, the company expanded quickly. By 2023, there were Forward offices in nineteen US cities.

Though Forward seemed to be thriving, Aoun wanted to "swing for the fences." To do this, he believed he needed to answer a central

---

* I was an adviser to Forward.

question that has long bedeviled healthcare pundits: What is the most scalable, least expensive physical space that can fill the gap between purely virtual care and a fully stocked physician's office? His answer was a self-service clinical kiosk, the size of a small home office, which he dubbed a CarePod. Patients would unlock the CarePod door with their phone, enter and settle into a comfy recliner, have their vital signs taken automatically, interact with a skin cancer screener and other digital tools, and receive AI-enabled symptom-based and preventive care, with remote MDs signing off on the plan later that day. When I tried out a CarePod before its public debut, a little trap door opened and out popped a Covid test kit; I stuck the kit back into the electronic drawer when I was done swabbing. It was designed to impress, and it did.

Aoun, who cultivated a "move fast and break things" persona in his public appearances, likened the experience to interacting with a bank's automatic teller machine. "An ATM doesn't do everything," he said in a 2023 interview. "We still have doctors behind the scenes, but now those doctors aren't doing 100% of the care, they are just doing that last 5% or focusing on the complex care." Aoun's goal was to install hundreds of CarePods in malls and office buildings across the nation. It was an audacious plan.

Then, in late 2024, unable to raise a new round of financing and outpaced by his burn rate, the company abruptly ran out of cash. On November 12, Forward members received a curt note: "We will be closing our Forward locations, canceling scheduled visits, and shutting down our mobile application, effective immediately."

What had doomed Forward? In the end, the company couldn't afford to build the CarePods (at an average cost of $1 million per Pod). There were also logistical and operational challenges, ranging from problems with self-service blood draws to patients getting stuck inside the Pods. Forward also couldn't offer the full range of services that patients often need, including access to subspecialists. Aniq Rahman, CEO of a health tech start-up and a Forward patient, put it this way: "For me, the lesson is, think through how to reach consumers in a way that feels new and novel, but do it in a way that actually fits the paradigm of how healthcare is delivered." In other words, try for singles, maybe doubles, with your spiffy new digital tools, but don't swing for the fences.

ANOTHER HIGH-PROFILE FAILURE was that of Babylon Health, founded in the UK in 2013 by Iranian-born healthcare entrepreneur Ali Parsa. Unlike Forward's model, Babylon care was virtual-only, combining AI with telemedicine-based consults delivered through a mobile app. The company raised over $1 billion from a variety of investors, and, in 2019, the UK's National Health Service rolled Babylon out as a core offering. The start-up also began making substantial inroads in the US, buying a couple of large medical practices and going public in 2021 through a complex merger valued at $4.2 billion.

Everything seemed to be going swimmingly for Babylon but for one small detail: The technology didn't work very well. The company used a pre-GPT rules-based AI model, which, as you'll recall, tends to stumble when presented with the type of complex cases that real humans often have. Doctors found that the app gave incorrect medical advice in 10 to 15 percent of cases. "The focus was on building fast and getting things out the door," a staffer told

Forbes in 2019. According to the article, Babylon's in-house doctors struggled to make their voices heard even when addressing safety concerns, while data scientists "were treated like rock stars." Bob Kocher, the Venrock investor, gave Babylon a spin. "It would take ten minutes and then it always said, 'Now go see a doctor.' I felt like it probably led to more visits than less because it was tuned to be so conservative."

In 2022, the company lost more than $200 million and began selling off its parts. The AI-based care platform, which former UK health secretary Matt Hancock called "revolutionary" in 2018, declared bankruptcy in 2023. By then, its price per share, which peaked at $272 in 2022, had fallen to two cents.

THE DEMISE OF Forward and Babylon—while vividly demonstrating that revolutionizing primary care is tough sledding—has not completely nailed the coffin on AI-based primary care. There are several hardy companies that soldier on in this space. One of them is Curai Health, whose founder and CEO is Neal Khosla, a thirty-one-year-old computer scientist and son of the legendary Silicon Valley investor Vinod Khosla.*

When Curai was founded in 2017, Neal Khosla's pitch was that the company would transform primary care by acquiring large clinical datasets and then building AI-based software tools to support practicing physicians. What he found, however, was that clinicians weren't keen on upending their workflow around a new tech tool. "Going to a health system and saying 'Change all your stuff to

---

* I am an adviser to Curai.

work around this new technology' is a losing proposition," Khosla told me.

With that recognition, Curai pivoted to building its own virtual-only ecosystem—hiring clinicians, retraining them, and codeveloping software with them. Now, when a Curai patient submits a text message with symptoms or a request, the AI is "mostly there to deliver a recommendation to the physician, not the patient," said Khosla.

The failure of companies like Forward and Babylon is never far from Khosla's mind. He's also clear-eyed about how hard it is to change people's habits, pointing out that the default for most patients is to google their symptoms and go to a nearby urgent care center. His aim is to build online tools that will save patients from making that trip—to deliver not only a diagnosis but a treatment, all virtually. "Our whole thesis only works if you believe that patients want to start with these kinds of tools," he said.

To create a viable business model, Khosla believes, small efficiency improvements (say, having the AI suggest and tee up a prescription so that the doctor simply needs to endorse it) won't be enough. Instead, the technology needs to increase the efficiency of a primary care physician about tenfold. Yet if physicians remain the final (and legally responsible) decision-makers, their minds can only do so much cogitating while running on a rapidly spinning, AI-enabled hamster wheel. "The switching costs of moving faster between patients, just the brain fatigue associated with this—it's very, very hard to create ten times more productive physicians when they're still involved in the task."

This brings him—and us—back to one of the central questions in healthcare AI: Rather than trying to speed up every part of the process, are there discrete tasks that AI can safely take off the doctor's plate while triaging only the higher-risk, more complex ones to the physician? While I have no doubt that a company will someday crack that code, the tech world is learning how hard it is.

MEANWHILE, THE PRIMARY CARE crisis continues. As far as I can tell, the only practices that seem to satisfy both patients and clinicians are not ones in which AI has been the special sauce. Rather, they are practices in which patients pay a yearly fee—ranging from the few thousand dollars my eighty-nine-year-old mom pays to see a terrific physician in Little Silver, New Jersey, to nearly $50,000 for a boutique San Francisco–based practice called Private Medical. These concierge practices provide their physicians with generous support staff and cutting-edge technology—luxuries that insurance payments alone can't support. The practices are also able to create panel sizes of a few hundred patients per physician, not the two thousand or so it takes for a standard primary care practice to remain economically viable. This smaller panel translates into appointments that last thirty to sixty minutes (or more), rather than the fifteen-minute fire drill that most patients and PCPs have come to expect. Jordan Shlain, physician and founder of Private Medical, contrasts the conditions his doctors work under with those of the average PCP. "Doctors used to be empathic," he told me, "but the system has sucked the soul out of everybody."

Yet while concierge-level care for everyone would be ideal, healthcare economics make this impossible. For the vast majority of patients who can't afford concierge services, access to quality primary care remains a critical gap in the American healthcare system. AI will undoubtedly play a role in addressing this challenge. However, without accompanying reforms in payment and policy—including incentives for preventive care, competitive compensation to attract new physicians to primary care, and sustainable patient panel sizes and visit durations—technology alone won't solve this problem.

While it won't be the entire solution, I *am* convinced that AI will play a key role in addressing our primary care crisis. In fact, as I'll discuss in chapter 7, I predict that our future system for delivering primary and urgent care will involve a different kind of tiering—not between usual and concierge care, but between usual and AI-enabled care.

Mayo and the Transformation of Clinical Care

"The future is already here; it's just not evenly distributed," the writer William Gibson famously said. I've found throughout my career that a visit to the world-renowned Mayo Clinic is the surest way to get a sense of healthcare's future.

The Mayo Clinic was founded in 1889 in Rochester, Minnesota, by two brothers, both physicians, Will and Charlie Mayo. Their big idea was this: People deserved the world's best healthcare, and the only way to deliver that care was to build teams of outstanding physicians and place those teams in a system laser-focused on clinical excellence. Mayo's combination of nearly 150 years of proud heritage, a relentless drive to improve systems of care, a culture of innovation, and nearly unlimited money (a steady stream of private jets from around the world keeps tiny Rochester International Airport hopping) helps the organization peer around corners to see the future, and act—often boldly though never recklessly—on that vision.

Among Mayo's many contributions is the modern medical record. In 1907, Mayo's Henry Plummer introduced a new method of assigning patients their own ID number and documenting all clinical observations about them in a unique record. While this seems obvious today, Plummer's system replaced the traditional one in which each doctor recorded information about each patient, one after another, in his personal "doctor's journal." That system made it nearly impossible to follow the course of an individual patient over time, to mine the medical record for research, or to share patient information with other physicians.

Mayo also recognized the importance of information capture and flow, though in pre-computer days this assumed a very different form than it does today. Beginning early in the twentieth century, the Mayo Clinic built a remarkable network of pneumatic tubes to move its paper charts and X-rays up, down, and between its many hospital and outpatient buildings in Rochester. At its peak, Mayo had approximately ten thousand pneumatic tubes covering more than ten miles. The longest, connecting its two main hospitals, spanned nine city blocks.

But healthcare is about far more than chronicling patient data and moving it to the right place at the right time. Mayo has long seen its ability to analyze and interpret patient information as a strategic asset, in both the care of individual patients and as an enabler of medical research. For example, many of the seminal studies on blood disorders like multiple myeloma were conducted by Mayo investigators, who were able to review decades of symptoms, test results, and pathology samples from thousands of patients. As parts of the medical record became computerized—first laboratory tests and billing records, later clinical notes and X-rays—Mayo digitized these records, adding rich new layers of data, such as genomic assays and retinal scans, as soon as they became available.

MAYO IS CURRENTLY led by a sixty-one-year-old gastroenterologist named Gianrico Farrugia. You met him on the first page of this book, when he introduced me to Mayo's digital twin program. A native of Malta, Farrugia came to Mayo in 1988 for a three-year residency in internal medicine. He never left. After a fellowship in gastroenterology, he joined the faculty, building a robust academic and leadership track record until being named CEO in January 2019.

The digital twin program is a key piece of Farrugia's vision for Mayo's future. But it's far from the only one. When he became CEO, Farrugia also recognized that the lack of diversity in Mayo's patient population would hamper the clinic's ability to conduct research and develop AI algorithms. The homogeneity isn't just about the fact that Rochester's population is approximately 75 percent white. (They also have data from their Arizona and Florida campuses, where the local populations are more diverse.) The bigger issue is that patients who travel to Mayo for clinical care are different from the average patient—sicker, better educated, and wealthier. They are also more likely to have uncommon diseases; we physicians call these diseases "zebras,"* and a hospital full of them is sometimes

---

* The term comes from a medical maxim that reminds us that common diseases are common: "When you hear hoofbeats, think horses, not zebras."

colorfully described as a "zebra garden." Mayo's garden is probably the world's most abundant.

Farrugia came to believe that the creation of a secure and trusted data ecosystem—a Mayo Clinic–led digital platform—could solve the problem of nondiverse data. He also recognized that non-Mayo healthcare organizations might seek a safe place to pool their data with others, and that a growing "lake" of diverse, secure data could entice start-ups and tech giants alike to jump in—as they, too, would need access to rich clinical datasets to build and test digital tools. Farrugia knew he needed an unusual person to turn this ambitious vision into reality. The job description might have read something like this:

> The Mayo Clinic seeks an engineer and computer scientist with forty years of digital transformation experience, an advanced degree in public policy, a robust track record working with local, state, and federal governments, unmatched connections with US and international tech companies, investors, researchers, health systems, insurance companies, and policymakers, and an interest in leading an audacious program designed to transform healthcare. Applicants must be willing to travel half a million miles a year.

As far as I know, there is only one person in the world who fits those specs, and that is who Farrugia chose: the sixty-two-year-old physician-informatician and policy expert John Halamka, whom we've already met a few times in this book. In the buttoned-up and change-resistant healthcare sector, he may well be, as the saying goes, the most interesting man in the world.

ᴏᴧₒ

JOHN HALAMKA WAS born in Des Moines, Iowa; his family relocated to Southern California when he was a child. John won his elementary school's fourth-grade science fair by building a linear accelerator (a grainy photo shows a bespectacled, adorable kid standing next to a glass column topped by a brass cylinder; the caption reads, "The Latest Electrostatic Atom Smasher"). He was an early computer geek, spending his free time dumpster diving in the alleyways behind SoCal electronics stores and the offices of defense contractors, pulling out parts and manuals to teach himself programming.

When he arrived at Stanford as an undergraduate in the early 1980s, Halamka found himself surrounded by innovation. Companies like Apple, Oracle, Atari, and Adobe were being born or taking their baby steps just miles from his dorm room. Inspired by these companies and their founders, Halamka's interest in computers grew. One day, he wandered over to Stanford's law library to see if there was a computer program to help people do their taxes. There wasn't. He thumbed through the US tax code and had an idea. He wrote a program ("I didn't think it was too complicated," he told me—probably the only person ever to make that assessment) that he sold out of his dorm room, surviving an IRS audit triggered when the feds saw that a twenty-year-old had declared tens of thousands of dollars in business deductions for shipping costs. The program ultimately became a predecessor to TurboTax; he sold it a few years later to his senior partners for a handsome sum.

At Stanford, he met Kathy Anne Greene, whom he would soon marry. "I was math, science, engineering, black and white, digital

0's and 1's, Zen, and monk-like asceticism," he wrote in 2010. "She was art, music, culture, color, analog, Victorian clutter, and joie de vivre." His right brain and her left meshed perfectly. Together, they had a daughter and took in a few pets—actually, some 250 of them—including alpacas, llamas, horses, ponies, sheep, cows, goats, pigs, and a vast collection of birds (but no zebras), hosted on the largest animal sanctuary in Massachusetts, Unity Farm, which they founded in 2016.

In 1984, Halamka began medical school at my institution, UCSF, where he also enrolled in our PhD program. The typical path for young physician-scientists—basic science research in a laboratory—held little attraction. Instead, he chose to pursue graduate-level training in bioengineering at UC Berkeley. He told his thesis advisers, UCSF's Michael Bishop and Harold Varmus, that he wanted to transform healthcare by building digital tools. Neither of the future Nobel Prize winners thought this was wise; Bishop was particularly mortified, telling Halamka that "it was the stupidest thing he'd ever heard."

In 1997, fresh out of training, Halamka was hired to be a physician-informaticist at Beth Israel Hospital (now Beth Israel Deaconess), one of Harvard's teaching hospitals. Within a few years, he had built one of the nation's first electronic health records: a homegrown, web-based system that Beth Israel used for twenty-five years. In 2001, he was named chief information officer of Harvard University. By then, he had become a legendary figure in digital health.

Halamka had no thoughts of leaving Harvard, although he was increasingly frustrated by the organization's internal politics—particularly the growing tension between the healthcare delivery systems (mostly the leviathan now known as Mass General Brigham) and Harvard Medical School. The two entities are owned by separate corporations and can, at best, be described as frenemies. This tension, combined with Harvard's philosophy of individual entrepreneurship among its faculty, made it extremely difficult to carry out his vision for digital transformation—which requires high levels of trust between doctors and their health system, and often a subjugation of individual preferences and egos to the common good, not something Harvard is known for.

All of this led him to answer the call in 2019 when he was asked to consider a role as president of the newly created Mayo Clinic Platform, the digital ecosystem envisioned by Farrugia. After about forty interviews, Mayo decided that Halamka was the ideal person for the job. And Halamka decided that Mayo was uniquely positioned to bring this vision to reality.

When Halamka arrived at Mayo, he traded in his Steve Jobsian black turtleneck for a nice Midwestern uniform of shirt, tie, and jacket, all in muted colors. As an homage to Mayo's storied tradition in data science, he also began wearing the same style of circular eyeglass frames worn a century earlier by Mayo's medical record pioneer, Henry Plummer.

THE MAYO CLINIC Platform idea is a bit technical, but it's worth taking a moment to appreciate what Halamka and his colleagues have built. "We started with Mayo Clinic data, de-identified it, built in security, privacy, and put the data behind glass," explained Steve Bethke, the Platform's vice president. The clinic then inked partnerships with health systems from around the world, including St. Louis's Mercy Hospital, Aga Khan University in Pakistan, SingHealth in Singapore, and Sheba in Israel. To complete the circle, more than seventy-five start-ups joined as "solution developers," using the Platform's growing dataset to build and test their AI tools.

In addition to the Platform's de-identified data, Mayo offers a suite of services to participants. For the companies, there's help with tool validation, advice on preparing submissions for the FDA or local governance committees, and assistance in integrating their tools into clients' electronic health records. Participating healthcare organizations get access to Mayo specialists and the digital tools on the Platform. The idea is to create what tech executives call a flywheel—a system that gets better and more useful over time as more hospitals and companies join the parade.

In most healthcare organizations, even generally progressive ones, the central bureaucracy often seems spring-loaded to thwart innovation, constantly fretting about the possibility of data breaches, lawsuits, or some other cataclysm. At Mayo, on the other hand, I found that the leaders of every clinical department—cardiology, surgery, pathology, radiology—were excited about AI and how it might transform their ability to care for patients. And central departments like legal and HR, including people whose job it is to minimize organizational risk, were seen as enablers, not obstructionists. "When I worked at Harvard," Halamka told me, "the lawyers would say no." At Mayo, he says, "I approach them as helpful friends and colleagues, not as adversaries." It makes a difference.

ALL THIS INFRASTRUCTURE and culture is well and good, but what is Mayo actually developing in the AI space? Like everyone else, they're implementing things like digital scribes and chart summarization (in partnership with Epic and Abridge). I also saw many other examples of AI-fueled innovations at the Mayo Clinic.

The first comes from the field of pathology, which has been poised to go digital for decades but hasn't quite managed to do so. When people think of the work of pathologists, they focus on the reading of pathology slides but fail to consider all that comes before that: the laborious and expensive process of taking a piece of human tissue, cutting it precisely, sticking it on a glass slide, staining it with the proper reagents, and having it land on a pathologist's microscope stand. You'd think that companies would emerge to streamline and digitize this process, but most hospitals can't see an economic case for the investment, which means that no companies have been built to tackle the problem. It's a classic market failure, which Mayo is trying to fix by launching companies that specialize in building a digitally enabled pathology supply chain.

The logistical complexity is only part of what's held digital pathology back. Like all physicians, pathologists are traditionalists—they learned their craft by peering through the eyepiece of a microscope, not at a video monitor. While there are massive advantages to digital pathology, there is also a slight loss of image quality—digital images are a smidgen less sharp than ones viewed through the microscope. Although one would think that the added efficiency and flexibility of a digital system would more than compensate for a tiny loss of image fidelity, at least until now, they haven't.

Labor shortages may finally tip the scales. Not only is it wildly expensive to staff the glass slide assembly line, but—echoing an increasingly common refrain for healthcare writ large—even Mayo is having problems finding enough staff to do the work. Moreover, AI-generated time savings for the pathologist can be enormous.

Consider a glioma, a common brain tumor whose behavior can range from relatively benign to rapidly fatal. A neuropathologist seeing a glioma in the microscope "might make the diagnosis five seconds after looking at the slide," Mayo pathologist Andrew Norgan told me. But to properly classify the tumor, which informs prognosis and guides treatment, the pathologist needs to count the number of cells undergoing division (mitosis). Counting mitoses is painstaking and tedious work that takes twenty to thirty minutes for a single glioma specimen; it's like counting buzzing bees in a large flowering garden. "With AI doing the reading, it takes thirty seconds," added Norgan.

A second striking example comes from cardiology. Mayo's automated EKG readings now not only describe traditional outputs like heart rhythm (e.g., normal sinus rhythm or atrial fibrillation) and evidence of a prior heart attack; they also include AI-generated estimates of patients' ejection fraction (the squeezing ability of the heart), future risk of atrial fibrillation, and physiologic (as opposed to chronological) age. The physiologic age estimate is prognostically salient—the fifty-five-year-old patient with a sixty-five-year-old-appearing heart on EKG has, on average, the life expectancy of a sixty-five-year-old. Interestingly, Mayo researchers have found that the physiologic age of the recipient of a heart transplant falls somewhere between their chronological age and that of the donor.

Of course, there's a real world out there, and these magical technologies sometimes hit a wall when they butt up against it. For example, most patients with known atrial fibrillation are treated with anticoagulants to lower the risk of blood clots; the evidence strongly supports this approach. However, when patients are identified as being *at risk* for atrial fibrillation, doctors can't currently assume they will benefit from early use of blood thinners, a treatment that carries its own risk. Another example: Insurance companies may balk at paying for an echocardiogram to confirm the presence of a low ejection fraction detected on an AI-enhanced EKG in an asymptomatic patient. We can't forget that effectively implementing AI-enabled tools and practices requires painstaking clinical research, as well as modifications of workflows, culture, and, at times, payment and regulatory systems.

MAYO IS ALSO pioneering remote surgeries and cardiac procedures. Where does AI fit in? As Mayo electrophysiologist Samuel Asirvatham explained to me, there is a challenge if a Mayo cardiologist in Minnesota is performing an ablation procedure—cauterizing a twitchy part of the heart muscle responsible for an arrhythmia—on a patient in Prague, 4,500 miles away. The problem is a slight time delay; at that distance, a signal to ablate heart tissue that originates in Minnesota won't arrive in the Czech Republic for about thirty-five milliseconds, at which time the heart is in a different place in its contraction cycle and the wrong part of the heart might get zapped. Mayo cardiologists are using AI to determine when the impulse should fire to ensure that it reaches the heart in Europe at precisely the right moment.

Another impressive technology is the AI-enabled stethoscope, developed at Mayo and commercialized by a company called Eko Health. Mayo research has shown that, like the AI-EKG analysis, this stethoscope can accurately estimate a patient's ejection fraction, something regular stethoscopes cannot do. Farrugia told me, "One of our physicians, working with a group in Nigeria, figured out you could put the algorithm in a stethoscope and give it to a nurse in Nigeria, and it will detect peripartum cardiomyopathy," a failing heart in pregnant or recently pregnant women.

I heard a version of the Africa story from several people during my time at Mayo—they're clearly proud of it. Halamka recalled that when he was hired by Farrugia, the CEO gave him a mandate "to touch the lives of three billion people. And I said, 'What does that mean?' And Gianrico said, 'This isn't about selling algorithms to Kenya. It's about empowering Kenyans to create algorithms that can help Kenyans.'" In this model, Halamka added, "Mayo is just an enabler of an ecosystem, not a provider of products." He then offers the usual platform analogy: How many cars does Uber own? How many hotel rooms does Airbnb own? The answer to both questions, of course, is zero.

MY VISIT TO Mayo left me energized, but also a bit frustrated with the pace of change elsewhere. Would the rest of us come up to speed? Or would the Mayos of the world—and perhaps a handful of others—emerge as national or even international brands, providing healthcare services to everyone everywhere, putting local hospitals and clinics out of business? If so, who would be left to provide the few services that had to remain in the community—like the emergency room, labor and delivery, and surgery? Could your local bookstore survive on coffee and chitchat if people ordered all their books through Amazon? As exciting as the innovations in AI and digital platforms are, we need to consider some of the unanticipated consequences they will inevitably spawn.

When I think about scaling digital tools to transform industries, my first thought is that the winners are likely to be digital titans—the Googles, Amazons, Microsofts, and Apples—all of whom have set their sights on healthcare. I asked Aaron Neinstein, chief medical officer of the AI start-up Notable, about the battle to become healthcare's platform of choice. "My bias always is, how can Amazon and Google lose?" he said. "And yet they always do. They perpetually underestimate healthcare. I think they're actually at a big disadvantage, because success is workflow-dependent, and they just are so far away from the frontline workflows."

Who would he bet on now, I asked—the Amazons of the world or the Mayos? "Mayo," he said without hesitation. "It's brand, trust, focus, and data."

I ASKED FARRUGIA whether he worried about going too fast and making a major misstep. After all, given Mayo's brand, there's plenty to lose. Farrugia's shirts are monogrammed with Mayo's famous three-shield logo; like the pope, he dons his vestments each morning with years of history balancing on his shoulders. "I think the risk of not going fast enough is far greater at this point than the risk of going too fast," he said.

But wasn't he concerned that some of Mayo's 80,000 employees, including 7,300 physicians, might worry about their job security—particularly if Mayo rushes, full steam ahead, into an unknowable AI future? "When we're no longer busy doing what we're doing now, we'll create much more technically demanding things that we didn't think were possible," he replied. "And we're going to create cures for diseases that are going to require physical interventions, that are going to require hospitals."

Still, I persisted, people will naturally fret, won't they?

"We've got to get people who worry about the worst-case scenario to go see a psychologist," he said.

NYU and the Reimagining of Medical Education

Medical education has long grappled with several daunting challenges. There is an enormous body of knowledge to master, and it's growing at a head-spinning pace. In 1950, medical information doubled every fifty years. Today, it's every couple of months. The modern diagnostic workup and management of diseases ranging from heart failure to stroke is entirely different from what I learned in medical school and residency. And the breadth of knowledge we expect from our medical trainees is hard to overstate: competence in the scientific disciplines that underlie health and disease, skills ranging from how to remove a gall bladder to how to tell a patient they have cancer, and comfort delivering care in settings ranging from homeless clinics to modern ICUs.

In 1910, in response to the haphazardly organized and often fraudulent medical training programs of the era, a major study, the Flexner Report, delivered a scathing critique and a blueprint for a new system for medical education in the United States. More than a century later, the Flexner Report remains the foundation for medical education. Most of a medical student's first two years are spent learning the scientific underpinnings of medical practice—biochemistry, immunology, pathophysiology, anatomy, and the like, gradually progressing to more practical courses in areas such as infectious diseases, pharmacology, and medical interviewing. Only after demonstrating mastery of those subjects do students fully transition to the clinical setting, where an apprenticeship of sorts begins. Through rotations in a variety of clinical specialties, they gradually climb their learning curve, moving from novice to expert through supervised learning and graded responsibility. After four years of medical school, students graduate to residency (in fields like internal medicine or surgery), and later—if they choose to subspecialize in areas like cardiology or neonatology—fellowship.

The Flexner Report also helped give rise to the modern academic medical center, which fused the educational and research missions of a medical school with a clinical delivery system. Those of us who have spent our careers working at AMCs find this entirely unexceptional (we routinely talk of our "tripartite mission": patient care, teaching, and research), but it's worth reflecting on just how unusual this is. Law schools don't run law firms, business schools don't run businesses. Most medical schools, on the other hand, are embedded in and tightly linked to healthcare delivery systems—hospitals and clinics—and there is near-total mutual interdependence. The healthcare systems rely on the medical school faculty and trainees to deliver care, while the faculty and trainees rely on the clinical enterprise as their platform to train the next generation of physicians, to conduct clinical research, and to generate flexible dollars.

While a system whose core structure was invented 115 years ago can hardly be called innovative, recent efforts to rethink medical training have begun to bear fruit. Most medical schools, including my own, now introduce students to actual patients relatively early in their first year (after starting with practice on simulators and actor-patients, you'll be pleased to hear). Skills that were ignored during my training—breaking bad news, working in interdisciplinary teams, improving systems of care, and addressing health disparities—are now standard features of most curricula. There are fewer lectures (some schools have abolished them entirely) and more case-based discussions.

Yet the bones of medical training remain fundamentally unaltered, and they are increasingly problematic. Competency is determined more by elapsed time—four years for medical school and, say, three years for an internal medicine residency—than by data-driven appraisals. When there is an assessment of a trainee's work, it is often drawn from proxy measures of performance. For example, we rarely observe students taking a patient's history but rather extrapolate their level of competence from a review of their written summary or their oral presentation of the case. This would be like trying to judge a student's skills as a pianist by having them leave the recital and describe how it went.

As we've discussed throughout this book, in clinical medicine we now collect all our data digitally but have been abysmal at turning these data into insights, then converting these insights into actionable steps that improve health and healthcare. In medical education, we also have boatloads of data about our trainees but have done precious little to convert those data into tangible improvements.

Just as AI is poised to revolutionize clinical care, there is enormous potential for AI to transform medical education. I set out to find the institution that seemed to best appreciate the need to collect and analyze educational data and apply modern methods, including AI, to the process of minting a physician. I found it in the heart of Manhattan, at New York University.

I VISITED NYU's urban medical campus over two warm September days in 2024. My host was Marc Triola, a fifty-two-year-old professor and director of NYU's Institute for Innovations in Medical Education. Triola is a warm, enthusiastic, and articulate man who looks more like a square-jawed off-Broadway actor than the nerd he tells me he sees in the mirror.

NYU's medical school and health system, known as NYU Langone Health (Ken Langone, the founder of Home Depot, is NYU's chief benefactor), are housed in a cluster of buildings near the East River, about ten blocks south of the United Nations. A major expansion of the hospital in 2018 required a unique design, since the East Side Access rail yard courses underneath the site en route to Grand Central Terminal, making it dangerous to sink a foundation directly beneath the building. The architects devised an ingenious cantilever structure that straddles the rail yard below. The hospital tower seems to float above this foundation, with patient rooms rising skyward from a sixth-floor structural bridge while the operating rooms are delicately suspended beneath it.

This bridge is a nice metaphor for NYU's organizational structure, which is unique among top academic health systems. In 2007, NYU's medical enterprise was foundering, partly because of an extreme version of a problem endemic to academic medicine: tensions and misaligned incentives between the School of Medicine and the health system. A gutsy decision was made by the board of directors that year to merge the two entities and put a single leader in charge, a major departure from the usual structure in which a dean runs the medical school and a CEO leads the health system. The leader they chose, a sixty-year-old neuroradiologist named Robert Grossman, became potentate over NYU's medical empire. By bridging the gulf between medical school and health system, the merger set the stage for the organization's preeminence in the digital transformation of medical education.

Thirteen years earlier, in 1994, Marc Triola had arrived at NYU's medical school after completing a BA in biology at Johns Hopkins. During orientation, students were asked to jot down their interests on an index card. Fatefully, he wrote "computers," and was assigned a mentor—an NYU professor named Marty Nachbar, who, as it happened, was a pioneer in educational informatics. Triola had no real interest in making education his career focus—virtually all young physician-informaticists, then and now, choose to focus on the digital transformation of clinical care. But he spied an opportunity. "All the time-motion studies reveal that sitting in front of a computer is 45 to 65 percent of every physician's day," Triola told me. Yet all those hours go unexamined and unaddressed when it comes to medical education. "Imagine if I could teach you about something that's going to impact 65 percent of your day. Wouldn't we want to focus on this?"

Following clinical training, Triola completed an informatics fellowship and then joined NYU's faculty. As Nachbar approached retirement, he asked Triola to help lead NYU's work in educational innovation. "I knew nothing about medical education at that point other than having been a student and a resident," Triola said. "But I loved [Nachbar], and I wanted to help."

Importantly, the merger of the school and health system not only elevated the educational mission in NYU's firmament (education usually takes a back seat to the clinical mission, mostly because the latter is where the money is), but also broke down the usual barriers between the healthcare delivery system and educational IT. Because the school and the health system were now led by the same person, investments in developing data warehouses and dashboards for clinical care could be readily adopted by the educational enterprise—a level of synergy absent at other academic medical centers.

Triola remembers the excitement that swirled around integrating clinical care and medical education through technology and data. "We had a new dean and CEO who said, 'Medical education needs to change dramatically. . . . Your mission is to destroy the status quo,'" he recalled with a smile. "What do informaticists love? Disequilibrium, in which we can insert new ways of thinking about and doing things." Triola built out his institute's infrastructure, including an unmatched education-focused data warehouse, and hired a crack team of informaticists and educators to rethink the way doctors are trained.

Triola and his team faced an enormous challenge. Evaluating how a student was doing, providing meaningful feedback, and sorting out whether the student was seeing an optimal mix of patients (i.e., not seeing too many with diabetes and too few with lupus) depended on analyzing mostly text-based sources, whether in the form of written evaluations by faculty or clinical notes in the EHR. I asked him what he thought when he first tried ChatGPT in late 2022. "I immediately thought, 'This is the answer to so many of the barriers that limit our ability to effectively educate and train in the way we want.' . . . Here we have this magical thing, and it's available on everybody's phone!"

Some of NYU's approaches to transforming education using generative AI are standard fare: hosting conferences and town halls to educate all fifty thousand NYU Langone employees about AI's benefits and risks; creating self-service AI tools for students and educators to use; holding "prompt-a-thons" to teach trainees how best to deploy AI in their work. But they also set out to develop and study AI-based tools to reimagine various aspects of medical education.

Take the admissions process. NYU's medical school gets a lot of applications—not surprisingly, the number surged when the school became tuition-free in 2018 after a $100 million donation from

Langone. Currently, NYU's Grossman School of Medicine (the school was renamed for the dean/CEO in 2019) receives nearly 10,000 applications each year for 104 slots, about 100 applicants per available position. Screening these applications took about six thousand hours of faculty time. Using data from five years of applications, Triola and team built an AI algorithm that essentially replicated the results of the faculty review. In their 2019 admission season, they tested the AI "virtual screener" against traditional faculty review, and found extremely high concordance, including equivalent handling of female and minority applicants. Triola published these results in 2023; the topic is controversial enough that "this was the first manuscript I had to get approved by chief legal counsel," he recalled. "Anything related to admissions, people freak out." But the data were sufficiently compelling that today, NYU's med school application screening process is entirely done by AI.

Much of this assessment is of numerical data like grades and board scores. But the AI now also "reads" the students' essays ("I like science and I want to help people" is the oft-parodied stock essay theme). In the past few years, the team has found that the language in essays has changed—including a major uptick in the use of the word "delve," a tell that many essays are being drafted, and possibly written, by AI. Just as physicians are using AI to draft prior authorizations and insurance companies are having their AI reject them, Triola predicts that "every school will soon have AI reading AI-generated essays. It's kind of farcical."

⌒∧⌒

NYU'S MOST AMBITIOUS goal is the promotion of so-called precision education. We've already discussed the idea of precision *medicine*:

taking advantage of detailed measurements of patients—not only their diseases, symptoms, and lab and X-ray results but also their genetics, social factors, and more—to create personalized treatment plans supported by rigorous research.

Precision education seeks to customize training by applying similar techniques. The paradigm aims to create standards for defined areas of knowledge, skill, and attitude, measure students' progress against these standards, provide customized coaching to help them meet the goals, and use the achievement of competency rather than elapsed time as the arbiter of when they're ready to move on. It is still early, but these are sound principles, and I suspect that their program will ultimately have a striking impact on medical education.

Where does AI fit into the vision for precision education? AI can monitor students' progress against goals by reviewing everything from their clinical notes to their attending evaluations. It can develop customized feedback and educational tools to increase the odds of meaningful improvements. It can monitor the patients that trainees are seeing, adjust the flow of patients to create a balanced clinical portfolio, and even deliver simulated experiences in areas where they haven't seen enough actual patients.

None of this is straightforward. For example, if the intern doesn't "need" to see another patient with a heart attack but one comes into the ER when she is the only person on call, the patient's welfare will trump the educational goals. But the overall direction seems right to me.

THE VENN DIAGRAM of AI and medical education raises two additional questions, both of which get at the very heart of what it means to be a physician. Namely, are there new skills that trainees should learn in order to practice in a healthcare system suffused with AI? And, even harder, are there elements of today's curriculum that trainees no longer need to master?

Determining what new things to learn seems relatively easy. Many training programs are now encouraging students and residents to use AI tools, teaching how to write good prompts, and introducing issues like how to be the human in the loop, how to spot hallucinations and bias, and how to manage ethics and compliance issues.

The harder question is what we should teach *less* of. Said Triola, "Rote memorization and fact regurgitation are just going to be less important." I'll buy that, although no one has the time to look everything up, and a physician needs to know enough facts and clinical reasoning strategies to catch, or at least suspect, an AI hallucination or error. For example, in the case of the patient with fever, back pain, and a new murmur mentioned earlier in the book, two facts are central to understanding why GPT's diagnosis of bacterial endocarditis may not be right: One can't fully trust that a "new" murmur is actually new, and pyelonephritis (kidney infection) is far more common than endocarditis (heart valve infection). After listening to countless hours of debate on curricular purging, I have found near-universal agreement on only one point: We should abolish the mandatory memorization of the Krebs cycle. This consensus likely stemmed more from physicians' collective trauma over learning this biochemical energy pathway in med school than from any rigorous assessment of its educational merit.

But what about core functions like learning how to take a patient history and write a clinical note? Do we stop teaching the latter because we're reasonably confident that everybody will have a digital scribe in a few years? Triola wrote a policy for NYU that said that, as a general philosophy, students should have access to AI scribes if their supervising physicians do. But he left some wiggle room in the policy, allowing final decisions to be made by the director of each rotation. "And many of the clerkship directors said, 'No way,'" Triola told me. I asked him what their rationale was. "'Because the students need to learn clinical reasoning,' they said. And now I'm thinking: How do I convince them that that's not the way of the future?"

This may be the hardest question of all in medical education— and perhaps across all of education. If you believe that AI will ultimately take over many physician functions, do you stop teaching them to medical students and residents? Or do you recognize that— at least for the foreseeable future—there *will* be a physician in the loop, and they better have mastered the core skills or they won't be effective in their role? Even worse, by actively promoting de-skilling you may be creating a doom loop in which the AI surpasses physician performance partly because the latter is degraded by an impoverished educational experience.

Ezra Klein, the *New York Times* opinion writer known for his incisive analyses, has grappled with this issue for several years. Here he is on his podcast in 2024:

> The obvious thing that technology does for you is automate the early parts of the creative process. The part where you're supposed to be reading something difficult yourself? Well, the AI can summarize it for you. The part where you're supposed to sit there with a blank page and write something?

Well, the AI can give you a first draft. . . . I believe a lot of what makes humans good at thinking comes in those parts. . . .

This, to me, is actually a really big branching path, right? Do I want my kids learning how to use AI or being in a context where they're using it a lot. Or do I want to protect them from it as much as I possibly can so they develop more of the capacity to read a book quietly on their own or write a first draft? I actually don't know.

Triola leans toward exposing trainees to current practice as it is being transformed by AI. Jesse Burk-Rafel, a young physician-informaticist who leads research for Triola's group, comes down on the other side. "So Marc's argument would be, 'Okay, we should be using what they're going to be using right off the bat. We should not mess around with any of the developmentally appropriate models or things that start with baby steps, to force you to do the thinking.' But I think there's value in the synthesis."

I spoke to Nina Singh, a recent graduate of NYU's medical school and now a resident in UCSF's internal medicine program. During her time at NYU, she did research with Triola and his group and greatly admires their work. She, like Burk-Rafel, leans toward the "continue to teach the basics" side of this argument. "I know I could type the details of a case into ChatGPT, but I feel like it's been more helpful to learn things the traditional way," she said. "AI currently seems most helpful to people who already have a lot of baseline knowledge in that domain so that they can tell if what the AI is saying makes sense or if it's missing something."

At this stage, I also lean more toward Burk-Rafel's and Singh's viewpoint than Triola's. Since the pace of AI implementation is so uncertain and the need for human oversight is likely to be great, removing foundational skills from the curriculum too quickly seems like a risky bet. And so much remains unpredictable. Just remember AI pioneer Geoffrey Hinton's 2016 admonition that we should stop training new radiologists. Thank goodness we didn't listen.

Triola and Burk-Rafel do agree that the pace of change is outstripping our ability to think these complex issues through fully. "What's funny about AI, as opposed to any other advance in healthcare, is that it has outpaced curriculum development," said Triola. "We haven't had the chance to take a breath and say, 'What's the etiquette?'"

They also agree, as do I, that AI will inexorably change the role of the physician—with some of today's tasks being carried out by AI or by lesser-trained colleagues who have been upskilled by AI. But even here, even among experts, the future is murky. "We're teaching medical students and residents to know how to play violin, how to play bassoon, how to play viola bass. Instead, we should be teaching them how to conduct," Triola told me in our parting discussion at NYU.

"What does that *mean*?" I asked.

"I don't know. It just sounded great."

Epic, Oracle, and the Titans of Data

At a 2023 Oracle conference in Las Vegas, Larry Ellison, the company's founder and executive chairman, told the audience why Oracle had decided the prior year to purchase Cerner—the struggling electronic health records company—for $28.3 billion. "You have this wealth of data that will help doctors make much better decisions of what therapeutics to give you, and that will deliver better outcomes at a much lower cost," Ellison said. "I'm not sure there's anything we're working on here at Oracle that's more important than this."

"There was just one problem," *Business Insider* reported in 2024. "Cerner was a total mess . . . failing at the most elementary tasks of data management." The company had landed a $10 billion contract with the US Department of Veterans Affairs in 2017, but that contract was put on hold in 2022 following numerous blunders. These included the disappearance of more than eleven thousand physician orders in an "unknown queue," the system's failure to contact patients known to be suicidal who had missed clinic appointments, a medication ordering process that had metastasized into one that sometimes required thirty different steps, and frequent blackouts.

Even as Oracle quickly abandoned the Cerner name (the new brand was Oracle Health) and promised a shiny new EHR, the company continued to lose clients to Epic, the industry leader. Incredibly, Oracle senior executives claimed ignorance of the depths of the problems they had inherited. "There's always things that you discover after the fact," Mike Sicilia, the Oracle executive in charge of Cerner, said in a tense congressional hearing on the VA fiasco. "We certainly had read things that were publicly disclosed. But there's nothing like owning something to fully understand what's going on."

Oracle's hope was that, by combining Cerner's legacy EHR, clinical data, and healthcare know-how with Oracle's world-class cloud technology and engineering capabilities, the company would produce a product that Epic couldn't match. Seema Verma, the former head of the Centers for Medicare & Medicaid Services under the first Trump administration, now leads Oracle Health. "Our theory is that you can't solve healthcare's problems with thirty-year-old technology that was built in somebody's garage," she said. This is a double-barreled barb directed at Epic, which was famously built on an aging computer language called MUMPS (although, as you'll see, Epic was born not in a garage, but in a basement).

Oracle released its redesigned ambulatory EHR in 2024, a down-to-the-studs redo, meaning that current Cerner clients will need to decide whether to ditch their old system and adopt the new Oracle version. They just might—it has built-in cloud and AI capabilities and is designed so that much of the navigation is driven by voice command. David Feinberg, Oracle Health's chairman, described it to me: The EHR "summarizes my patient, uses ambient listening, I can interact in the middle of the visit. 'Hey Oracle, what's the person's hemoglobin A1C [a measure of diabetes control]? And how has it changed based on their metformin [a diabetes medication]?' Then all the actions are done. Billing, coding, referrals, the note to the patient, all with the human in the loop. AI is built into the whole thing. And we'll beat Epic because it's all integrated, you don't pay extra for it."

As Oracle began to disassemble and retool the Cerner chassis and infuse a healthy dose of AI, Feinberg expected that Oracle's seasoned engineers would be able to apply many of their skills from working on prior non-healthcare projects. But even he was still surprised by how often Oracle's previous projects proved relevant to healthcare. He recalled discussing the registration and check-in process for a new clinic patient with the programmers. He assumed it would take them months to build it out, but they had it done in no time. "I said to the Oracle guys, 'How long did you take to build it?' They're like, 'We didn't build it,'" implying that they had found an off-the-shelf solution from a prior project. Feinberg asked them where this module came from. "'Oracle is the market leader in prisons,'" they told him. "'And when you come to the prison, you've got to get undressed, you've got to go over there, you've got to get this and that done. And then you go out, you need stuff.' And I'm like, of course!"

In other words—and this is a bit sobering, though perhaps not surprising to anyone who has had a recent outpatient appointment—the procedure for a patient checking in for a clinic visit is like that of a convict being processed into the prison system.

MEANWHILE, AS ORACLE was coming to terms with its dog-caught-the-car issues, Epic continued to grow and, mostly, thrive. Though Oracle/Cerner does have a robust international business and a strong presence among small-to-midsize US hospitals, Epic has continued to dominate the US market. As of 2025, every one of the twenty hospitals on *U.S. News & World Report*'s Top Hospitals list uses Epic, including my own, UCSF. Two long-standing and prestigious Cerner clients, Intermountain Health and the University of Pittsburgh, announced in 2023 that they were switching to Epic, not content to wait for Oracle to reboot a mediocre Cerner product that they'd lost confidence in.

While Epic's history is well known to healthcare insiders, the story is worth a brief retelling. Judy Faulkner was born in 1943 in New Jersey and received her undergraduate degree in mathematics from Dickinson College in Carlisle, Pennsylvania. She then completed a master's degree in computer science from the University of Wisconsin. In 1979, a few years after graduating, UW's psychiatry department hired her to write a program to computerize its records and track its patients. She and her three employees worked in the basement of an off-campus apartment building outfitted with used furniture, the spinning disk drives in her Data General 16-bit mini-computer sounding like a clothes dryer tossing around a pair of wet sneakers. "You couldn't touch it because it would corrupt the data," Faulkner later recalled.

Faulkner and a colleague scraped together $70,000 from friends and family to launch a company they called Human Services Computing; they later renamed it Epic. Her cofounder, a UW psychiatrist named John Greist, left the company in 1983 after a fallout with Faulkner over her vision—specifically over control. "Part of my difficulty with her was me saying, 'Gosh, why don't we get some venture capital and we can build it faster,'" Greist recounted in a 2021 interview. "And she said, 'No, we're not going to do that. Because we'll lose control.' And certainly, that's been her policy. And she has lived it out and proven it. I was wrong. She was right."

That's an understatement. Today, Faulkner's company sits on 1,700 acres of rolling farmland in Verona, 11 miles outside of Madison and 2,100 miles away from Silicon Valley. The company now has fourteen thousand employees, thousands of clients, and yearly revenues of over $5 billion. More than 250 million people—about three out of four Americans—have at least some of their health data in an Epic record, and more than half the hospital beds in the US are serviced by the company's EHR.

Faulkner's theory of the case was that only by maintaining complete control over everything could Epic produce an integrated product that reliably served its users' needs. Over the years, she has rebuffed myriad offers to buy the company, take it public, or accept Wall Street financing. Faulkner's plan after she dies—she is currently eighty-two years old—is to place her shares into a trust controlled by family members and employees; they cannot be sold.

Even before the 2022 introduction of ChatGPT, Epic recognized the importance of AI to its business. The company set out to hire AI engineers, which meant convincing them that living and working in south-central Wisconsin would beat living and working in Palo Alto. They certainly try. The company's motto is "Do good. Have fun. Make money," and its dress code is "When there are visitors, you must wear clothes." Epic's campus is peppered with whimsical sculptures, including Humpty Dumpty, the Tin Man from *The Wizard of Oz*, and Dr. Seuss's Cat in the Hat. "How do we expect people to develop software that's going to be beautiful for our users if we keep them in a boring, sterile environment?" asks Faulkner.

Epic's yearly users' meeting is legendary for its size and, as you'd guess, quirkiness. Every summer, Verona's population swells from fifteen thousand to nearly twice that, as eleven thousand users descend on Epic's "Intergalactic Headquarters" and jam the five-story "Deep Space" auditorium to hear what the company is up to. In 2024, the theme was, of course, AI. "If you think we've done a lot of creative things in the last year, hold on to your hat. You ain't seen nothing yet!" Faulkner gushed to an admiring crowd.

As she does at every year's conference, Faulkner came out in costume; in 2024 it was a Mother Goose outfit, befitting the session's theme of "Storytime." The reference was to Epic's AI story: more than one hundred AI initiatives already rolled out or in development, covering virtually every use case I've touched on in this book, including ambient scribes, inbox drafts, prior auths, clinical decision support, precision medicine, scheduling, billing, patient flow, and clinical trials matching. In addition, the company is leveraging its database of more than one hundred million de-identified patient records to facilitate clinical research. The initiative, which Epic calls

Cosmos, can also provide treatment recommendations based on the experience of patients in the database with similar clinical profiles.

While VC-funded Silicon Valley start-ups promise speed and nimbleness, one thing they can't compete with Epic on is trust—not necessarily that the AI tools will function perfectly out of the box (since, at least so far, most have not), but trust that Epic's AI will be seamlessly integrated into their EHR's workflow and that the company will still be around in five years. "Every hospital customer and prospect knows what it's getting with Epic: trust, predictability, collaboration, and security. Innovation with Epic may take time, but it can be trusted," wrote Seth Joseph in a 2024 *Forbes* profile of the company's AI ambitions. The Epic sepsis decision support tool's sloppy debut (chapter 4) rocked the company, mostly because it had the potential to shatter this hard-won trust.

OVER ITS NEARLY half century in business, Epic has gone from scrappy start-up to the King Kong of the healthcare industry. Several companies have built specialty-specific ambulatory EHRs for fields like dermatology and orthopedics, but only Oracle is taking aim at Epic's core business—the electronic health record for large hospitals and health systems. Today, the competition centers not so much on which EHR to install (since nearly everybody already has one) but on whether to place your big AI bet on your EHR vendor or on a plug-and-play strategy—with your EHR serving as a backbone while software built by third parties provides AI solutions for specific problems.

An obvious analogy is Apple's App Store, a model for the smooth integration of products built by an army of third-party developers. While Apple is "open," the company is obsessive about *how* it integrates with other tools—nobody can just join without paying Apple a hefty fee and adhering religiously to its integration standards. This, of course, has helped Apple become one of the world's most valuable companies and created an ecosystem of apps that deliver a generally positive and predictable user experience.

Judy Faulkner recognizes that pressure from third-party creators and health systems—and now federal law—requires that she open her notoriously closed system to competitors. She professes to be unconcerned. "I think that what will happen is that a few of them will do very well. And the majority of them won't," she told *Forbes* in 2021. "It's not us as much as the health systems who have to respond to the patient saying, 'Send my data here,' or 'Send my data there.'"

The *Forbes* profile outlined seven Epic tactics—ranging from noncompete restrictions to picking companies to partner with—that seem either monopolistic or at least "raise questions." You'll recall from chapter 4 that Epic chose Nuance's DAX and Abridge as its favored AI scribe affiliates. They were part of an Epic program initially called "Partners and Pals," which was later rebranded to "Workshop," likely on the advice of corporate attorneys who worried that the term "partners" might be problematic in antitrust litigation. "A big question ultimately comes down to whether Epic's conduct can be interpreted as fair play—simply part of the 'rough and tumble of the marketplace'—or exclusionary and anti-competitive in nature, pursued primarily for the purpose of advancing Epic's control," wrote *Forbes*'s Seth Joseph.

While one can appreciate both sides of the argument, there is no doubt that the cumulative effect of Epic policies and practices is to beat back competitive threats. I spoke to several health system technology leaders who told me they lean toward using Epic's AI offerings even when they know there are better third-party tools out there. In considering the purchase of AI tools from an outside vendor, "they have to be extraordinarily better than Epic's," one leader who wished to remain anonymous told me. (Virtually every health system leader I spoke with who had anything critical to say about Epic insisted on anonymity, which tells you much of what you need to know about Epic's stranglehold on the industry.)

The reasons some health systems favor Epic's AI offerings go beyond economics, integration, and codependency. Most healthcare IT leaders don't really want to deal with 120 decibels of "innovation noise." As one chief information officer lamented, "I have fifty vendors reaching out a week. Which one do I listen to?" Going—and sticking—with Epic for your AI needs has become the safe choice, echoing the maxim about a colossus from a previous generation: "Nobody ever gets fired for buying IBM."

In 2025, Epic introduced a new pricing option that—while helping its clients employ the company's AI tools at scale—would discourage customers from wandering off into the broader AI marketplace. In addition to its traditional à la carte model, health systems could now pay a single fee to access Epic's *entire* AI portfolio. The system that has paid for the complete Epic menu is unlikely to shell out additional dollars for a third-party AI tool, no matter how much better it might be.

At Epic's annual users' meeting in August 2025, the company made several announcements that illustrated its ongoing push to dominate the AI market among its EHR users. First, as I mentioned earlier, Epic announced that it would release its own AI scribe product, in partnership with Microsoft. More significantly—given the growing focus on agentic AI—it announced a suite of AI agents integrated directly into the EHR: "Art" for clinicians, "Penny" for administrators, and "Emmie" for patients.

While many start-ups maintained their bravado ("The bottom line is that we're building an AI platform for healthcare that's much broader than building an AI feature in an EHR," insisted Suki CEO Punit Soni), Epic's relentless moves continued to challenge the intrepid start-ups. Though Epic's new tools haven't been fully vetted as of this writing, the threat was clear. I heard one health system IT executive colorfully describe Epic's approach as being like that of the kid who "licks all the cookies" before friends arrive at his birthday party—and the cookie jar keeps getting bigger.

Given Epic's commanding position and its comprehensive efforts to maintain it, one could have guessed that an antitrust lawsuit wouldn't be far behind. In September 2024, a company named Particle Health filed a lawsuit against Epic in the Southern District of New York, claiming that Epic was engaged in monopolistic, anticompetitive practices that hampered Particle's effort to compete in the provider-payer marketplace. Epic punched back, claiming that Particle was violating patient privacy by selling EHR data to other companies under false pretenses.

The Biden administration, under Federal Trade Commission chair Lina Khan, took an aggressive stance against monopolistic business practices, though it had not weighed in on Epic or the Particle lawsuit by the end of its term. As of this writing, while it seems unlikely that Trump's team will aggressively pursue Epic, it seems equally unlikely that the Particle lawsuit will be the last legal challenge to Epic's corner on the market. In fact, in May 2025, CureIS, a company specializing in technology solutions for government healthcare programs, filed suit in federal court, alleging that Epic was engaged in a "scheme to destroy" its business.

In the end, the question may turn on whether we should allow *any* private company to dominate something as important as our healthcare data. "There's a need for broader reform," Adam Gaffney, past president of Physicians for a National Health Program, told *The American Prospect* magazine in 2024. "Handing the keys over to a private monopoly doesn't make sense. You need to think of a national medical record system as a public service."

GIVEN HIS WIDE variety of leadership roles, David Feinberg may well have a better view of the healthcare digital landscape than anyone. He's run two large health systems (UCLA and Geisinger), led Google Health for two years, and became CEO of Cerner in 2021, orchestrating the company's sale to Oracle the following year. Perhaps just as important, he's a trained psychiatrist. I asked him how he characterizes the Epic-Oracle competition, one in which, at this point, Oracle is the clear underdog. "Epic was the wrong strategy with brilliant execution, and Cerner was the right strategy with shitty execution. And now our execution is insane," he gushed. "I meet with Larry Ellison every week. He says, 'We are now a health company.'"

Nevertheless, it will be an uphill climb for Oracle. Epic literally owns the market sector composed of marquee health systems and teaching hospitals in the US, which means that nearly all young doctors will use Epic during their training—and thus will expect to use it when they begin practice. Feinberg is counting on Oracle's

VA installation to dampen Epic's advantage, since 70 percent of trainees also rotate through VA hospitals. He anticipates a future in which "every doc rotates at a VA and has an amazing experience and then goes back to their academic hospitals and says, 'Hey, I want what's over there.'" You have to admire his moxie, but that feels like a stretch to me, particularly since no Epic customer has ever traded out its system, except after hospital mergers or acquisitions.

WHILE EPIC AND ORACLE are battling with each other to be the EHR (and, by extension, the AI platform) of choice, their greatest competition may come from their flanks. As technological breakthroughs— as well as lawsuits, government pressure, and ultimately health system and maybe even patient demand—make it easier to buy and integrate apps built by third parties, many of the best AI tools won't be ones built by the EHR companies themselves; they'll be ones developed by AI-focused companies and organizations. If that's the case, Epic's competition may come less from Oracle and more from the Abridges and Hippocratics of the world, or the OpenAIs and Microsofts. Or the Mayos.

In fact, moving toward a more pluralistic digital ecosystem is how most industries evolve over time. Rather than being worried, Feinberg thinks this offers Oracle another leg up. Epic is beginning to open itself up, but it is doing so reluctantly and after a long history of obsessing over control. Oracle's corporate DNA, in contrast, is oriented toward being the sturdy Christmas tree on which many digital ornaments can hang. "There's no industry where the end user is working on the system of record except healthcare," Feinberg said. "So not only do we have to fix the EHR; the real play—because I think they become a commodity—is the platform."

The example here comes from aviation. While you are interacting with sleek web- and app-based tools from Expedia or United Airlines, the underlying system of record is actually Sabre, the aviation scheduling, pricing, and reservations database built by American Airlines and IBM in the late 1950s. Astonishingly, Sabre remains aviation's database of record, humming in the background, although virtually no end user interacts directly with it.

In an interview with Bryan Roberts, the prominent healthcare investor, I raised the question of how outside companies, particularly healthcare AI start-ups, will compete against the Epics of the world. "I think Epic starts out running the hundred-yard dash five yards ahead of everybody else," he said. "The EHR could be the user interface, or it could just become the clinical database [akin to Sabre]. I think [the EHR companies] will fight like hell not to just become the clinical database, and they should."

As you can see, the real competition in the AI-for-healthcare marketplace has far more angles than a simple contest between one remarkable company built on Wisconsin farmland by an intrepid entrepreneur who became the nation's wealthiest self-made woman and a digital behemoth owned by the world's second-richest person, hell-bent on topping off his legacy by fixing healthcare through the purchase—and remaking—of a struggling EHR company. Nevertheless, there is clearly a mano a mano aspect to the competition between the two giants. I asked Feinberg about his own relationship with Epic's iconic leader. "I say to Judy, 'I love you, Judy, and I will never say anything bad about you or Epic.' And she goes, 'Dave, I love you. I'll never say anything bad about you.'"

6

Payment, Policies, and Politics

Show Me the Money

I had a wise and battle-scarred mentor who once said to me, "Whenever anybody tells you, 'It's not about the money,' you can assume it's about the money." You've surely gotten a sense that AI's march through hospital wards and clinics will not be determined solely by the pursuit of healing, but also by the hunt for profit. Let's dive a bit deeper into this dance between the values of Hippocrates and those of Gordon Gekko.*

We'll begin with four basic truths. The first is that most of the AI in healthcare will be built and purchased by organizations that are driven, in large part, by the desire to be profitable. This is true even for organizations like UCSF, a nonprofit health system with a strong social mission, but one that nonetheless would have to shut down if our expenses exceeded our revenues for more than a few months.

---

* "Greed is good," he infamously said in the 1987 Oliver Stone film *Wall Street*.

The second is that the economics of health AI are influenced by the labyrinthine flow of dollars through the health system—with employers, government, insurers, providers, and patients all vying to get the best value for their money, and a motley assortment of middlemen thrown in just in case things aren't confusing enough. This mishmash of a system distorts the usual economic relationship between vendor and purchaser in crucial ways.

The third is that AI, in healthcare and elsewhere, is being propelled by a gigantic bubble, with sky-high valuations and huge investments by venture capitalists and some of the wealthiest companies on the planet. The AI market appears to be following the path of the famous Gartner Hype Cycle, with healthcare AI currently near the cycle's "Peak of Inflated Expectations." This means that it's likely to pass through the "Trough of Disillusionment" on its way—if all goes well—to the "Plateau of Productivity." "You can already see the writing on the wall," Ali Ghodsi, CEO of Databricks, a data analytics company, said in 2024. "It doesn't matter how cool it is what you do—does it have business viability?"

The fourth is that the eye-popping investments in AI—the ones with a dollar sign followed by twelve digits and three commas—won't be healthcare-specific. Rather, they are outlays that traditional tech giants like Google, Amazon, Microsoft, and Meta, and new entrants like OpenAI and Anthropic, are making to build and test foundation models like Gemini, GPT, and Claude. These businesses hope to recoup their investments in part when smaller companies, including those in healthcare, license their technologies or store their data in the giants' corporate clouds, attracted in part by the AI capabilities unlocked by those choices.

While these behemoths are not thinking exclusively about healthcare in planning their AI strategies, with healthcare accounting for nearly 20 percent of the US economy, it's not far from front of mind. As of this writing, I don't see signs of an impending bursting bubble ("Whether we burn $500 million a year or $5 billion—or $50 billion a year—I don't care," said OpenAI CEO Sam Altman in 2024), although the emergence of the Chinese AI model DeepSeek in 2025 did challenge one fundamental assumption about generative AI: that building advanced AI models demands virtually unlimited capital and the world's most cutting-edge chips. If gen AI foundation models become a commodity, it won't just be the start-up puppies that need to worry about their defensible moats. The big dogs may as well.

While DeepSeek will amp up competition for the "Magnificent Seven"* (the tech titans powering the stock market's surge in the 2020s), the industry's fundamentals remain solid. If anything, the democratization of AI may advance the whole field, including in healthcare, by making better tools available at lower cost. Of course, anything can happen to an industry in a bubble, particularly with something as novel and rapidly changing as gen AI. "Reporters have successfully called 25 of the last three bubbles," quipped tech journalist Casey Newton.

Even amid today's AI hype and the inevitable market shakeout, healthcare AI's economic potential will probably track with its transformative power over time. AI is not another blockchain or crypto fad—it's a massively powerful, genuinely useful, constantly improving, widely accessible, and relatively understandable innovation that is highly likely to deliver tangible value to an industry plagued by unmet needs and staggering inefficiencies. While the

---

* Apple, Microsoft, Alphabet (Google), Amazon, Nvidia, Tesla, and Meta (formerly Facebook).

AI bubble may eventually deflate somewhat, in healthcare at least, it's built on too solid a foundation to burst entirely.

oᴸₒ

THE PURCHASING DECISIONS for most AI tools in healthcare will be based on end users' assessments of the costs and benefits of bringing in the technology. This is certainly true for things like digital scribes and chart summarization, where the payoff, health systems hope, will come through seeing more patients, better billing, and happier clinicians. In other cases, particularly when the AI is an adjunct to existing (and billable) services, the question arises: Should there be a separate, add-on payment for the use of AI? And, if there is, whose bank account should the dollars come from?

These questions usually boil down to whether the additional cost of an AI-enabled service will be covered by a private insurance company or a government payer like Medicaid or Medicare. There are a handful of cases in which a payer has added an AI-specific reimbursement, such as when Medicare decided in 2020 to pay a supplemental fee for the use of Viz LVO, an AI tool that reviewed specialized CT scans to triage patients with suspected strokes. Similarly, in 2024 Medicare increased its reimbursement for an AI-enabled system that uses biopsy and imaging data to predict risk and guide therapy for patients with prostate cancer.

In contrast, as of this writing insurers have not agreed to pay for AI-enhanced mammograms. Nevertheless, many radiologists are offering them, asking patients to pay an additional $40 to $100 per scan out of pocket for the promise of a modest increase in detection rates. When offered this option, more than one-third of women chose the enhanced screening protocol, according to a 2024 study of nearly 750,000 patients.

Some companies have flamed out while waiting for their AI payment ship to come in. Pear Therapeutics was a Boston-based company that built an AI-based tool to help people with opiate addiction. Despite a relatively modest cost ($300 for twelve weeks of therapy), approval from the FDA, and some data showing the tool's value, Pear filed for bankruptcy in 2023 after failing to secure reimbursement from government and private payers. "As a digital therapeutics company, you have to go to the FDA, go to the insurers, then you actually have to go and get people to use it to get revenue," Keith Figlioli of the investment firm LRV Health, told *Politico*. "That is so much friction to get a company off the ground."

There is clearly a delicate balance to be struck: Failure by insurers to pay for the use of effective AI tools will discourage adoption, while locking in overly generous insurance reimbursements may encourage overuse. "The goal cannot be to capture all of the savings associated with an AI-enabled service," wrote health economists Anna Zink, Michael Chernew, and Hannah Neprash in a 2024 *JAMA* article. Instead, the insurance payments must "be sufficient to allow AI firms to set a price that clinicians and patients can afford (taking AI-induced savings into account) and still promote innovation." Some—probably most—of the AI we'll use in everyday practice, such as decision support tools, will *not* be associated with additional payments, their costs absorbed by health systems as a new price of doing business and their leaders hoping against hope to see a positive ROI when all the numbers are in.

Sorting out the economics of AI-enabled healthcare in our fee-for-service payment system will become increasingly cumbersome.

Tacking on extra fees for the use of AI in clinical care may not be a viable long-term solution—over time, it will be like buying a car and being charged additional fees for an AI-enabled steering wheel, mirrors, pedals, and wipers. Assuming that our political system is acting rationally (a risky assumption), AI should accelerate the shift toward global- and population-based payment systems. In a world brimming with AI tools, having a clinical practice receive risk-adjusted payments for the overall care of a population of patients seems more sensible than paying for each service separately. Under a global payment model, healthcare organizations will have an incentive to implement AI that improves their quality, access, satisfaction, and efficiency.

ALL THE PLAYERS in the healthcare system have incentives and worldviews that influence their decisions. Brian Silverstein, a physician and strategist at Innovaccer, a health tech solutions company, told me, "Health insurance works on a one-year cycle. So, unless you have a program for me that I can make money on in a year, I'm not really going to do it. I'll give it lip service because I don't want to sound like a pariah, but ultimately, I'm just not interested."

Ami Parekh, chief medical officer of Included Health, which coordinates care for large companies, sees a similar problem. Her company is rapidly adopting AI tools to improve member services and decrease administrative load, but investments in clinical care are stunted because of the payment system. Take, for example, tools to aid in diagnosis. "AI can do a great job at diagnosis. But is anyone going to be willing to pay for that?" she asks rhetorically. "Because we never made the transition to value-based payment or paying for outcomes, we're going to struggle to adopt the coolest parts of AI." While the healthcare system is moving toward payment models that reward improved outcomes and cost-effectiveness, the pace of that transformation is somewhere between sluggish and glacial.

THE VENTURE CAPITAL companies investing in healthcare AI are also central actors in this grand narrative. One of the most acclaimed is Hemant Taneja, CEO of General Catalyst (GC), a $32 billion investment fund based in Silicon Valley. About a decade ago, soon after *The Digital Doctor* was published, Taneja called me to ask for a tutorial on how doctors think about healthcare and how hospitals function. No surprise, I found him to be a fast study. In late 2024, I asked him to assess the rapidly evolving healthcare AI space.*

Taneja anticipates that much of the change wrought by AI will be in nonclinical areas, like HR, billing, and legal services. He predicts that AI will allow much of this work, which in the past two decades has been offshored, to be brought back to the US. "The biggest thrust right now is in places where we took advantage of globalization and offshore labor for cost improvements. We're going to surpass that with onshore productivity using AI."

As important as the operational and business efficiencies are, Taneja recognizes that AI's biggest impact will be in transforming tasks like diagnosing and prescribing. But, he cautions, "This is people's health and life. So you need to make sure these things are

---

* I advise Commure, a company funded by General Catalyst.

trained specifically for healthcare." While he's the lead investor in Hippocratic AI—you'll recall its founder's celebration of autonomous AI—Taneja believes that the human in the loop will remain important in most clinical scenarios for the foreseeable future. "A nurse making a mistake will be much more acceptable, emotionally, than an AI, for a while," he said. "I think you need to build confidence by having it be supervised."

While Taneja has invested in several healthcare AI companies tackling a variety of use cases, he thinks that integration—accomplished through digital platforms—is ultimately the North Star. He recalled that a decade ago, "it seemed like everybody was trying to innovate around the edges. And I was like, no. Not a bunch of point solutions that don't talk to each other. The main thing is to make the main thing the main thing. And so we've got to get into the guts of it and change how we operationalize the interactions between employees and administration and the clinical workforce."

While General Catalyst could encourage each of its founders to build and test their individual tools and then try to weave them into a holistic platform for health systems, Taneja worried that this approach wouldn't create a truly integrated solution. He decided to go big—really big. In February 2025, General Catalyst finalized its purchase of Summa Health, a midsize health system based in Akron, Ohio—the first instance of a health system being fully acquired by a venture capital company. While some of the motivation was for Summa to serve as a test bed for various AI tools built by GC-funded start-ups, Taneja also wants to make the hospital a poster child for profitability, patient and clinician experience, and responsible use of data and AI. "I want it to become what everybody else wants to be," he said. "We wanted a place where the community and the system were aligned, and the leaders [at Summa] are keen on it. We'll see, it'll be very hard. I'm not being naive, but if we don't try, we're not going to change things."

After a presentation on the Summa–General Catalyst relationship at GC's 2024 Napa conference, I chatted with one of the attendees, a leader at another GC-funded company. We both agreed that the marriage of a Bay Area–based venture capital firm and an Akron, Ohio, health system was exciting and gutsy. But, she added, "You have a Midwestern flyover town and a bunch of wealthy coastal elites flying in to 'help.' What could go wrong?"

WHILE THE GC-SUMMA relationship represents an audacious bet, it's not a careless one. In fact, having taken a deep dive into the world of VCs and digital health start-ups a decade ago when I was researching *The Digital Doctor*, I've been impressed by how much more sophisticated and realistic the start-up founders and investors are today.

This isn't to say that they've completely purged hyperbole from their pitch decks, or that they truly understand the world of clinical medicine. John Halamka, the Mayo Clinic digital guru, told me why he no longer attends HIMSS, the massive health IT industry conference. "Imagine if you have five thousand twenty-two-year-olds that can't spell HIPAA but are absolutely convinced they can disrupt healthcare. And then you have five thousand venture capitalists that think that, if they can just find the right twenty-two-year-old, they'll make 5x on their investment," he said.

Of course, two things can be true at the same time: This kind of hype can make an amusing caricature, and this kind of optimistic risk-taking is needed if healthcare is ever to be truly transformed.

Regulation

When ChatGPT hit the public's radar screen on November 30, 2022, most people were astonished by the capabilities of the new tool. But Rob Califf, commissioner of the US Food and Drug Administration, was unfazed. In between his two stints at the FDA (under Obama from 2016 to 2017 and Biden from 2022 to 2025), he spent "five years in the bowels of Google," helping to lead both Google Health and the company's life sciences incubator, Verily. At Google, he had a chance to see generative AI take shape, which prepared him for the concerns it would cause once it was released into the wild. "The big question [within Google] was not, 'Is it going to happen?'" he told me. "The question was what were the risks of unleashing it on society?"

I spoke to Califf a few weeks before he ended his second tenure as FDA commissioner. Given the attitude of the incoming Trump administration toward regulation and federal bureaucracy, he worried about his FDA colleagues; many were planning to take early retirement or look for new jobs. He also feared that a large hit to FDA's budget and morale would have dire consequences for the health of Americans—not just in medicine but in the huge swath of the US economy that the FDA regulates. Califf argued that the agency needs *more* resources to carry out its functions, particularly as new AI tools become ubiquitous features of clinical care.

Healthcare regulators have always walked a precarious tightrope. Too much regulation, and you might stifle innovation to the point of blocking lifesaving treatments from reaching patients. Too little, and you risk erosion of public trust—or worse, actual harm to patients.

As challenging as this balancing act is under normal circumstances, at least drugs and medical devices are relatively stable targets. Generative AI is different—it's a technology that could transform itself overnight, that could hallucinate one day and perform flawlessly the next, that could do everything from revolutionizing healthcare to creating bioweapons. As Ethan Mollick says, today's AI is the worst you'll ever use. I certainly hope that's true, but who's to say that tomorrow's AI might not be more dangerous? The traditional regulatory paradigm and toolbox seem woefully inadequate.

YOU'LL RECALL MY description of NYU's AI tool to screen applicants for its training programs. After rigorous studies proved the value and safety of the tool when used to review medical school applications, the team tried the algorithm on residency applications. The results were equally impressive.

In 2023, New York City passed a law governing the use of AI in employment decisions. The law didn't ban AI hiring tools outright. Instead, it required annual independent audits to ensure these tools weren't introducing bias. While this sounds reasonable, here is where good intentions collide with real-world complexity: Residents and fellows—at NYU and elsewhere—exist in a gray area between students and employees. Faced with legal uncertainty and the expense of compliance, NYU's lawyers recommended yanking the plug on the use of the AI screener for the residents and fellows. Poof: Several thousand hours of faculty time were back on applicant-screening duty and could no longer be applied to seeing patients, conducting research, or educating trainees. (NYU continues to use the AI screener for medical students, who are unambiguously not employees.)

When I shared this story with Micky Tripathi, the chief health AI officer of the United States at the time, he shook his head in frustration. "That's the kind of thing that scares me a lot," he said. "We should always keep in mind, 'How does the technology compare to what humans are doing today?' Let's not pretend that the machine has to be perfect."

Rob Califf saw nuance rather than error in the New York authorities' actions. After I described the NYU case to him, he said, "You just encapsulated why enforcement discretion"—the regulator's ability to selectively choose which cases to pursue—"drives people crazy, but why it's so important. Because what if an institution in New York City was using AI to discriminate against people with Jewish backgrounds, or something similar?"

Before you choose sides in the light- versus heavy-touch regulation debate, it's worth recalling that the modern FDA was born from tragedy—specifically, the thalidomide disaster of the late 1950s and early 1960s. While other countries witnessed thousands of horrific birth defects from the heavily marketed sedative, the US was largely spared, thanks to a diligent FDA reviewer named Frances Oldham Kelsey who refused to rush the drug's approval. Later disasters involving drugs like Vioxx and fen-phen, plus the devastating opioid epidemic, remind us that although the risks of overregulation are very real, too little oversight can kill.

THE STORY OF healthcare regulation begins in the fifth century BCE, in ancient Greece, with what might be considered the world's first medical regulation: the Hippocratic oath. This voluntary ethical code was a noble start, but as medicine grew more complex, good intentions proved insufficient. Over the last century, a web of oversight has emerged: licensing and board certification for doctors, accreditation for hospitals and medical schools, federal regulations for medications and devices, and guardrails around patient privacy through laws like HIPAA. Each of these oversight bodies has its own approach, authority, and funding sources, and all struggle to find the right balance.

Generative AI has thrown an enormous wrench into this long-established machinery. Unlike traditional medical tools, gen AI doesn't produce consistent outputs—ask the same question twice, you may get different answers. It can evolve over time, potentially introducing new biases or "algorithmic drift." It's not limited to a single function—a gen AI tool can diagnose diseases, summarize medical records, or predict patient outcomes. Its reasoning can be as opaque as a black box, even to its creators. Its benefits and risks may be very different when implemented in different organizations, driven by factors ranging from patient population to organizational culture.

Under Califf's leadership, the FDA approached these challenges with gritty determination and, at least for a massive federal agency, some creativity. The organization started by adapting its existing playbook—after all, the FDA has been certifying medical software since 1995, when it approved PAPNET, an AI tool for detecting suspicious cells in Pap smears. Over the years, the FDA developed Software as a Medical Device (SaMD) standards, authorizing more than one thousand AI-enabled medical devices, most of them in radiology.

One reason AI is a square peg to FDA's round holes is that the agency's own definition of a device involves screening for or diagnosing and treating *a disease*. As Christina Silcox, a Duke University expert on health regulation, explained to me, "It's the 'a disease' part that starts to trip them up." An AI-enabled tool to diagnose heart attacks or strokes fits neatly into the FDA's paradigm. An AI scribe, a chart summarizer, or a hospital length-of-stay predictor: not so much.

To Califf, the decision to require a full FDA review for adding AI to a previously regulated device like an MRI machine or a cardiac defibrillator was straightforward: "Of course." Health promotion and administrative tools—here, the decision was that no review was needed, since the risk was felt to be low. The most challenging cases were those in the middle—mostly clinical decision support tools that, while not dictating clinical care, surely shape it.

Interestingly, while much of the debate focuses on this middle category, Califf has second thoughts about the decision to exclude administrative AI tools from FDA oversight. He sees the big problem as the financialization of everything in the US, including healthcare. "The fundamental core values of clinical care have really lost out. AI doesn't have a soul," he says sadly. "If a car-driving algorithm gets you from point A to point B safely and quickly, that's pretty darn good. But if AI is optimized to maximize profit for the health system, that can hurt people." Thought of this way, AI that's used by an insurance company to deny payment for a certain procedure or treatment, or by a hospital to create access barriers for certain types of patients, should not evade regulatory scrutiny.

The FDA faces another important limitation: The organization's authority, at least for now, allows it to regulate only manufacturers, not end users like hospitals and health systems. "It is becoming increasingly evident that AI performance should be monitored in the environment in which it is being used," Califf and colleagues wrote in *JAMA* in 2024. They compared this need for ongoing, real-time monitoring to keeping tabs on patients in the intensive care unit.

The muddiest area on the regulatory football field is how to classify AI-enabled clinical decision support (CDS) tools, in part because the FDA has moved the goalposts. In 2019, the rules seemed straightforward: If a hospital implemented a CDS tool but the clinicians had the final say, could see the AI's reasoning, and weren't bound by its recommendations, FDA's blessing was not required. In 2022, however, the agency's guidance shifted. Now, any CDS tool producing specific outputs for urgent situations or relying on frequent vital sign measurements was considered high risk and thus subject to FDA oversight.

Duke's Mark Sendak and colleagues analyzed the implications of the new guidance for sepsis prediction tools. Their sobering conclusion? Under a strict reading of the 2022 guidance, virtually every acute care decision support tool used in American hospitals would require FDA clearance, including algorithms we routinely use to assess the likelihood that patients have pulmonary embolism, pneumonia, or stroke, and to triage those patients. "While a prevailing view may be that the FDA is unlikely to pursue enforcement action against healthcare delivery organizations (HDOs), this brings little comfort to risk-averse HDO leaders," wrote Sendak. He posited that if the FDA ever stepped up its enforcement, hospitals would simply turn off their clinical decision support tools, a decision that might harm patients, particularly as the tools become more accurate and useful.

In my conversations with Califf, he emphasized the idea of "enforcement discretion" several times. In his mind, the regulator sometimes sends a signal regarding something they're watching, rather than a clear warning that they're ready to pounce. He feels that it's the end users who often overreact, which sometimes represents a failure of leadership. "The lawyer can't tell you not to do something," he told me. "That's a decision the leaders of the health system are making. The lawyers can just advise you of the risk."

Califf appreciates that there's no way for the FDA to regulate all the AI-based decision support that will be employed in healthcare. He points to the Food Safety Modernization Act of 2011 as one potential model for relatively light-touch but broad-based regulation of a multiplayer ecosystem. There are ten rules that define the preservation of food safety as you go from farm to table, he explained. "These are not like ten commandments—they're rules. The expectation is that the farms, the suppliers, and the retail stores are all going to practice these rules. What the FDA and state regulators do is audit every three to five years, three if you're bad, five if you're good. And the system is dependent on people following those rules. We need that sort of a system in clinical decision support because it is going to be ubiquitous. I don't think there's any stopping it. And it's needed."

When I met with Micky Tripathi in 2024, even he—the government's chief health AI official—struggled to solve the regulatory puzzle. I asked him this: "If we throw a wrapper on GPT-4 and it gives me diagnostic advice when I'm seeing a patient—but I, as a physician, still need to sign off at the end—where does that live in the regulatory framework?" He paused for a moment and then said, "Dunno yet."

IN 2024, FORMER national coordinator for health IT David Blumenthal, writing with Google's chief of regulatory affairs, Bakul Patel, argued that regulating clinical decision support would be as problematic as regulating medical textbooks or journals—after all, they're just automating the application of existing medical knowledge. Blumenthal and Patel believe that gen AI's unique attributes demand a radical rethink. "How can the government regulate a single device that could be applied to any conceivable clinical problem, whose knowledge base dwarfs any human's and changes constantly, whose methods of reaching conclusions are beyond the comprehension even of its creators, and whose computing capacity grows by leaps and bounds?" they asked.

Their provocative recommendation: Treat AI more like we treat doctors than devices. They proposed a system—modeled on the licensing and certification of a new physician—in which AI tools must demonstrate appropriate training, pass clinical exams, undergo supervised practice (under human oversight, at least initially), and retrain for new clinical situations. The AI's performance would be publicly reported, just like we publish physician licensure and board certification status. I asked Califf what he thought about the idea. "I think the concept is not bad," he said, "but I wouldn't take it very literally. I mean, my God, we've got physicians now recommending that public health officials can't promote flu and Covid vaccines." In other words, it's not like our model for regulating physicians is perfect.

EVEN FOR AI TOOLS clearly within its jurisdiction, the FDA has struggled with the technology's shape-shifting nature. The FDA's traditional approach to medical device regulation was like evaluating a fixed snapshot, but AI tools are more like a constantly evolving live video feed. In response, in 2024 Califf announced a "total product lifecycle" approach. Under the new system, manufacturers can submit a Predetermined Change Control Plan (PCCP) at the time of their initial application, which allows them to retrain and retest their tools according to preapproved parameters. Between updates, the AI is locked down, just like any other medical device.

The FDA is also borrowing from the world of institutional accreditation, by assessing the manufacturer's culture and development processes—not just the product itself—in its oversight of certain healthcare AI tools. This resembles systems in aviation and financial services, in which the regulator focuses on whether firms are adhering to best practices in developing and monitoring their tools.

Not everyone is sold on these ideas. As Blumenthal and Patel pointed out, "The FDA would never delegate such authority to pharmaceutical manufacturers for a drug whose composition and/or performance characteristics might have changed significantly over time. It will take only a few missteps—intended or unintended—on the part of vendors to undermine trust . . . among clinicians, their patients, and Congress."

The regulatory web extends beyond the FDA—there's a veritable alphabet soup of additional players, each with their own authority and purview. I've largely spared you details regarding state regulatory authorities, the FTC, and the malpractice system, all of which play a supporting role on this cluttered stage. AI standards may come from the Joint Commission, which accredits most US hospitals, and Medicare, through its Conditions of Participation. The Office of the National Coordinator for Health IT oversees electronic health records, although its dominion regarding AI tools embedded in these systems is currently unclear. The Office for Civil Rights within the Department of Health and Human Services can intervene if an AI tool demonstrates bias—a prospect that kept developers awake at night in the pre-Trump era. However, the OCR has been defanged under the current administration.

Health law scholar Michelle Mello takes a thirty-five-thousand-foot view of the overall healthcare AI regulatory landscape. "I just think it's a hot mess. I don't think anybody has any idea who or how we ought to go about assuring safety."

GIVEN THESE COMPLEXITIES, many experts see a place for a new kind of public-private regulatory partnership. Enter the Coalition for Health AI (CHAI), founded in 2021. Now with more than three thousand member organizations—from tech giants to academic hospitals, AI start-ups to government agencies—CHAI represents a bold experiment in collaborative oversight. The organization's flagship project is a national network of "assurance labs," mostly based at academic health systems, designed to test and validate healthcare AI tools.

John Halamka is one of CHAI's leaders. (Of course he is.) He envisions something like a mattress tag for healthcare AI: Every algorithm would come with a "model card" detailing its specifications, training data, and limitations. The goal is a nationwide registry where potential AI buyers and users can review model cards, examine algorithms, and test AI tools on populations like their own using validated approaches. In June 2025, the Joint Commission announced a partnership with CHAI to update its hospital accreditation process for an AI-enabled world. The FDA might ultimately accept an assurance lab's blessing as sufficient certification for low-risk tools.

Former FDA commissioner Scott Gottlieb sees promise in CHAI's approach, writing in 2024 that it could "streamline the FDA's review process while enhancing the depth of expert oversight the agency can provide." Harvard law professor and ethicist Glenn Cohen agrees. "I tend to think that [the ideal solution] would be some form of third-party auditing and generating information about the quality of these products," he told me. "It would allow hospital systems and practices to become wise consumers."

Rob Califf also sees CHAI as a reasonable way of trying to balance innovation and safety in a fast-moving field with few precedents. "CHAI is one of many efforts to define an ecosystem that can begin to put into place the kind of assessments that we need," he said. He told me that one of his favorite sayings is "Educate before you regulate," and CHAI might contribute to that goal.

But CHAI also has its critics. Some doubt the model card approach will provide meaningful assurance that an AI tool is producing accurate and unbiased results. Others worry about potential conflicts of interest. "Working only with tech giants increases the risk of regulatory capture by these large companies, which will also hinder innovation down the line," argued Punit Soni, CEO of Suki, the AI scribe start-up. In 2024, several Republican congressmen raised concerns about CHAI's membership (which includes the likes of Google, Microsoft, and Amazon), warning the FDA that "partnering with CHAI would effectively put large organizations that are actively developing and commercializing AI models of their own in the position of evaluating AI programs developed by affiliated companies or competitors."

Halamka bristles at these accusations, particularly the ones focusing on conflicts of interest. "This is [three thousand] organizations coming together to do nonprofit goodness for society. Why do you need to keep trying to tear it down?" Yet people keep spinning conspiracy theories, he said—that Microsoft is plotting to control all AI, or that the Mayo Clinic is forcing every start-up to use its validation process. The frustration in his voice is palpable.

WHILE THE BROADER regulatory landscape takes shape, healthcare organizations can't afford to wait on the sidelines. Whether CHAI succeeds or fails, hospitals and health systems need their own processes for evaluating and implementing AI tools. Califf is in total agreement—he sees the end users, particularly health systems and doctors, as the major locus of control and safety. For most patient-facing AI tools, he said, "I think the key is recurrent local validation. Is it telling you to take a right turn when you should take a left? Is it leading clinicians to recommend the wrong treatment or the right treatment? You can't know that without knowing what happened to your patients."

Patient safety experts Dean Sittig and Hardeep Singh have outlined a framework for such health system oversight. Before implementing any AI tool, they argue, organizations need robust governance structures—like an AI control tower. They should demand strong evidence of effectiveness, not just accept vendor promises. Clinicians and patients need clear communication about what tools are in use, and what the tools can and can't do.

But the real work begins after implementation. Hospitals and clinics need systems to track AI performance, including regular checks for bias and algorithmic drift. They should measure the impact of their AI tools on outcomes, workflow, and satisfaction of both clinicians and patients. Most dramatically, Sittig and Singh advocate for a "kill switch" in case an AI system starts to threaten patient safety.

While the kill switch might sound like something from a sci-fi movie, it reflects a crucial reality: Regulation can only take us so far with something as novel, powerful, and inscrutable as generative AI. As Mustafa Suleyman, the DeepMind cofounder who now leads AI initiatives at Microsoft, warned in his sobering book *The Coming Wave*, "Governments fight the last war. Regulators regulate the things they can anticipate. This, meanwhile, is an age of surprises."

What's clear is that no single approach will be sufficient. We need a layered defense: federal oversight for high-risk applications, transparency from vendors to allow purchasers to make informed decisions, third-party validation through organizations like CHAI, robust local governance by healthcare organizations, and novel private-public partnerships to help protect patients from being harmed by dangerous patient-facing AI tools.

The challenge of healthcare AI isn't just about finding the right temperature for Goldilocks's regulatory porridge anymore. It's about crafting rules for bowls of porridge that are being eaten in restaurants and homes everywhere, and that can change their temperature, ingredients, and even their very nature without notice. As we navigate this unprecedented challenge, one thing seems certain: The regulatory solutions will require as much innovation and nimbleness as we're seeing in the technology itself.

7

Implications, Recommendations, and Predictions

HAVING BEGUN MY YEARLONG TOUR of the world of healthcare AI at a moment of peak hype, I expected to end it disappointed. But I didn't.

In fact, my hope that the new AI would usher in digital healthcare's "gradually, then suddenly" moment is being realized. My optimism isn't only because the AI has improved dramatically since ChatGPT's November 2022 debut—although it has. It's mainly because clinicians and healthcare organizations are implementing these tools thoughtfully and beginning to see tangible, positive results. Some patients are too.

Google cofounder Larry Page likes to evaluate new technology ideas with his "toothbrush test": Is this something that improves your life and that you'll use at least once or twice a day? For me, generative AI passes this test decisively. I use GPT and OpenEvidence several times a day when I'm seeing patients, and Claude, NotebookLM, and OpenAI's Deep Research have become invaluable partners in my writing and in my role as chair of a large medical department.

While we clearly need more experience and research to understand AI's full impact, I'm also convinced that it is improving patient care in my own health system. When I look around UCSF Health, I see widespread adoption of AI scribes, and early and careful rollouts of chart summarization, inbox message drafting, and billing assistance—the kind of relatively low-risk, high-feasibility tasks that make sense as early implementations. After its bumpy debut, decision support for sepsis has improved, and we're slowly adding similar support across other specialties and diseases. Some of our faculty, trainees, and staff are building specialized AI tools, such as chatbots that incorporate everything from UCSF policies to guidelines from professional societies. It's a little hither and yon, but the overall direction is encouraging, and we're just getting started.

While concerns about AI being deployed too rapidly are justified when it comes to society at large, healthcare's natural guardrails— our professional risk aversion, powerful incumbents, spring-loaded malpractice system, byzantine payment structures, and stringent privacy rules—produce ample amounts of brake-tapping. These constraints have created a healthy equilibrium—one in which we are gaining comfort with AI while implementing only reasonably well-vetted tools built by companies we trust.

When I wrote *The Digital Doctor* in 2015, virtually every doctor and nurse I interviewed told me stories of how the electronic health record had made their work harder and their lives worse. In my research for this book, the sentiment couldn't have been more different. While some clinicians remain neutral about AI or haven't even tried it, those who have experienced modern AI in areas ranging from scribing to curbside consults have come away somewhere between moderately impressed and wowed. I don't foresee another healthcare AI winter—this early buy-in suggests we're building a solid foundation for implementing more ambitious tools to address more challenging problems.

Patient perceptions of AI in healthcare are also positive—much more so than their views about AI in general. In a Gallup survey published in 2025, Americans expressed bleak views of AI overall, with majorities believing it will spread false information (72 percent), diminish social connections (64 percent), reduce job opportunities (60 percent), and harm national security (56 percent). The sole bright spot was medical diagnosis and treatment, where 61 percent of Americans viewed AI positively and only 26 percent viewed it negatively. Of course, this may be as much a statement about our healthcare system's sorry state as about AI's strengths.

LOOKING AHEAD, in fact, I see AI ushering in something of a golden age in healthcare. Our ability to diagnose and treat disease is accelerating, with AI poised to catalyze innovations in many fields of medicine—from interpreting X-rays and blood tests to developing smarter devices and effective new medications. AI's contributions build on the progress we were already seeing in medical science, as evidenced by breakthroughs in cancer, stroke, heart disease, vaccines, and obesity in the past decade.

With so many medical advances now at our disposal, this should be a glorious time to be practicing medicine. But it's not. While our scientific victories are remarkable, they ring hollow when clinicians buckle under mountains of paperwork, struggle to stay current with research, and lack the time to see patients who desperately need care. For the first time in years, though, we're beginning to see glimmers of hope on the horizon, in large part thanks to AI.

AI should improve not only the lives of clinicians but also of patients. Within a few years, I expect patient portals to seamlessly facilitate appointments, provide clear information about medical conditions and test results, handle prescription refills, and simplify health system navigation—in short, to deliver the kind of experience we've come to expect from consumer-friendly industries. Patients who opt for self-care will have tools to diagnose common ailments and receive guidance—sometimes avoiding unnecessary doctor visits. Digital wearables and sensors will collect more data, but more importantly, AI will transform that data into meaningful insights and actionable recommendations that should promote better health.

WHEN CONSIDERING AI TOOLS for healthcare, turning promise into reality requires far more than just buying the right technology. Healthcare organizations must fundamentally rewire themselves to take full advantage of the powerful tools. As you've seen, UCSF now has a chief health AI officer, a position we couldn't have imagined needing just two years ago. We've established new frameworks for assessing our needs, selecting use cases, analyzing ROI, vetting AI tools, training our staff, screening for bias, and addressing privacy concerns.

Academic health systems like mine also face the challenge of integrating AI into our educational and research enterprises. Here, too, there's progress. In medical education, we're beginning to embed AI in our systems for assessment, feedback, and coaching, while tackling the question of what new curriculum to add—and the harder question of what traditional content we can eliminate. In research, we've created safe environments to test AI tools and are training researchers in responsible use of the technology. I launched a new division in my department—the UCSF Division of Clinical Informatics and Digital Transformation (DoC-IT for short)—focused on research and education in AI-powered healthcare, and it's flourishing. In all these areas, we need to remain mindful of the Productivity Paradox of Information Technology—history repeatedly teaches us that reimagining the work and workflows is essential for successfully deploying general-purpose technologies. AI is no exception.

HEALTHCARE'S DIGITAL TRANSFORMATION can't happen without the involvement of companies, investors, and entrepreneurs. However, the business landscape remains dynamic and unforgiving. At a high-profile healthcare conference in January 2025, Jonathan Bush, a leading health tech entrepreneur, saw the coming year or two as make-or-break for many of the start-ups. "Maybe half the companies die, or two-thirds. . . . And, if you can't get there by yourself, you're going to need to merge." As of this writing, companies like Hippocratic AI and Abridge are thriving, while start-ups that overpromised and underdelivered—like Forward and Babylon—were punished mercilessly in the marketplace. There's a saying in economics that "equilibrium emerges from chaos," and that aptly describes today's healthcare AI market.

Healthcare systems' purchasing decisions will do much to shape the business environment. No health system will want to manage scores of single-purpose tools or juggle relationships with dozens of vendors. This means that start-ups whose AI solves a single problem—whether it's documentation, prior authorization, or diagnosis—will struggle to compete against those offering all-in-one solutions. While every Silicon Valley start-up claims to be "a platform"—able to solve multiple problems for its customers—only those that truly deliver integrated offerings will stand a fighting chance.

Examples of comprehensive platforms are emerging. I recently watched a demo showcasing a call center on Notable's platform in which multiple AI agents worked in concert to handle various healthcare tasks.* The scenario began with a mock patient phoning the call center to make an appointment to see a specialist. The AI agent verified the referral and then presented several scheduling options, one of which the patient accepted. Seamlessly, the conversation shifted to an outstanding balance on the patient's account, which the chatbot and patient resolved on the spot. When the patient requested a medication refill, the AI processed this too, sending it directly to his preferred pharmacy. Just before it ended, the conversation took a serious turn—the patient casually mentioned that he'd been experiencing chest pain and shortness of breath. Recognizing the gravity of the symptoms, the AI agent immediately directed the patient to call 911.

This could be the blueprint for scalable solutions in healthcare AI—starting with products that solve specific problems and then weaving them into end-to-end platforms serving broader patient and clinician needs. As Julia Adler-Milstein, the digital policy expert who leads DoC-IT at UCSF, explained, "It feels like the market is rewarding the unit of scale that is general enough to apply to a

---

* A reminder that I'm an adviser to Notable.

broad group of specialties, but also solves a very well-defined problem so that you can put it into a budget somewhere." Her observation captures the current market dynamics perfectly—start-ups must succeed and build trust with focused products, then rapidly pivot to creating platform-like offerings, either by themselves or through strategic partnerships.

The looming presence of electronic health record companies is a chronic source of unease for start-up founders and investors. This is because companies like Epic and Oracle Health have a natural platform advantage—once their EHRs are installed, virtually every transaction, clinical and administrative, flows through them. But as integration of third-party tools becomes easier through progress in both legislation and technology, this incumbency advantage could fade. If they can build superior tools, well-run AI-first companies may find opportunities to compete successfully with AI created by EHR vendors. Epic's decision to begin forming partnerships with outside companies, something it has long avoided, seems like a tip of the hat to this business reality.

In February 2025, a few days after watching Notable's call center demonstration, I witnessed a vivid illustration of the challenge facing many healthcare AI start-ups. Phil Lindemann, Epic's VP for Data and Research, showed me a demo of Epic's version of agentic AI. The scenario involved another mock patient; this one had undergone wrist surgery. On a video visit a few days after the procedure, Epic's AI called the patient to check in, first asking about the patient's pain. Then, instructing the patient to "hold your wrist like a waiter holding a tray," the Epic tool guided the patient through a wrist extension test, using machine vision to compare the angle of his wrist to many others in its database of post-op wrist patients. Based on the patient's better-than-average mobility, the AI agent determined that the patient could skip his one-week follow-up appointment.

Impressive as this was, there was a catch. Lindemann described the agentic platform as "aspirational," and emphasized its early stage—despite Epic having showcased this demo at its summer user's group meeting six months earlier. "We're going to be hopefully getting some of the first agentic workflows out later this year," he said, "but we're certainly not going to start patient-facing." Therein lies the dilemma: While Notable offers a sophisticated tool that's already in use, Epic's demo may lead many health systems to simply say, "We'll wait for Epic's version," even if it's years away.

Epic, of course, is far from the only behemoth competing for a slice of healthcare's AI dollar. The major cloud providers—Microsoft, Amazon, and Google—are guaranteed a spot at healthcare's AI table, as most healthcare systems will store their data in one of the Big Three's cloud platforms. But neither they nor AI powerhouses like OpenAI and Nvidia possess a deep enough understanding of healthcare, nor are they close enough to the action, to dominate my field as they do so many others. They will be formidable players in areas that leverage their existing strengths—Amazon Pharmacy is a prime (pun intended) example—but the last two decades have taught us that while these companies seem too big to fail when it comes to healthcare, they usually do.

At nearly 20 percent of the US gross domestic product, the healthcare market is large enough to support multiple winners. However, it will be important to create policies that promote a level playing field. In the end, health systems should be able to make rational decisions about how best to serve their AI needs, and EHR vendors should be compelled to support those choices. Epic's dominance in the EHR space—while achieved through legitimate market prowess—now threatens to stifle the competition needed to ensure the deployment of the most capable and cost-effective AI tools.

MOST HEALTH SYSTEMS have wisely begun their AI journey with low-risk applications like scribing and billing. However, even if these tools succeed, we can't be complacent—our patients' needs and healthcare's financial, logistical, and workforce challenges demand more ambitious uses of AI. True transformation will emerge through AI's ability to help diagnose illnesses, recommend treatments, coordinate care, facilitate precision medicine, and empower patients with self-management tools—not from solving important but relatively small-bore problems like documentation and prior auths. While it's premature to swing for the fences, we can't be content with bunts and singles.

Once healthcare systems successfully implement individual AI tools and begin creating platforms for cross-cutting initiatives, we'll face an even greater task: building an AI-enabled organizational central nervous system that connects all the parts to form a cohesive whole. What might this look like? Consider the young woman with multiple sclerosis I described way back in chapter 1. Her diagnosis, treatment recommendations, and care itinerary emerged from humans working in tandem with AI. In a fully AI-powered healthcare ecosystem, all the digital tools and databases—clinical, operational, HR, and financial—would be woven together. Such a system would not only prompt doctors to order the appropriate tests but would schedule radiology and clinic appointments based on system capacity and patient preference, adjust clinician and staff schedules in response to real-time demands, and modify supply

chain orders through ongoing monitoring. Moreover, with patients' permission, the AI would tap into wearable and home monitor data to deliver round-the-clock oversight—a clinical air traffic
control system that identifies problems early and even provides
digital nudges to the patients to encourage healthy behaviors.

In 2024, researchers at Tsinghua University in China announced
that they had created a small virtual AI hospital—populated by virtual doctors, nurses, and patients—and that it excelled in diagnosing and treating patients while rapidly learning from its experience.
"The [virtual doctor] is able to complete the diagnosis and treatment
of tens of thousands of patients within a few days, which would
typically take at least two years for a human doctor," they reported.
When you hear the Mayo Clinic's CEO discussing digital twin physicians or see a Silicon Valley VC firm buying a Midwestern health
system, you can bet they are envisioning a fully AI-enabled and
connected healthcare ecosystem. That vision no longer seems beyond reach.

THE CHALLENGES OF monitoring and regulating AI in healthcare
remain largely unresolved. While the FDA has an important role to
play in regulating high-risk tools with directive outputs (such as
those produced by radiology and cardiology AI devices), there will
simply be too many tools evolving too quickly for a single federal
regulator to be the entire solution—particularly an agency whose
authority extends only to vendors. We'll need a new healthcare AI
regulatory model that scans the entire landscape, establishing appropriate standards for manufacturers, health systems, clinicians,

and insurers. This regulatory framework will likely include non-governmental organizations and academic partners working alongside government agencies. While the exact shape of this oversight remains unclear, at this early stage I favor a relatively light regulatory touch as we learn more and the technology and markets mature.

Much of the oversight burden will fall to healthcare organizations, which must ensure that their AI tools function reliably and safely—and not just on day one. We'll need to develop practical approaches to ongoing monitoring, with AI likely serving double duty as both the subject and the agent of monitoring—a situation that will predictably raise concerns about foxes guarding henhouses. As we grapple with this conundrum, let's acknowledge that we've never excelled at ongoing monitoring of our *non*-AI-based systems.

TRUST REMAINS PARAMOUNT, especially since healthcare will inevitably face its "Cruise robotaxi moment"—when a high-profile AI failure (probably accompanied by bungled oversight by a human who was supposed to be "in the loop" but wasn't quite) triggers intense media scrutiny and calls for stricter regulation, just as it did when Cruise's driverless car ran over a woman, dooming the company. That's just the natural cycle of innovation in any high-stakes field. The deeper our reservoir of trust beforehand, the better healthcare AI will weather this storm.

My perspective on trust has evolved during the process of researching and writing this book. My initial focus was on trust in the AI tools and their developers. This, of course, continues to be fundamental. However, after deeply immersing myself in this subject for the past two years, I've found myself beginning to lose trust in healthcare providers and systems that haven't started to implement AI or reshape themselves to do so.

I don't mean that patients should immediately switch doctors or health systems based on their AI adoption. But the time for sitting on the sidelines—for stroking our collective beards as we ruminate over our "grave reservations"—has passed. Mayo Clinic CEO Gianrico Farrugia's observation that the risks of going too slowly exceed the risks of going too fast seems right to me. Just as we judge providers by their adoption of effective new medications, surgical techniques, or diagnostic tools, we should evaluate them on their willingness to adopt—and adapt—proven AI solutions. AI's capabilities are too advanced, its potential is too vast, and healthcare's challenges are too urgent to delay embracing this technology. I look forward to the day when a health system's highway billboards promote not its latest surgical laser or tummy tuck technique, but rather its thoughtful deployment of AI to enhance patient care.

Yet, as you've seen throughout this book, my enthusiasm for healthcare AI is tempered by realism about its current limitations. While hallucinations have decreased and reliability has improved, we still face significant challenges in addressing bias, workflow integration, privacy, security, and misinformation. Our experiences with sepsis decision support and liver transplant algorithms are sobering reminders that missteps are part of the journey. Although I remain convinced that AI's potential benefits in healthcare far outweigh its risks, we need to approach its implementation with both optimism and vigilance.

Even after AI smooths out much of the friction in today's healthcare system, we'll still face other, more fundamental challenges in healthcare: unsustainable costs, a dysfunctional payment structure, inequities in care and access, conflicts of interest, and our habitual focus on treatment over prevention, to name a few. As AI addresses many of today's tractable problems, it should create bandwidth to tackle the really hard stuff. I expect AI to help with these deeper problems as well, but—given their underlying societal, economic, and political drivers—that will take more time.

Finally, my overall optimism about AI in healthcare shouldn't be mistaken for a lack of concern about AI's potential negative impacts in areas like bioterrorism, threats to democracy, or climate change. Even if things work out reasonably well in healthcare, as I believe they will, there's plenty for all of us to worry about when it comes to AI in the rest of our lives.

TWO INTERRELATED CONCERNS arise in virtually every conversation about AI and healthcare: the balance between autonomy and human oversight, and the future of medical employment. Let's address each briefly here; I'll return to the "Will AI replace doctors?" question in the final chapter.

Rather than focusing on AI replacing entire jobs, we should examine whether it can replace specific *tasks*. This kind of deconstruction will be needed to determine how AI—whether acting as a copilot or an autonomous agent—can add value. In these early stages of healthcare's AI journey, it would be premature to hand over high-stakes tasks to autonomous agents without ironclad evidence of near-perfect performance. Of course, as we build copilot models, we need to be clear-eyed about the weaknesses in the human-in-the-loop paradigm—inattention, de-skilling, automation bias, and the like—and address them proactively.

With time, as the technology improves, certain large tasks will become candidates for autonomous AI. We should try to identify these tasks rather than insisting on human oversight that is pro forma, clinically meaningless, and sometimes even dangerous. We will almost certainly find that the universe of human-only tasks will shrink, and AI-capable tasks will expand. At that point, we may question whether we need humans at all for certain roles. For most healthcare jobs—including our most vulnerable ones, like radiologists and pathologists—I believe this transition is many years away. How many? Based on our AI adoption curve thus far, the pace of technological improvements, the strength of the counter- vailing forces, and our history with prior healthcare technologies, I'd bet on somewhere between ten and twenty years.

In fact, for the foreseeable future, I expect only modest job re- placement among clinicians, mostly because of a fortuitous set of competing trends. In the absence of AI, our aging population, de- clining birth rate, ambivalence about immigration, and burgeon- ing new treatments and technologies would have created insatiable demands for more clinicians and other healthcare personnel. The happy coincidence: Over the next decade at a minimum, I believe that AI's productivity gains will roughly match healthcare's unmet needs.

This balanced dynamic contributes to my prediction of a com- ing golden age in healthcare. If healthcare professionals faced the prospect of massive job losses, we'd confront not just the human toll of unemployed doctors and nurses but a powerful backlash that would significantly impede AI's progress. While some labor unrest over AI-driven job displacement is inevitable—particularly among nonclinical staff whose roles face greater automation risk—I expect healthcare's overwhelming needs will temper this response. Indeed, I believe most healthcare personnel will embrace AI's assistance, seeing it as a welcome solution to their demanding workload rather than a threat to their livelihoods.

Employment dynamics won't be the only economic factor shaping AI in healthcare. Take, for example, the question of whether patients will receive their primary care from a human physician or a virtual AI agent. In a world of exploding healthcare costs and massive shortages of primary care clinicians, I foresee the emergence of a tiered system, loosely analogous to our current system of concierge care, with many patients who have basic insurance plans being offered—or choosing, perhaps driven by easier access or lower co-pays—AI-first care. The AI would assess new symptoms, answer questions, and manage common conditions like hypertension, diabetes, high cholesterol, depression, and asthma—with a human clinician providing oversight in the background and an escalation path for complex cases.

In contrast, patients with more generous insurance plans, greater ability to pay, or particularly complex clinical needs will be offered human-first care—though some may prefer an AI-based option, particularly if it's more convenient. There are analogies to this kind of tiering in other industries. Many people use software programs to do their taxes when their needs are limited and their budget tight, while others see (increasingly AI-assisted) human professionals if they can afford to do so or have complex requirements. And, of course, most people accept the idea of business and economy classes on commercial flights—recognizing that safety remains equivalent despite the differences in service and amenities. I expect that many patients will also accept reduced personal interaction with doctors or other clinicians if an AI-first system can deliver high-quality care and convenience at a significantly lower cost—which I believe, in the next few years and in the right settings, it can.

ᴏᴧ̖ₒ

AS FOR THE FUTURE of healthcare jobs, while Geoffrey Hinton got it wrong in 2016 when he predicted the imminent downfall of radiologists, the threat of job replacement is real. Over the next several decades, in a world of driverless cars, it would be naive to claim that autonomous AI has no place in healthcare. Eventually, AI's productivity gains will outpace healthcare's growing needs, which will result in some clinical roles being displaced by technology.

Yet when I'm asked if I would encourage a child to pursue a career in medicine—and I get this question often—my answer is an emphatic yes. I'm convinced that AI will lift many of the bureaucratic burdens that weigh down today's medical practice, allowing us to rediscover what makes medicine profoundly satisfying: the privilege of helping people when they're most vulnerable. As AI-powered tools enable patients to handle routine healthcare tasks independently, clinicians will be freed to focus on more complex and humanistic aspects of care. And let's be realistic: If AI ever does significantly disrupt the medical profession, we won't be the first to face this shift—lawyers, consultants, writers, and accountants will have already blazed that distressing trail.

Questions about AI's impact on jobs run deep, and compelling arguments exist on both sides. Some envision a future where professional employment faces existential threats, while others foresee AI creating new roles over time, just as previous technological revolutions—from the printing press to electricity to the internet—

created brand new categories of employment. I think we'll see some of both. Depending on how this plays out in the coming decades, government intervention may be necessary to prevent technological advancement from triggering widespread unemployment and the social unrest that would surely accompany it. Yet amid these complex considerations, we must remember a fundamental truth: Healthcare's primary purpose isn't to provide jobs—it's to maximize human health.

8

On Being a Doctor
in the Age of AI

EARLY IN THEIR TRAINING, physicians learn to erect a psychological firewall—to approach cases clinically, not emotionally. You should know that this professional distancing is a survival technique. Fully absorbing the weight of our work would be debilitating—particularly for those of us who regularly deal with death. While we certainly experience sorrow when we lose a patient or deliver bad news, our ability to compartmentalize is what allows us to return the next day and carry on.

I've tried to apply a similar clinical detachment as I've gathered evidence, diagnosed implications, and recommended treatments for a new condition: the emergence of modern AI in healthcare. My North Star was as simple to state as it is hard to achieve: a health-care system that uses AI in ways that achieve the best care at the lowest cost. If the continued involvement of physicians helps reach that goal, splendid. If AI can do the job by itself or with far fewer doctors, then we should allow it to do so, with humans standing aside and finding something else to fill our days.

But I must confess that after forty deeply fulfilling years as an academic physician, it would be utterly disingenuous to say that I don't have a dog in the fight—that I'm truly indifferent to the impact of AI on physicians. I desperately want my daughter, son-in-law, and the other 183 young doctors currently in my internal medicine residency program to experience the profound satisfaction I've enjoyed in my career: the rich, fascinating, and complex interactions with patients; the intense collegiality with fellow physicians and other healthcare professionals; the joy of teaching brilliant and passionate trainees; the thrill of cracking a tough case. In short, while I truly appreciate the magic of AI, the idea that it might ultimately replace doctors saddens me terribly.

Having experienced healthcare from both sides of the exam table—as a clinician as well as a patient and family member—I remain skeptical that AI can fully supplant real live doctors and nurses without sacrificing something fundamental. But as AI becomes more capable, how do we measure and defend the value of flesh-and-blood professionals? What makes this analysis particularly hard is that the human dimension of healthcare—the quality that skilled clinicians bring to their patients—isn't something we can fully capture in metrics and spreadsheets.

For those of us rooting for the humans, watching the evolution of AI over the past few years has been sobering. My own journey began when I first witnessed ChatGPT's basic gifts on its launch day in 2022. Things escalated from there, as gen AI demonstrated sophisticated diagnostic reasoning and remarkable simulations of empathy. Then, watching in astonishment, I saw AI develop the ability to explain its reasoning process, avoid hallucinations, conduct PhD-level research, and now, execute complex tasks independently. While human performance inches forward, AI seems to get appreciably better with each passing month.

As I said in chapter 7, I think the net effect of AI in healthcare over the next ten to twenty years will be highly beneficial, for both patients *and* clinicians. And I predict that most clinical jobs will be secure for the next decade, at a minimum. But over a longer time horizon, the question still looms: Will AI ultimately render human physicians obsolete? While the only honest answer anyone can give is "I don't know," in February 2025 I conducted a thought experiment to illuminate my own crystal ball.

DURING A COUPLE of rainy winter weeks in San Francisco, I served as an attending physician on the hospital medicine service at UCSF Medical Center, working closely with a team of residents and medical students. This is a role I've played for nearly four decades—the first two of which involved practicing medicine without the benefits of an electronic health record, and the last two with an EHR but remarkably little assistance from AI. As I cared for about forty hospitalized patients during this stint on the wards, I not only took full advantage of all our digital tools, including modern AI, but I tried to imagine—to the degree mere mortals can—what future AI tools might be capable of.

As I've said, in chronic care, urgent care, and disease management, I *do* see opportunities to replace physicians with autonomous AI, or to upskill nonphysician providers to deliver care that previously required a doctor. In these areas, some of the medicine—though far from all—follows predictable patterns and fits neatly within established guidelines.

However, patients who require admission to a hospital are far from straightforward, offering me some welcome reality testing regarding the potential reach of healthcare automation. What I found was that, although AI could provide me with advanced knowledge tools, decision support, and some help accomplishing relatively straightforward tasks, the improvements seemed more incremental than revolutionary.

For example, one of my patients was a sweet ninety-seven-year-old woman with a blood clot in her leg, atrial fibrillation, and a recent gastrointestinal bleed.* GPT-4o laid out the pluses and minuses of starting her on a blood thinner to reduce the chance of a pulmonary embolism from her blood clot or a stroke from her A-Fib while minimizing the risk of recurrent bleeding. OpenEvidence provided a few useful references. In part based on AI's analysis, I ultimately chose to give her a blood thinner at a lower-than-usual dose.

Another patient was a sixty-seven-year-old woman with metastatic breast cancer and progressive leg weakness, now unable to climb the stairs in her home. I went down to the radiology department to review her MRIs. I described her history and physical examination to the neuroradiologist who, sitting with me in the darkened room, spent ten minutes toggling between the patient's current MRIs and several of her prior scans, obtained at variable intervals. Only after our discussion and this painstaking review did he determine that her tumor had spread and now was pepper-

---

* I've changed clinically irrelevant facts like ages and genders to ensure confidentiality.

ing the lining of her spinal cord. While the technology is not yet there, I could imagine an AI accurately reading the MRIs, and maybe even comparing her current scans to her old ones. But I couldn't see it replacing my back-and-forth dialogue with the radiologist; orchestrating my team's discussions with the patient's oncologist, neurosurgeons, and radiation oncologists to determine the treatment plan (she ended up with radiation therapy to her spine); or, most important, conducting the difficult conversations I had with the patient and her husband.

During my time on the wards, I tried using GPT-4o to help me prepare for sensitive discussions with patients and families about whether to pursue dialysis, consider ICU admission, accept another round of chemotherapy, or transition to hospice care. The AI tools offered me some wise tips and reminders; they undoubtedly would have been even more helpful for a novice. Yet despite their usefulness as a coach, I struggled to envision any patient or family feeling comfortable weighing these profound life decisions in discussion with an algorithm rather than a fellow human being.

In addition to thinking about how AI might change my own practice as a physician, I also considered the work of my nonphysician colleagues. Several of my patients were ready to be discharged from the hospital but were in no shape to go home. We sometimes had a physical therapist assess a patient's ability to walk, or a speech therapist assess their ability to swallow. While AI-based tools might effectively perform these tasks for a healthy patient at home with, say, a sports injury, I found it hard to imagine them doing so for a frail, elderly widower who spoke only Mandarin and lived in a second-floor Chinatown walk-up.

I could easily see how AI could improve the experience of

patients in the hospital. Food could be delivered by robots, as could medications. The confused patient might have a robotic sitter by her bedside, providing reassurance, conversation, and maybe even a gentle nudge if she tried to climb out of bed. Vital signs could be taken by sensors, transmitted automatically to the EHR, and analyzed for worrisome patterns. Patients and families would have ready access to current information about their disease and treatment plans (along with bios of all the strangers in white coats who kept popping into the room), and a robust tool for planning their post-hospital itinerary. The dreaded nurse call button—which often feels like a bridge to nowhere—would be replaced by a chatbot that could address many of the patient's needs and questions, particularly if linked to a multitasking robot. But there would still need to be a human nurse to comfort the patient, talk to families, get the patient to the commode, assess changes in clinical status, and respond to emergencies.

AT THE END of my time on the wards, I was more convinced than ever that current AI tools enhanced my capabilities as a physician, and that increasingly advanced ones would do even more in the coming years. When I asked AI for guidance on diagnosis or treatments, GPT and OpenEvidence nearly always provided reliable and helpful answers—they have truly become valued curbside consultants in my pocket. It was easy to envision how AI tools will help with scribing, chart summaries, medication management, and discharge planning—practical aids that will improve my efficiency and effectiveness and, quite likely, my demeanor.

But this kind of technological support, impressive as it was—or will soon be—touched only the edges of my daily work in the hospital. The core of clinical care remained an intricate web of countless decisions under uncertainty, delicate conversations with patients and families, hands-on procedures, and the time-sensitive orchestration of complex and shifting care teams. Yes, AI made me better at my work, but perhaps by 5 to 10 percent, not 80 percent. A decade from now, I suspect that figure might be 25 percent—which, if scaled to all of healthcare, would be an incredible boon. But I'd still have a job.

And then there's the human element. I tried to imagine a chatbot—even one with superintelligence—navigating the complex, sometimes gut-wrenching discussions I had with patients and families in their most vulnerable moments. I tried to picture how the AI would handle situations where there's no clear "right" answer, where we struggled to choose the better of two bad options, each with its own risks and trade-offs. I tried to envision how the AI would gather and orchestrate the input of a primary physician, specialists, nurses, case managers, family members, and the patient herself into a coherent care plan that respected everyone's input. These aren't merely technical puzzles to solve—they're profoundly human ones, and they require empathy, intuition, experience, and wisdom. I believe they'll remain so, at least as far as I can see into healthcare's future.

TOWARD THE END of my time on the wards, I cared for a twenty-two-year-old woman with severe autism who was nonverbal at baseline. She was brought to the ER by her mother for fever, cough, and lethargy. In her case, the diagnosis of pneumonia was straightforward, as was the choice of treatment: IV fluids and standard antibiotics. I had no doubt that AI could have easily replaced my clinical decision-making.

Still—and perhaps I'm being selfish—I treasure having been part of this young woman's care. As she emerged from her near-comatose state, her mother's face brightened as she proudly told us that her daughter was back to her "sassy" self. Thinking of my own experience as a parent, I tried to put myself in this mom's place. I was awed by her resilience—her ability to find delight in loving a child who would never speak a word, for whom life's conventional milestones would always be out of reach. Lost in these thoughts, I turned toward my patient, only a bit younger than my team of residents and students standing by her bedside. Just then, the patient flashed us a radiant smile and blew kisses to me and my team.

As I hope I've made clear, I *am* convinced that AI's breathtaking and rapidly expanding capabilities will transform healthcare in ways we can barely imagine today, bringing enormous benefits to patients and clinicians, and turning our healthcare system into one that, for once, functions reasonably well. By handling myriad administrative chores, allowing patients to accomplish many healthcare tasks independently, and permitting clinicians to be more capable versions of their professional selves, AI is poised to make our system better, safer, more convenient, and less expensive.

But I am equally convinced that—particularly for patients with acute and complex chronic conditions—there will always be a need for a human guide: someone with not only deep medical knowledge and refined clinical judgment but also the emotional intelligence to recognize and address their unspoken fears, the leadership skills to orchestrate their care across diverse teams, the patience and wisdom to navigate the inherent uncertainties of medicine and healthcare's bureaucratic cul-de-sacs, the uniquely human capacity for deep compassion that transcends both the practical and the algorithmic. And someone to be on the receiving end of a speechless patient's kisses.

They will need a doctor.

Acknowledgments

ON FEBRUARY 20, 2024, I received an email from Casey Ebro, who had edited the paperback version of *The Digital Doctor* nearly a decade earlier at McGraw Hill. Now an executive editor at Portfolio, Penguin Random House's prestigious nonfiction imprint, she wondered if I'd consider writing a new book on AI and healthcare.

I hesitated at first—ChatGPT had been out for about a year, and there were already several books on generative AI and medicine. Not only did the market seem saturated, but the field's breakneck pace of change made me wonder if anything I wrote would quickly become obsolete. But Casey, my agent Jim Levine, and several trusted friends and colleagues helped me see that my unique position and background might allow me to write something both timely and enduring—a book that would not only document this remarkable moment in healthcare and technology but illuminate its deeper meaning and long-term implications. The task, I came to realize, demanded examining the subject through multiple lenses—clinical and technological, of course, but also economic, historical, cultural, political, sociological, and philosophical.

One challenge was trying to process the daily deluge of AI information—from academic papers to news articles, podcasts to videos, tweets to notices in the *Federal Register*. Moreover, separating wheat from chaff and shiny pennies from game changers was a major test. It was clear that I needed to gather many different perspectives to appreciate all facets of the narrative. I'm deeply grateful to the more than one hundred people I interviewed for this book—every conversation yielded valuable insights, and many of the stories that animate the book emerged from these discussions.

I'm indebted to Jim Levine, my assistant Samantha Santiago, and my UCSF colleagues, particularly Michelle Mourad, Maria Novelero, and Michael Chen, who frequently covered my responsibilities while I—or at least my brain—was elsewhere. Special thanks to Joe Hiatt, Aaron Neinstein, Adnan Alseidi, Peter Lee, and Sara Murray for their thoughtful feedback on early drafts. Casey Ebro, Leila Sandlin, and Niki Papadopoulos of Portfolio expertly guided the book through the publishing process, striking just the right balance between attaboys and "this can be cut."

Writing a book about AI is, of course, a play within a play. While every word is mine, I did find GPT-4o useful for research, Claude for wordsmithing and idea generation, NotebookLM as a repository and synthesizer of interviews, and OpenEvidence for its clinical insights. These tools enhanced my writing process, just as they're reshaping healthcare. I remain convinced that truly understanding AI's capabilities and limitations requires hands-on experience, both at home and at work.

As always, my deepest gratitude goes to my wife, Katie Hafner, who somehow managed to edit this book while writing her own—

her ninth book and second novel. (As I've learned, writing about real people—even with the odd digital twin thrown in—is far simpler than conjuring them up in your imagination.) Having a brilliant journalist and novelist who also deeply understands both healthcare and technology as my in-house editor—not to mention my wife, co-parent, and best friend—is my life's greatest gift.

Notes

Preface

xv **Gianrico Farrugia, the chief executive:** Gianrico Farrugia, interview by author, October 31, 2024.

xix **medical student licensing exam:** Tiffany H. Kung et al., "Performance of ChatGPT on USMLE: Potential for AI-Assisted Medical Education Using Large Language Models," *PLOS Digital Health* 2, no. 2 (2023): e0000198, https://doi.org/10.1371/journal.pdig.0000198.

xix **performed at a level equal:** Zahir Kanjee, Byron Crowe, and Adam Rodman, "Accuracy of a Generative Artificial Intelligence Model in a Complex Diagnostic Challenge," *JAMA* 330, no. 1 (2023): 78–80, https://doi.org/10.1001/jama.2023.8288.

xx **In 2023, a study showed:** John W. Ayers et al., "Comparing Physician and Artificial Intelligence Chatbot Responses to Patient Questions Posted to a Public Social Media Forum," *JAMA Internal Medicine* 183, no. 6 (2023): 589–96, https://doi.org/10.1001/jamainternmed.2023.1838.

xx **researchers at Google showed:** Mariana Lenharo, "Google AI Has Better Bedside Manner Than Human Doctors—and Makes Better Diagnoses," *Nature* 625, no. 7996 (2024): 643–44, https://doi.org/10.1038/d41586-024-00099-4.

xxi **Approximately one out of three:** Health Affairs Research Brief, "The Role of Administrative Waste in Excess US Health Spending," *Health Affairs,*

October 6, 2022, https://www.healthaffairs.org/content/briefs/role-administrative-waste-excess-us-health-spending.

xxi **Nearly one million Americans:** David E. Newman-Toker et al., "Burden of Serious Harms from Diagnostic Error in the USA," *BMJ Quality & Safety* 33, no. 2 (2024): 109–20, https://doi.org/10.1136/bmjqs-2021-014130.

xxiv **physician burnout had skyrocketed:** Lisa S. Rotenstein et al., "Prevalence of Burnout Among Physicians: A Systematic Review," *JAMA* 320, no. 11 (2018): 1131–50, https://doi.org/10.1001/jama.2018.12777.

xxiv **I wrote a book:** Robert Wachter, *The Digital Doctor: Hope, Hype, and Harm at the Dawn of Medicine's Computer Age* (McGraw Hill, 2015).

xxv **reminds us in his book:** Ethan Mollick, *Co-Intelligence: Living and Working with AI* (Portfolio, 2024).

xxvii **wrote the philosopher Annette Baier:** Annette C. Baier, "Trust," *The Tanner Lectures on Human Values*, delivered at Princeton University, March 6–8, 1991, https://www.coursehero.com/file/212723453/baier92pdf.

xxvii **In December 2022, he tweeted:** Sam Altman, "ChatGPT is incredibly limited, but good enough at some things to create a misleading impression of greatness. It's a mistake to be relying on it for anything important right now. It's a preview of progress; we have lots of work to do on robustness and truthfulness," Twitter (now X), December 10, 2022, https://x.com/sama/status/1601731295792414720.

xxix **"There's a group of people":** Mark Smith, interview by author, June 5, 2024.

Chapter 1 | An Overnight Revolution, Fifty Years in the Making

1 *The Sun Also Rises:* Ernest Hemingway, *The Sun Also Rises* (Scribner's, 1926).

4 **A major talking point:** RAND Corporation, *Computerizing Medical Records Could Save $81 Billion Annually and Improve the Quality of Medical Care*, September 14, 2005, https://www.rand.org/news/press/2005/09/14.html.

5 **account for 8 percent:** Greg Rosalsky, "Are Doctors Overpaid?," *Planet Money* (blog), March 12, 2019, https://www.npr.org/sections/money/2019/03/12/702500408/are-doctors-overpaid.

6 **they were spending:** Christine Sinsky et al., "Allocation of Physician Time in Ambulatory Practice: A Time and Motion Study in 4 Specialties," *Annals of Internal Medicine* 165, no. 11 (2016): 753–60, https://doi.org/10.7326/M16-0961.

6 **Physician burnout reached alarming levels:** Sara Berg, "The COVID-19 Emergency's Over, but 1 in 2 Doctors Report Burnout," *AMA News Wire*, June 23, 2023, https://www.ama-assn.org/practice-management/physician-health/covid-19-emergency-s-over-1-2-doctors-report-burnout.

6 **two hundred million patient-users:** Seth Joseph, "The Travel Industry Offers Hospitals a Warning About MyChart," *STAT*, February 17, 2025, https://www.statnews.com/2025/02/17/epic-systems-mychart-hospitals -patient-communication-online-travel-agencies.

6 **US law even gave patients:** "U.S. Federal Rule Mandates Open Notes," *OpenNotes*, accessed January 12, 2025, https://www.opennotes.org/onc -federal-rule.

7 **Benjamin Vipler recounted:** Benjamin Vipler, "'What's Lymphoma?' Risks Posed by Immediate Release of Test Results to Patients," *New England Journal of Medicine* 390, no. 12 (2024): 1064–66, https://doi.org/10.1056 /NEJMp2312953.

8 **family physician was soon spending:** Brian G. Arndt et al., "More Tethered to the EHR: EHR Workload Trends Among Academic Primary Care Physicians, 2019–2023," *Annals of Family Medicine* 22, no. 1 (2024): 12–18, https://doi.org/10.1370/afm.3047.

9 **concluded that the actual savings:** Reed Abelson and Julie Creswell, "In Second Look, Few Savings from Digital Health Records," *New York Times*, January 10, 2013.

9 **Brynjolfsson coined the term:** Erik Brynjolfsson, "The Productivity Paradox of Information Technology," *Communications of the ACM* 36, no. 12 (1993): 66–77, https://doi.org/10.1145/163298.163309.

10 **Robert Solow quipped:** Robert M. Solow, review of *Manufacturing Matters: The Myth of the Post-Industrial Economy*, by Stephen Cohen and John Zysman, *New York Times Book Review*, July 12, 1987.

10 **Research by Brynjolfsson and others:** Erik Brynjolfsson and Andrew McAfee, *The Second Machine Age: Work, Progress, and Prosperity in a Time of Brilliant Technologies* (W. W. Norton, 2014).

10 **calls these changes "complementary innovations":** Erik Brynjolfsson, Daniel Rock, and Chad Syverson, "The Productivity J-Curve: How Intangibles Complement General Purpose Technologies," Working Paper No. 25148 (National Bureau of Economic Research, October 2018), https:// www.nber.org/papers/w25148.

11 **"A new scientific truth":** Max Planck, *Scientific Autobiography and Other Papers* (Philosophical Library, 1949).

11 **said John Glaser:** Aaron Ricadela, *Re-envisioning Electronic Health Records* (Oracle Corp., 2025).

12 **the fastest-growing profession:** Kelly Gooch, "20 Fastest-Growing Occupations: Nurse Practitioner Is No. 1," *Becker's Hospital Review*, August 7, 2023, https://www.beckershospitalreview.com/workforce/20-fastest -growing-occupations-nurse-practitioner-is-no-1.html.

12 **relentless expansion of healthcare jobs:** MGMA Staff, "Nearly All Medical Groups Still Feeling the Squeeze of Rising Operating Expenses,"

MGMA Stat, June 26, 2024, https://www.mgma.com/mgma-stat/nearly-all-medical-groups-still-feeling-the-squeeze-of-rising-operating-expenses.

12 **According to recent analyses:** Alejandra O'Connell-Domenech, "The US Is Suffering a Healthcare Worker Shortage: Experts Fear It Will Only Get Worse," *The Hill*, September 28, 2023.

16 **In a 1971 article:** Howard L. Bleich, "The Computer as a Consultant," *New England Journal of Medicine* 284, no. 3 (1971): 141–47, https://doi.org/10.1056/NEJM197101212840307.

16 **The AI of the day:** Michael D. Howell, Greg S. Corrado, and Karen B. DeSalvo, "Three Epochs of Artificial Intelligence in Health Care," *JAMA* 331, no. 3 (2024): 242–44, https://doi.org/10.1001/jama.2023.25057.

18 **Larry Fagan, one such pioneer:** Larry Fagan, interview by author, August 7, 2014.

18 **"our new computer overlords":** John Markoff, "Computer Wins on 'Jeopardy!': Trivial, It's Not," *New York Times*, February 16, 2011.

19 **"may be the first job":** Ken Jennings, "My Puny Human Brain," *Slate*, February 16, 2011.

19 **estimated at $3 billion:** Steve Lohr, "IBM Is Selling Off Watson Health to a Private Equity Firm," *New York Times*, January 21, 2022.

20 **suggested that a cancer patient:** Angela Chen, "IBM's Watson Gave Unsafe Recommendations for Treating Cancer," *The Verge*, July 26, 2018.

20 **conjure up cancer patients:** Casey Ross and Ike Swetlitz, "IBM's Watson Supercomputer Recommended 'Unsafe and Incorrect' Cancer Treatments, Internal Documents Show," *STAT*, July 25, 2018, https://www.statnews.com/2018/07/25/ibm-watson-recommended-unsafe-incorrect-treatments.

22 **digital platform, told me:** John Halamka, interview by author, May 17, 2024.

Chapter 2 | The Power and the Pitfalls

23 **the 2017 landmark paper:** Ashish Vaswani et al., "Attention Is All You Need," *Advances in Neural Information Processing Systems* 30 (2017): 5998–6008, https://doi.org/10.48550/arXiv.1706.03762.

23 **Marche in *The New Yorker*:** Stephen Marche, "Was Linguistic A.I. Created by Accident?," *New Yorker*, August 23, 2024.

25 **determine a patient's ejection fraction:** Zachi I. Attia et al., "Screening for Cardiac Contractile Dysfunction Using an Artificial Intelligence–Enabled Electrocardiogram," *Nature Medicine* 25 (2019): 70–74, https://doi.org/10.1038/s41591-018-0240-2.

25 **"fraught with peril":** John Halamka, interview by author, May 17, 2024.

26 **a guest on *GeriPal*:** Alex Smith and Eric Widera, *GeriPal*, podcast, episode 307, "The Promise and Pitfalls of AI in Medicine: Bob Wachter," April 18, 2024, https://podcasts.apple.com/us/podcast/the-promise-and-pitfalls-of-ai-in-medicine-bob-wachter/id1164272877?i=1000652823254.

26 **Smith mentioned recent research:** Mariana Lenharo, "Google AI Has Better Bedside Manner Than Human Doctors—and Makes Better Diagnoses," *Nature* 625 (2024): 643–44, https://doi.org/10.1038/d41586-024-00099-4.

28 **exhausted all the data:** Cade Metz et al., "How Tech Giants Cut Corners to Harvest Data for A.I.," *New York Times*, April 6, 2024.

28 **the development of synthetic datasets:** Alison Snyder, "This Is AI's Brain on AI," *Axios*, July 27, 2024, https://www.axios.com/2024/07/27/synthetic-ai-data-effects.

28 **smaller, more focused models:** Dean DeBiase, "Why Small Language Models Are the Next Big Thing in AI," *Forbes*, November 25, 2024.

29 **so-called inference learning:** Ethan Mollick, "Scaling: The State of Play in AI," *One Useful Thing* (blog), September 16, 2024, https://substack.com/@oneusefulthing/p-148908313.

29 **model called DeepSeek:** Cade Metz, "What to Know About DeepSeek and How It Is Upending A.I.," *New York Times*, January 27, 2025.

31 **Doctors and their staff spend:** Mariah Taylor, "Prior Authorization Is 'Wreaking Havoc': AMA Survey," *Becker's Hospital CFO Report*, June 18, 2024.

31 **CEO Jeff Tangney told me:** Jeff Tangney, interview by author, September 13, 2023.

31 **having their own AI reject:** Noah Tong, "UnitedHealth, CVS and Humana Increasingly Deploy AI and Deny Post-Acute Care Claims, Senate Report Finds," *Fierce Healthcare*, October 17, 2024, https://www.fiercehealthcare.com/payers/unitedhealth-cvs-humana-increasingly-deploy-ai-and-deny-prior-auth-claims-senate-report.

33 **depicted the early American presidents:** Megan Morrone, "Google Pauses AI Image Generation amid Diversity Controversies," *Axios*, February 23, 2024, https://www.axios.com/2024/02/23/google-gemini-images-stereotypes-controversy.

33 **attorneys submitted a legal brief:** Benjamin Weiser, "ChatGPT Lawyers Are Ordered to Consider Seeking Forgiveness," *New York Times*, June 22, 2023.

33 **"AI Overview" feature recommended:** Liv McMahon and Zoe Kleinman, "Glue Pizza and Eat Rocks: Google AI Search Errors Go Viral," *BBC*, May 24, 2024, https://www.bbc.com/news/articles/cd11gzejgz4o.

33 **In a 2005 book:** Harry G. Frankfurt, *On Bullshit* (Princeton University Press, 2005).

35 **told me about this tendency:** Peter Lee, interview by author, September 30, 2024.

36 **known as reinforcement learning:** Paul Christiano et al., "Deep Reinforcement Learning from Human Preferences," preprint, *arXiv*, February 17, 2023, https://doi.org/10.48550/arXiv.1706.03741.

36 **founder and CEO of OpenEvidence:** Daniel Nadler, interview by author, October 22, 2024.

37 **known as Retrieval-Augmented Generation:** Karen Ka Yan Ng, Izuki Matsuba, and Peter Chengming Zhang, "RAG in Healthcare: A Novel Framework for Improving Communication and Decision-Making by Addressing LLM Limitations," *NEJM AI* 2, no. 1 (2025), https://doi.org/10.1056/AIra2400380.

37 **Peter Lee explained to me:** Peter Lee, email to author, January 9, 2025.

38 **In early 2025, OpenAI:** Cade Metz and Karen Weise, "A.I. Is Getting More Powerful, but Its Hallucinations Are Getting Worse," *New York Times*, May 5, 2025, https://www.nytimes.com/2025/05/05/technology/ai-hallucinations-chatgpt-google.html; Kyle Wiggers, "OpenAI Explains Why ChatGPT Became Too Sycophantic," *TechCrunch*, April 29, 2025, https://techcrunch.com/2025/04/29/openai-explains-why-chatgpt-became-too-sycophantic.

41 **There were lots of examples:** Ethan Mollick, "Getting Started with AI: Good Enough Prompting," *One Useful Thing* (blog), November 24, 2024, https://www.oneusefulthing.org/p/getting-started-with-ai-good-enough.

41 **most googled new job category:** Justinas Vainilavičius, "AI Prompt Engineer Top New Job—Report," *Cybernews*, June 28, 2023, https://cybernews.com/tech/ai-prompt-engineer-top-job/.

41 **a February 2024 riff:** "Jon Stewart on the False Promises of AI," *The Daily Show*, February 16, 2024, YouTube, https://www.youtube.com/watch?v=20TAkcy3aBY.

42 **As always, Stewart was prophetic:** Dina Genkina, "AI Prompt Engineering Is Dead," *IEEE Spectrum*, March 6, 2024, https://spectrum.ieee.org/prompt-engineering-is-dead.

42 **recently shifted his advice:** Mollick, "Getting Started with AI."

43 **AI's "jagged frontier":** Fabrizio Dell'Acqua et al., "Navigating the Jagged Technological Frontier," Working Paper No. 24-013 (Harvard Business School, September 22, 2023), https://www.hbs.edu/ris/Publication%20Files/24-013_d9b45b68-9e74-42d6-a1c6-c72fb70c7282.pdf.

43 **study found that Black patients:** Knox H. Todd et al., "Ethnicity and Analgesic Practice," *Annals of Emergency Medicine* 35, no. 1 (2000): 11–16, https://doi.org/10.1016/s0196-0644(00)70099-0.

44 **clinical scenario, a white man:** Kevin A. Schulman et al., "The Effect of Race and Sex on Physicians' Recommendations for Cardiac Catheterization," *New England Journal of Medicine* 340, no. 8 (1999): 618–26, https://doi.org/10.1056/NEJM199902253400806.

44 **University of Toronto researcher:** Don Redelmeier, interview by author, May 31, 2024.

44 **bias is algorithmic drift:** Raj M. Ratwani, Karey Sutton, and Jessica E.

Galarraga, "Addressing AI Algorithmic Bias in Health Care," *JAMA* 332, no. 13 (2024): 1051–52, https://doi.org/10.1001/jama.2024.13486.

44 **In a 2022 exposé:** Casey Ross, "AI Gone Astray: How Subtle Shifts in Patient Data Send Popular Algorithms Reeling, Undermining Patient Safety," *STAT*, February 28, 2022, https://www.statnews.com/2022/02/28 /sepsis-hospital-algorithms-data-shift.

45 **unwieldy term "algorithmovigilance":** Peter J. Embi, "Algorithmovigilance— Advancing Methods to Analyze and Monitor Artificial Intelligence–Driven Health Care for Effectiveness and Equity," *JAMA Network Open* 4, no. 4 (2021): e214622, https://doi.org/10.1001/jamanetworkopen.2021.4622.

45 **described what happens:** Ross, "AI Gone Astray."

45 **described by Ziad Obermeyer:** Ziad Obermeyer, interview by author, November 22, 2024.

45 **influential 2019 paper, Obermeyer:** Ziad Obermeyer et al., "Dissecting Racial Bias in an Algorithm Used to Manage the Health of Populations," *Science* 366, no. 6464 (2019): 447–53, https://doi.org/10.1126/science.aax2342.

46 **"to Black patients were weird":** Obermeyer, interview.

47 **Civil Rights issued a rule:** US Department of Health and Human Services, "HHS Issues New Rule to Strengthen Nondiscrimination Protections and Advance Civil Rights in Health Care," April 26, 2024, https://www .hhs.gov/about/news/2024/04/26/hhs-issues-new-rule-strengthen -nondiscrimination-protections-advance-civil-rights-health-care.html.

47 **In an editorial that year:** Michelle M. Mello and Jessica L. Roberts, "Antidiscrimination Law Meets Artificial Intelligence—New Requirements for Health Care Organizations and Insurers," *JAMA Health Forum* 5, no. 8 (2024): e243397, https://doi.org/10.1001/jamahealthforum.2024.3397.

47 **asked Mello if she thought:** Michelle Mello, interview by author, July 25, 2024.

48 **Cohen, a health law scholar:** Glenn Cohen, interview by author, August 6, 2024.

48 **raised the specter of bias:** Halamka, interview.

49 **erosion in the bond of trust:** Clare Ansberry, "Why We Don't Trust Doctors Like We Used To," *Wall Street Journal*, February 23, 2025.

49 **2024 *New York Times* essay:** Daniela J. Lamas, "Skepticism Is Healthy, but in Medicine, It Can Be Dangerous," *New York Times*, April 24, 2024.

50 **A 2024 survey found:** Edelman Trust Institute, "2024 Edelman Trust Barometer Special Report: Trust and Health," *Edelman Trust Barometer*, accessed May 15, 2025, https://www.edelman.com/trust/2024/trust -barometer/special-report-health.

50 **"generation that wants to know":** Timothy Lynch, "Being a Trustworthy Professional in an Untrusting World," *2024 ABIM Foundation Forum Summary Paper* (ABIM Foundation, Philadelphia, PA, 2024).

51 **the outputs of gen AI:** Boris Babic et al., "Beware Explanations from AI in Health Care," *Science* 373, no. 6552 (2021): 284–86, https://doi.org/10.1126/science.abg1834.

52 **"nobody ever clicks the button":** Kevin Johnson, interview by author, June 17, 2024.

52 **agrees that explainability is overrated:** Vardit Ravitsky, interview by author, July 31, 2024.

52 **Pierre Elias told me:** Pierre Elias, interview by author, June 18, 2024.

53 **highlight a crucial tension:** See Amina Adadi and Mohammed Berrada, "Peeking Inside the Black-Box: A Survey on Explainable Artificial Intelligence (XAI)," *IEEE Access* 6 (2018): 52138–60, https://doi.org/10.1109/ACCESS.2018.2870052.

53 **capacity for "chain of reasoning":** Gladys Rama, "OpenAI Launches 'Reasoning' AI Model Optimized for STEM," *THE Journal*, September 12, 2024.

54 **some basis for their reasoning:** Thomas Savage et al., "Diagnostic Reasoning Prompts Reveal the Potential for Large Language Model Interpretability in Medicine," *npj Digital Medicine* 7, no. 20 (2024), https://doi.org/10.1038/s41746-024-01010-1.

55 **I tweeted about the thousands:** Bob Wachter, "13/ 3rd concern: misinformation. Below: if we vaccinate 10M Americans, how many will develop a serious illness in 2 months after they got their shots. Answer: many thousands (& I've only included 4 illnesses, plus death). And the vaccines will have zero to do with any of them," Twitter (now X), December 2, 2020, https://x.com/Bob_Wachter/status/1333966348972539904.

55 **Betty White, Bob Saget:** Bella Otte, "No, Bob Saget and Betty White's Deaths Were Not Due to the COVID-19 Vaccine," *Poynter*, March 2, 2022, https://www.poynter.org/tfcn/2022/no-bob-saget-and-betty-whites-deaths-were-not-due-to-the-covid-19-vaccine.

55 **Matthew Perry:** Ciara O'Rourke, "Claims That Matthew Perry Died Because of COVID-19 Vaccine Are Unfounded, Lack Evidence," *PolitiFact*, October 30, 2023, https://www.politifact.com/factchecks/2023/oct/30/instagram-posts/claims-that-matthew-perry-died-because-of-covid-19.

55 **Hank Aaron:** Rick Rojas and Denise Grady, "Never Mind the Skeptics, Officials Say: Hank Aaron's Death Had Nothing to Do with the Covid-19 Vaccine," *New York Times*, January 31, 2021.

56 **318,000 Americans died:** Global Epidemics Team, "New Analysis Shows Vaccines Could Have Prevented 318,000 Deaths," *GlobalEpidemics*, May 13, 2022, https://globalepidemics.org/2022/05/13/new-analysis-shows-vaccines-could-have-prevented-318000-deaths.

56 **infodemic of mis- and disinformation:** David Scales, Jack Gorman, and

Kathleen H. Jamieson, "The Covid-19 Infodemic—Applying the Epidemiologic Model to Counter Misinformation," *New England Journal of Medicine* 385, no. 8 (2021): 678–81, https://doi.org/10.1056/NEJMp2103798.

57 **A 2023 study found that:** Christopher Doss et al., "Deepfakes and Scientific Knowledge Dissemination," *Scientific Reports* 13 (2023): 13429, https://doi.org/10.1038/s41598-023-39944-3.

58 **ability to microtarget individuals:** Francesco Salvi, Manuel H. Ribeiro, and Riccardo Gallotti, "On the Conversational Persuasiveness of Large Language Models: A Randomized Controlled Trial," preprint, *arXiv*, March 21, 2024, https://doi.org/10.48550/arXiv.2403.14380.

58 **"conspiratorial rabbit holes":** Kashmir Hill, "They Asked an A.I. Chatbot Questions. The Answers Sent Them Spiraling," *New York Times*, June 13, 2025, https://www.nytimes.com/2025/06/13/technology/chatgpt-ai-chatbots-conspiracies.html.

58 **Physician-investor Bob Kocher:** Bob Kocher, interview by author, June 18, 2024.

59 **New York City's health system:** Dave Chokshi, interview by author, September 18, 2024.

59 **"The Library of Babel":** Kevin Roose and Casey Newton, *Hard Fork*, podcast, episode 104, "A Flood of A.I. Slop + Searching for Satoshi + the Hot Mess Express Returns," *New York Times*, October 11, 2024, https://www.nytimes.com/2024/10/11/podcasts/ai-slop-bitcoin-hot-mess.html. See also Jorge Luis Borges, *The Library of Babel*, translated by Andrew Hurley (David R. Godine, 2000).

60 **using "real-world evidence":** Julia Gehrmann et al., "What Prevents Us from Reusing Medical Real-World Data in Research," *Scientific Data* 10, no. 459 (2023), https://doi.org/10.1038/s41597-023-02361-2.

61 **"working on ad optimization":** Presentation by Ziad Obermeyer, November 22, 2024.

61 **Marzyeh Ghassemi recalled:** Presentation by Marzyeh Ghassemi, November 22, 2024.

62 **technical grounds, a lawsuit:** Mindy Nunez Duffourc, Sara Gerke, and Dipl-Jur Univ, "Health Care AI and Patient Privacy—*Dinerstein v. Google*," *JAMA* 331, no. 11 (2024): 909–10, https://doi.org/10.1001/jama.2024.1110.

62 **Feinberg about the differences:** David Feinberg, interview by author, December 5, 2024.

63 **the situation to me this way:** Halamka, interview.

63 **passed the 21st Century Cures Act:** Department of Health and Human Services, "21st Century Cures Act: Interoperability, Information Blocking, and the ONC Health IT Certification Program," *Federal Register* 85, no. 85 (2020), https://www.federalregister.gov/documents/2020/05/01/2020

-07419/21st-century-cures-act-interoperability-information-blocking
-and-the-onc-health-it-certification.

64 **2019 conference, Seema Verma:** Heather Landi, "Verma Takes a Shot at
Epic for Using Privacy Concerns to 'Hold Patient Data Hostage,'" *Fierce
Healthcare*, January 29, 2020, https://www.fiercehealthcare.com/tech/cms
-seema-verma-throws-shade-at-epic-and.

64 **now leading Oracle Health:** Discussion with Seema Verma, September
24, 2024.

64 **In a 2024 blog post:** Micky Tripathi, "Getting Real About Information
Blocking and APIs," *HealthITBuzz*, October 8, 2024, https://www.healthit
.gov/buzz-blog/electronic-health-and-medical-records/interoperability
-electronic-health-and-medical-records/getting-real-about-information
-blocking-and-apis.

65 **Faulkner's attitude is:** Micky Tripathi, interview by author, September 25,
2024.

65 **While he has a point:** Aaron Neinstein, email to author, January 26, 2025.

66 **the health insurer Anthem:** SpyCloud Team, "Surviving a Data Breach
at Anthem: A CISO's Perspective," *SpyCloud*, September 16, 2020,
https://spycloud.com/blog/surviving-a-data-breach-at-anthem-a-cisos
-perspective/.

66 **The 2017 WannaCry ransomware attack:** NHS England, "NHS England
Business Continuity Management Toolkit Case Study: WannaCry Attack,"
April 21, 2023, https://www.england.nhs.uk/long-read/case-study-wannacry
-attack/.

66 **single medical record can fetch:** Brian Stack, "Here's How Much Your
Personal Information Is Selling for on the Dark Web," *Experian*, December 6,
2017, https://www.experian.com/blogs/ask-experian/heres-how-much-your
-personal-information-is-selling-for-on-the-dark-web.

66 **suffered a ransomware attack:** Energy & Commerce Chairman Guthrie,
"What We Learned: Change Healthcare Cyber Attack," May 3, 2024,
https://energycommerce.house.gov/posts/what-we-learned-change
-healthcare-cyber-attack.

66 **approximately $3 billion:** Giles Bruce, "Change Healthcare Cyberattack
Costs to Reach $2.87B," *Becker's Health IT*, October 16, 2024, https://www
.beckershospitalreview.com/cybersecurity/change-healthcare-cyberattack
-costs-to-reach-2-87b.html.

Chapter 3 | In the Loop

69 **Ethan Mollick tells the story:** Ethan Mollick, "Gradually, Then Suddenly:
Upon the Threshold," *One Useful Thing* (blog), July 4, 2024, https://www
.oneusefulthing.org/p/gradually-then-suddenly-upon-the.

70 **"Executing a left turn":** Frank Levy and Richard J. Murnane, *The New*

Division of Labor: How Computers Are Creating the Next Job Market
(Princeton University Press, 2004).

71 **observed journalist Alexis Madrigal:** Alexis Madrigal, "By the Time Your
Car Goes Driverless, You Won't Know the Difference," *All Tech Considered*,
NPR, March 4, 2014, https://www.npr.org/sections/alltechconsidered/2014
/03/04/285740673/.

71 **lessons from Waymo's experience:** Justin G. Norden and Nirav R. Shah,
"What AI in Health Care Can Learn from the Long Road to Autonomous
Vehicles," *NEJM Catalyst*, March 7, 2022, https://catalyst.nejm.org/doi
/abs/10.1056/CAT.21.0458.

72 **safer than human-driven ones:** Timothy B. Lee, "Human Drivers Are to
Blame for Most Serious Waymo Collisions," *Understanding AI*, September
10, 2024, https://www.understandingai.org/p/human-drivers-are-to-blame
-for-most.

72 **video is on YouTube:** "Waymo: Encountering an Elderly Lady Chasing a
Duck in a Wheelchair," posted September 1, 2018, YouTube, https://www
.youtube.com/watch?v=weXDUc5Osto.

72 **a remote human operator:** Cate Metz et al., "When Self-Driving Cars
Don't Actually Drive Themselves," *New York Times*, September 11, 2024.

73 **A Cruise robotaxi:** Kevin Truong, "Cruise Hid Video of Woman Being
Dragged Along San Francisco Street, DMV Says," *San Francisco Standard*,
October 24, 2023, https://www.sfstandard.com/2023/10/24/cruise-robotaxi
-dmv-suspension-video.

73 **CEO Kyle Vogt resigned:** Brad Templeton, "Kyle Vogt Resigns as CEO of
GM's Cruise Robotaxi Unit," *Forbes*, November 19, 2023, https://www
.forbes.com/sites/bradtempleton/2023/11/19/kyle-vogt-resigns-as-ceo-of
-gms-cruise-robotaxi-unit.

73 **its robotaxi ambitions:** Nathan Bomey, "GM Ending Cruise Robotaxi
Program amid 'Increasingly Competitive' Market," *Axios*, December 10, 2024,
https://www.axios.com/2024/12/10/gm-cruise-robotaxi-general-motors
-self-driving-cars.

76 **doublespeak as only he can:** "Jon Stewart on the False Promises of AI,"
The Daily Show, April 1, 2024, YouTube, 10 min., 15 sec., https://www
.youtube.com/watch?v=20TAkcy3aBY.

76 **venture fund General Catalyst:** Munjal Shah, interview by author, August 6,
2024.

77 **Health IQ, imploded:** Aditi Ganguly, "Andreessen Horowitz and Others
Poured $200 Million into Startup Health IQ—Now It's Bankrupt," *Yahoo!
Finance*, September 30, 2023, https://finance.yahoo.com/news/andreessen
-horowitz-others-poured-200-171609893.html.

77 **vaunted label of "unicorn":** Heather Landi, "Hippocratic AI Banks $141M
Series B, Hits 'Unicorn' Status as It Rolls Out AI Agent App Store," *Fierce*

Healthcare, January 9, 2025, https://www.fiercehealthcare.com/ai-and
-machine-learning/hippocratic-ai-banks-141m-series-b-hits-unicorn
-status-it-rolls-out-ai.

80 **"It has to 'work-work'":** Landi, "Hippocratic AI Banks $141M."

83 **objection to "unproven AI":** Emma Beavins, "National Nurses United
Pushes Back Against Deployment of 'Unproven' AI in Healthcare," *Fierce
Healthcare*, June 3, 2024, https://www.fiercehealthcare.com/ai-and-machine
-learning/national-nurses-united-pushes-back-against-deployment-ai
-healthcare.

85 **"AI won't completely replace humans":** Peter Lee, interview by author,
September 30, 2024.

85 **a doctor—to patients:** Muthu Alagappan, interview by author, October 1,
2024.

86 **Sounds perfect, right?:** Julia Adler-Milstein, Donald A. Redelmeier, and
Robert M. Wachter, "The Limits of Clinician Vigilance as an AI Safety
Bulwark," *JAMA* 331, no. 14 (2024): 1173–74, https://doi.org/10.1001/jama
.2024.3620.

86 **most famously Teslas:** Ian Duncan and Andrew Gregg, "Crashes
Involving Tesla's Full Self-Driving Prompt New Federal Probe," *Washington Post*, October 18, 2024.

87 **"The pilots were flying":** Sully Sullenberger, interview by author, May 12,
2014.

87 **"We are locked into a spiral":** William Langewiesche, "The Human
Factor," *Vanity Fair* (October 2014).

88 **pilots in a flight simulator:** Kathleen L. Mosier et al., "Automation Bias:
Decision Making and Performance in High-Tech Cockpits," *International Journal of Aviation Psychology* 8, no. 1 (1998): 47–63, https://doi.org
/10.1207/s15327108ijap0801_3.

89 **a tragic incident unfolded:** Federal Aviation Administration, "Tupolev
TU154M and Boeing 757-200," July 1, 2002, https://www.faa.gov/lessons
_learned/transport_airplane/accidents/RA-85816.

89 **"people believe that is correct":** Jim Fallows, interview by author, June 21,
2024.

89 **Jonathan Chen recalled seeing:** Jonathan Chen, interview by author, June
29, 2024.

90 **he was conducting with colleagues:** Ethan Goh et al., "Large Language
Model Influence on Diagnostic Reasoning: A Randomized Clinical Trial,"
JAMA Network Open 7, no. 10 (2024): e2440969, https://doi.org/10.1001
/jamanetworkopen.2024.40969.

90 **recalled a case:** Kim Kallianos, interview by author, December 27, 2024.

91 **flag this for double-checking:** Noémie Elhadad, interview by author,
September 19, 2024.

91 **if there's significant uncertainty:** Eric Horvitz, discussion with author, January 22, 2024.

91 **bombs into the agents' displays:** "Tougher TSA Bomb Tests Raise Stakes for Screeners," Aviation Pros, October 17, 2007, https://www.aviationpros .com/home/news/10384740/tougher-tsa-bomb-tests-raise-stakes-for -screeners.

92 **"Which AI use case":** Sara Murray, interview by author, April 27, 2024.

93 **more than two hundred thousand:** Brian W. Patterson et al., "Call Me Dr. Ishmael: Trends in Electronic Health Record Notes Available at Emer-gency Department Visits and Admissions," *JAMIA Open* 7, no. 2 (2024): ooae039, https://doi.org/10.1093/jamiaopen/ooae039.

93 **variety of chart review tasks:** Scott L. Fleming et al., "MedAlign: A Clinician-Generated Dataset for Instruction Following with Electronic Medical Records," preprint, *arXiv*, December 24, 2023, https://doi.org /10.48550/arXiv.2308.14089.

94 **"It's also a billing problem":** Bob Kocher, interview by author, June 18, 2024.

94 **CEO of The Doctors Company:** Richard Anderson, interview by author, June 5, 2024.

95 **technology, psychology, and religion:** Nicholas Christakis, interview by author, June 25, 2024.

Chapter 4 | Healthcare AI in Action

97 **doctor spent about six hours:** A. Jay Holmgren, Robert Thombley, Christine A. Sinsky, and Julia Adler-Milstein, "Changes in Physician Electronic Health Record Use with the Expansion of Telemedicine," *JAMA Internal Medicine* 183, no. 12 (2023): 1357–65, https://pubmed.ncbi.nlm .nih.gov/37902737.

97 **now average fifteen hours:** Athenahealth, "Almost All U.S. Physicians Surveyed Feel Burned Out on a Regular Basis," press release, February 21, 2024, https://www.athenahealth.com/press-releases/us-physicians-surveyed -feel-burned-out-on-a-regular-basis.

98 **2014 experiment, Cornell researchers:** Aner Tal, Aviva Musicus, and Brian Wansink, "Eyes in the Aisles: Why Is Cap'N Crunch Looking Down at My Child?," *Environment and Behavior* 47, no. 7 (2015): 715–33, http:// dx.doi.org/10.2139/ssrn.2419182.

100 **Smith recalled a 2024 appointment:** Mark Smith, interview by author, June 5, 2024.

100 **the physician and VC leader:** Bob Kocher, interview by author, June 18, 2024.

101 **Rao's journey to founding Abridge:** Shiv Rao, interview by author, May 30, 2024.

103 **"a dime a dozen":** Bryan Roberts, interview by author, June 12, 2024.

104 **healthcare's "Pepsi Challenge":** Katie Palmer, "Health Care's 'Pepsi Challenge': Doctors' Offices Are Testing AI Tools in Head-to-Head Pilots," *STAT*, July 30, 2024, https://www.statnews.com/2024/07/30/generative-ai-health-care-adoption-ambient-scribes/.

104 **Nabla, a French start-up:** Anastassia Gliadkovskaya, "Medical AI Scribe Startup Nabla Rolling Out Tool to the Permanente Medical Group Docs in Northern California," *Fierce Healthcare*, October 9, 2023, https://www.fiercehealthcare.com/health-tech/medical-scribe-startup-nabla-rollout-tool-kaiser-permanente-docs.

104 **Abridge won Kaiser's Pepsi Challenge:** Heather Landi, "Kaiser Permanente Rolls Out Abridge's Gen AI Clinical Tech Across 40-Hospital System," *Fierce Healthcare*, August 14, 2024, https://www.fiercehealthcare.com/health-tech/kaiser-permanente-rolls-out-abridges-gen-ai-clinical-tech-across-40-hospitals-60.

104 **arrangement with Epic:** Heather Landi, "Abridge Inks Epic Partnership, Emory Healthcare Tie-Up for Its Generative AI Tech," *Fierce Healthcare*, August 16, 2023, https://www.fiercehealthcare.com/health-tech/abridge-inks-epic-partnership-emory-healthcare-tie-its-generative-ai-tech.

104 **other scribe partner is Nuance:** Andrea Fox, "Nuance AI Copilot Now Fully Embedded in Epic EHR," *Healthcare IT News*, January 19, 2024, https://www.healthcareitnews.com/news/nuance-ai-copilot-now-fully-embedded-epic-ehr.

105 **"as this technology becomes":** Sara Murray, text message to author, June 19, 2025.

105 **Ng, the CEO of Ambience:** Mike Ng, interview by author, July 31, 2024.

106 **Conant, a geriatrician at UCSF:** Rebecca Conant, interview by author, September 13, 2024.

106 **In one study from Kaiser:** Aaron A. Tierney et al., "Ambient Artificial Intelligence Scribes to Alleviate the Burden of Clinical Documentation," *NEJM Catalyst* 5, no. 3 (2024), https://doi.org/10.1056/CAT.23.0404.

106 **"I'm so happy":** Unnamed physician quoted in Diane Sliwka, *One Good Thing* (newsletter at UCSF), no. 227, December 6, 2024.

107 **112 primary care clinicians:** Tsai-Ling Liu et al., "Does AI-Powered Clinical Documentation Enhance Clinician Efficiency? A Longitudinal Study," *NEJM AI* 1, no. 12 (2024), https://doi.org/10.1056/AIoa2400659.

107 **few have seen greater gains:** Matthew J. Duggan et al., "Clinician Experiences with Ambient Scribe Technology to Assist with Documentation Burden and Efficiency," *JAMA Network Open* 8, no. 2 (2025), https://jamanetwork.com/journals/jamanetworkopen/fullarticle/2830383.

109 **Prior auth requirements have exploded:** Jeannie Fuglesten Biniek, Nolan Sroczynski, and Tricia Neuman, "Use of Prior Authorization in

Medicare Advantage Exceeded 46 Million Requests in 2022," *KFF*, August 8, 2024, https://www.kff.org/medicare/issue-brief/use-of-prior -authorization-in-medicare-advantage-exceeded-46-million-requests -in-2022.

109 **companies have responded in kind:** Casey Ross, "AI Versus AI: The Emerging Arms Race over Health Insurance Denials," *STAT*, December 12, 2024, https://www.statnews.com/2024/12/12/artificial-intelligence -appealing-health-insurance-denials/.

109 **2023 investigative piece in *STAT*:** Casey Ross and Bob Herman, "Denied by AI: How Medicare Advantage Plans Use Algorithms to Cut Off Care for Seniors in Need," *STAT*, March 13, 2023, https://www.statnews.com /2023/03/13/medicare-advantage-plans-denial-artificial-intelligence/.

110 **"the beneficiary," said the director:** Bob Herman and Casey Ross, "UnitedHealth Discontinues a Controversial Brand amid Scrutiny over Algorithmic Care Denials," *STAT*, October 23, 2023, https://www.statnews .com/2023/10/23/unitedhealth-optum-navihealth-rebranding-algorithm/.

110 **Systems, built an AI program:** Aaron Weitzman, "1 Big Thing: Automat-ing Health Care Calls," *Axios Pro*, October 24, 2024, https://www.axios .com/pro/health-tech-deals/newsletters/2024/10/24/health-tech-automating -phone-calls.

110 **has gotten into the act:** Tanya Albert Henry, "Prior Authorization Fixes Earn Majority Support in Congress," *AMA News Wire*, November 21, 2024, https://www.ama-assn.org/practice-management/prior-authorization /prior-authorization-fixes-earn-majority-support-congress.

111 **Health has connected its EHR:** Marc Zarefsky, "With the EHR, Half of Prior Authorizations Get Instant Approval," *AMA News Wire*, June 5, 2024, https://www.ama-assn.org/practice-management/prior-authorization /ehr-half-prior-authorizations-get-instant-approval.

111 **solutions at Elevance, told me:** Catherine Gaffigan, interview by author, September 22, 2024.

112 **colleagues went even further:** Leslie A. Lenert, Steven Lane, and Ramsey Wehbe, "Could an Artificial Intelligence Approach to Prior Authorization Be More Human?," *Journal of the American Medical Informatics Associa-tion* 30, no. 5 (2023): 989–94, https://doi.org/10.1093/jamia/ocad016.

112 **a 2023 *JAMA* article:** Michael Stillman, "Death by Patient Portal," *JAMA* 330, no. 3 (2023): 223–24, https://doi.org/10.1001/jama.2023.11629.

113 **Patient-generated inbox:** Brian Halstater and Maribeth Kuntz, "Using a Nurse Triage Model to Address Patient Messages," *Family Practice Management* 30, no. 4 (2023): 7–11, https://www.aafp.org/pubs/fpm/issues /2023/0700/patient-messages.html.

114 **more than fifty each day:** Jane F. Fogg and Christine A. Sinsky, "In-Basket Reduction: A Multiyear Pragmatic Approach to Lessen the Work Burden

of Primary Care Physicians," *NEJM Catalyst* 4, no. 5 (2023), https://doi.org
/10.1056/CAT.22.0438.

115 **researchers from UC San Diego:** H. C. Eschenroeder et al., "Associations
of Physician Burnout with Organizational Electronic Health Record
Support and After-Hours Charting," *Journal of the American Medical
Informatics Association* 28, no. 5 (2021): 960–66, https://doi.org/10.1093
/jamia/ocab053.

115 **results with Chris Longhurst:** Chris Longhurst, interview by author, June
20, 2024.

115 **Sara Murray told me that:** Sara Murray, interview by author, April 27,
2024.

116 **had a characteristically positive:** Heather Landi, "Epic Touts New AI
Applications to Streamline Charting and Bring Research Insights to the
Point of Care," *Fierce Healthcare*, August 21, 2024, https://www.fiercehealth
care.com/ai-and-machine-learning/epic-touts-new-ai-applications
-streamline-charting-and-bring-research.

116 **One study of AI-generated answers:** Shan Chen et al., "The Effect of
Using a Large Language Model to Respond to Patient Messages," *Lancet
Digital Health* 6, no. 6 (2024): e379–81, https://doi.org/10.1016/S2589
-7500(24)00060-8.

117 **for the company, told me:** Garrett Adams, interview by author, January 29,
2025.

117 **to *The New York Times*:** Teddy Rosenbluth, "That Message from Your
Doctor? It May Have Been Drafted by A.I.," *New York Times*, September 24,
2024.

117 **currently favors disclosure:** Vardit Ravitsky, interview by author, July 31,
2024. A group from UC San Diego also argued for disclosure in 2025:
Marlene Millen, Ming Tai-Seale, and Christopher Longhurst, "A Call for
Disclosure When Using AI for Patient Communications," *NEJM AI* 2,
no. 6 (2025), https://doi.org/10.1056/AIp2401167.

118 **In an intriguing 2025 study:** Joanna S. Cavalier et al., "Ethics in Patient
Preferences for Artificial Intelligence–Drafted Responses to Electronic
Messages," *JAMA Network Open* 9, no. 3 (2025): e250449, https://doi.org
/10.1001/jamanetworkopen.2025.0449.

118 **Permanente has tried to address:** Vincent X. Liu et al., "Content of
Patient Electronic Messages to Physicians in a Large Integrated System,"
JAMA Network Open 7, no. 4 (2024): e244867, https://doi.org/10.1001
/jamanetworkopen.2024.4867.

118 **Corewell Health West:** Alexis Kurek et al., "The 'Inboxologist': A Novel
Approach to In-Basket Management in Primary Care," *NEJM Catalyst* 5,
no. 10 (2024), https://doi.org/10.1056/CAT.24.0133.

120 **in a 2024 panel discussion:** Peter Lee, *DealBook Summit*, podcast, episode 1, "The A.I. Revolution," *New York Times*, December 11, 2024, https://dealbook-podcast.simplecast.com/episodes/20241211-1-veijDuI7.

120 **spoke to Lee in 2024:** Peter Lee, interview by author, September 30, 2024.

122 **Autopsy studies have found:** Kaveh G. Shojania et al., "Changes in Rates of Autopsy-Detected Diagnostic Errors over Time: A Systematic Review," *JAMA* 289, no. 21 (2003): 2849–56, https://doi.org/10.1001/jama.289 .21.2849.

122 **eight hundred thousand Americans:** David E. Newman-Toker et al., "Burden of Serious Harms from Diagnostic Error in the USA," *BMJ Quality & Safety* 33, no. 2 (2024): 109–20, https://doi.org/10.1136/bmjqs -2021-014130.

122 **diagnostic mishaps remain:** Ali S. Saber Tehrani et al., "25-Year Summary of US Malpractice Claims for Diagnostic Errors 1986–2010: An Analysis from the National Practitioner Data Bank," *BMJ Quality & Safety* 22, no. 8 (2013): 672–80, https://doi.org/10.1136/bmjqs-2012-001550.

126 **first sentence in *Anna Karenina*:** Leo Tolstoy, *Anna Karenina* (Oxford University Press, 1878).

128 **at Harvard, is also surprised:** Adam Rodman, interview by author, October 21, 2024.

128 **that "diagnostic brain" has evolved:** Pat Croskerry, "A Universal Model of Diagnostic Reasoning," *Academic Medicine* 84, no. 8 (2009): 1022–28, https://doi.org/10.1097/ACM.0b013e3181ace703.

129 **in describing one such study:** Adam Rodman, "Actual clinical reasoning isn't anything like that at all. . . . it's about collecting clinical information, sifting through a lot of noise, and organizing this information into differentials and treatment plans under uncertainty," Twitter (now X), April 3, 2024, https://x.com/AdamRodmanMD/status /1775612056491704510. The study he's referring to is Zahir Kanjee, Byron Crowe, and Adam Rodman, "Accuracy of a Generative Artificial Intelligence Model in a Complex Diagnostic Challenge," *JAMA* 330, no. 1 (2023): 78–80, https://doi.org/10.1001/jama.2023.8288.

130 **Jeff Dean, a longtime leader:** Jeff Dean, interview by author, August 2, 2024.

130 **Today, two-thirds of patients:** W. N. Schoening et al., "Twenty-Year Longitudinal Follow-Up After Orthotopic Liver Transplantation: A Single-Center Experience of 313 Consecutive Cases," *American Journal of Transplantation* 13, no. 9 (2013): 2384–94, https://doi.org/10.1111/ajt.12384.

131 **That's when things went sideways:** Arvind Narayanan and Sayash Kapoor, "Does the UK's Liver Transplant Matching Algorithm Systematically Exclude Younger Patients?," *AI Snake Oil*, November 11, 2024, https://www.aisnakeoil.com/p/does-the-uks-liver-transplant-matching.

132 **The fatal flaw was:** "Algorithms Are Deciding Who Gets Organ Transplant: Are Their Decisions Fair?," *Financial Times*, November 8, 2023, https://www.ft.com/content/5125c83a-b82b-40c5-8b35-99579e087951.

133 **traumatized my neighbors at Stanford:** Eileen Guo and Karen Hao, "This Is the Stanford Vaccine Algorithm That Left Out Frontline Doctors," *MIT Technology Review*, December 21, 2020.

133 **In a 2023 paper:** Angelina Wang et al., "Against Predictive Optimization: On the Legitimacy of Decision-Making Algorithms That Optimize Predictive Accuracy," *ACM Journal of Responsive Computing* 1, no. 9 (2024): 1–45, https://doi.org/10.1145/3636509.

134 **tend to overestimate survival:** Nicholas Christakis, interview by author, June 25, 2024.

134 **the patients entering hospice:** Kathleen T. Unroe et al., "Variation in Hospice Services by Location of Care: Nursing Home Versus Assisted Living Facility Versus Home," *Journal of the American Geriatrics Society* 65, no. 7 (2017): 1490–96, https://doi.org/10.1111/jgs.14826.

135 **Zeke Emanuel and I drew:** Ezekiel J. Emanuel and Robert M. Wachter, "Artificial Intelligence in Health Care: Will the Value Match the Hype?," *JAMA* 321, no. 23 (2019): 2281–82, https://doi.org/10.1001/jama.2019.4914.

136 **advertorial in *Time* magazine:** Sam Altman and Arianna Huffington, "AI-Driven Behavior Change Could Transform Health Care," *Time*, July 7, 2024.

136 **Warzel was unimpressed:** Charlie Warzel, "AI Has Become a Technology of Faith," *The Atlantic*, July 12, 2024.

137 **receives more than sixty messages:** Hardeep Singh et al., "Information Overload and Missed Test Results in Electronic Health Record–Based Settings," *JAMA Internal Medicine* 173, no. 8 (2013): 702–4, https://doi.org/10.1001/2013.jamainternmed.61.

137 **90 percent of alerts:** Siru Liu et al., "Why Do Users Override Alerts? Utilizing Large Language Model to Summarize Comments and Optimize Clinical Decision Support," *Journal of the American Medical Informatics Association* 31, no. 6 (2024): 1388–96, https://doi.org/10.1093/jamia/ocae041.

138 **tapped into the bedside monitors:** Barbara J. Drew et al., "Insights into the Problem of Alarm Fatigue with Physiologic Monitor Devices: A Comprehensive Observational Study of Consecutive Intensive Care Unit Patients," *PLOS One* 9, no. 10 (2014): e110274, https://doi.org/10.1371/journal.pone.0110274.

138 **told me about a chat:** Barbara Drew, interview by author, June 19, 2014.

142 **cry from Epic's rosy claims:** Andrew Wong et al., "External Validation of a Widely Implemented Proprietary Sepsis Prediction Model in Hospitalized Patients," *JAMA Internal Medicine* 181, no. 8 (2021): 1065–70, https://doi.org/10.1001/jamainternmed.2021.2626.

142 **Colorado Health system struggled:** Casey Ross, "Epic's Overhaul of a Flawed Algorithm Shows Why AI Oversight Is a Life-or-Death Issue," *STAT*, October 24, 2022, https://www.statnews.com/2022/10/24/epic -overhaul-of-a-flawed-algorithm.

143 **"The way we had":** Ross, "Epic's Overhaul."

143 **retuned Epic's algorithm:** Michiel Schinkel, Tom van der Poll, and W. Joost Wiersinga, "Artificial Intelligence for Early Sepsis Detection: A Word of Caution," *American Journal of Respiratory and Critical Care Medicine* 207, no. 7 (2023): 853–54, https://doi.org/10.1164/rccm.202212-2284VP.

144 **A 2025 survey showed that:** Paige Nong et al., "Current Use and Evaluation of Artificial Intelligence and Predictive Models in US Hospitals," *Health Affairs* 44, no. 1 (2025): 90–98, https://doi.org/10.1377/hlthaff .2024.00842.

144 **published guidelines dictate the systolic:** Giuseppe Mancia et al., "2023 ESH Guidelines for the Management of Arterial Hypertension: The Task Force for the Management of Arterial Hypertension of the European Society of Hypertension," *Journal of Hypertension* 41, no. 12 (2023): 1874–2071, https://doi.org/10.1097/HJH.0000000000003480.

147 **Kocher has invested in Lyra:** Bob Kocher, interview by author, June 18, 2024.

148 **"Artificial pancreas" systems:** Francis J. Doyle III et al., "Closed-Loop Artificial Pancreas Systems: Engineering the Algorithms," *Diabetes Care* 37, no. 5 (2014): 1191–97, https://doi.org/10.2337/dc13-2108.

148 **described one tool:** Longhurst, interview.

149 **the most mind-blowing:** John D. Birkmeyer et al., "Surgical Skill and Complication Rates After Bariatric Surgery," *New England Journal of Medicine* 369, no. 15 (2013): 1434–42, https://doi.org/10.1056/NEJMsa1 300625.

149 **told *MIT Technology Review*:** Simar Bajaj, "This AI-Powered 'Black Box' Could Make Surgery Safer," *MIT Technology Review*, June 7, 2024.

151 **Carla Pugh has been studying:** Carla Pugh, interview by author, September 19, 2024.

152 **Albom in *Tuesdays with Morrie*:** Mitch Albom, *Tuesdays with Morrie: An Old Man, a Young Man, and Life's Greatest Lesson* (Doubleday, 1997).

152 **relatively brief feedback:** Frank J. Overdyk et al., "Remote Video Auditing with Real-Time Feedback in an Academic Surgical Suite Improves Safety and Efficiency Metrics: A Cluster Randomised Study," *BMJ Quality and Safety* 25, no. 12 (2016): 947–53, https://doi.org/10.1136/bmjqs-2015-004226.

152 **OR costs about fifty dollars:** Tyler Smith et al., "Cost of OR Time Is $46.04 per Minute," *Journal of Orthopaedic Business* 2, no. 4 (2022): 10–13, https://doi.org/10.55576/job.v2i4.23.

152 **In 2010, two simulation tasks:** Melina C. Vassiliou et al., "FLS and FES:

Comprehensive Models of Training and Assessment," *Surgical Clinics of North America* 90, no. 3 (2010): 535–58, https://doi.org/10.1016/j.suc .2010.02.012.

153 **survey of 165 practicing surgeons:** M. Morino, V. Festa, and C. Garrone, "Survey on Torino Courses: The Impact of a Two-Day Practical Course on Apprenticeship and Diffusion of Laparoscopic Cholecystectomy in Italy," *Surgical Endoscopy* 9, no. 1 (1995): 46–48, https://doi.org/10.1007/BF00187884.

154 **Alseidi, a leading surgical educator:** Adnan Alseidi, interview by author, January 10, 2025.

155 **Envision a virtual operating room:** Chris Varghese et al., "Artificial Intelligence in Surgery," *Nature Medicine* 30 (2024): 1257–68, https://doi .org/10.1038/s41591-024-02970-3.

157 **for pre-cancerous lesions:** Shenghan Lou et al., "Artificial Intelligence for Colorectal Neoplasia Detection During Colonoscopy: A Systematic Review and Meta-Analysis of Randomized Clinical Trials," *The Lancet eClinicalMedicine* 66 (2023): 102341, https://doi.org/10.1016/j.eclinm .2023.102341.

157 **Goldberg, an economist and engineer:** Ken Goldberg, interview by author, February 4, 2025.

157 **uses the term "augmented dexterity":** Ken Goldberg and Gary Guthart, "Augmented Dexterity: How Robots Can Enhance Human Surgical Skills," *Science Robotics* 9, no. 95 (2024), https://doi.org/10.1126/scirobotics.adr5247.

158 **AI-enabled surgical "black box":** Bajaj, "This AI-Powered 'Black Box.'"

158 **OR team failed to follow:** Amr I. Al Abbas et al., "The Operating Room Black Box: Understanding Adherence to Surgical Checklists," *Annals of Surgery* 276, no. 6 (2022): 995–1001, https://doi.org/10.1097 /SLA.0000000000005695.

159 **"you work as a radiologist":** Geoff Hinton, "On Radiology," Creative Destruction Lab, November 24, 2016, YouTube, https://www.youtube.com /watch?v=2HMPRXstSvQ.

159 **a career in radiology:** Samantha M. Santomartino and Paul H. Yi, "Systematic Review of Radiologist and Medical Student Attitudes on the Role and Impact of AI and Radiology," *Academic Radiology* 29, no. 11 (2022): 1748–56, https://doi.org/10.1016/j.acra.2021.12.032.

160 **shortage, not a surfeit:** Elizabeth Y. Rula, "Radiology Workforce Shortage and Growing Demand: Something Has to Give," *American College of Radiology Bulletin*, July 3, 2024, https://www.acr.org/Clinical-Resources /Publications-and-Research/ACR-Bulletin/Radiology-Workforce -Shortage-and-Growing-Demand-Something-Has-to-Give.

161 **patients with dark skin:** Rebecca Fliorent et al., "Artificial Intelligence in Dermatology: Advancements and Challenges in Skin of Color," *Interna-*

tional Journal of Dermatology 63, no. 4 (2024): 455–61, https://doi.org/10.1111/ijd.17076.

161 **but physicians do too:** Roni Caryn Rabin, "Dermatology Has a Problem with Skin Color," *New York Times*, August 30, 2020.

162 **why he still had a job:** John Mongan, interview by author, May 30, 2024.

162 **neuroradiologist Bradley Erickson added:** Bradley Erickson, interview by author, November 1, 2024.

164 **Bredella recalled seeing a demo:** Miriam Bredella, interview by author, December 15, 2024.

166 **tools entered community practice:** Joshua J. Fenton et al., "Influence of Computer-Aided Detection on Performance of Screening Mammography," *New England Journal of Medicine* 356, no. 14 (2007): 1399–1409, https://doi.org/10.1056/NEJMoa066099.

166 **common cause of successful lawsuits:** Jeremy S. Whang et al., "The Causes of Medical Malpractice Suits Against Radiologists in the United States," *Radiology* 266, no. 2 (2013): 548–54, https://doi.org/10.1148/radiol.12111119.

166 **will likely recommend a biopsy:** Joann G. Elmore and Christoph I. Lee, "Artificial Intelligence in Medical Imaging—Learning from Past Mistakes in Mammography," *JAMA Health Forum* 3, no. 2 (2022): e215207, https://doi.org/10.1001/jamahealthforum.2021.5207.

166 **In a 2023 Swedish study:** Kristina Lång et al., "Artificial Intelligence–Supported Screen Reading Versus Standard Double Reading in the Mammography Screening with Artificial Intelligence Trial (MASAI)," *Lancet Oncology* 24, no. 8 (2023): 936–44, https://doi.org/10.1016/S1470-2045(23)00298-X.

167 **New AI models:** Jonas Gjesvik et al., "Artificial Intelligence Algorithm for Subclinical Breast Cancer Detection," *JAMA Network Open* 7, no. 10 (2024): e2437402, https://jamanetwork.com/journals/jamanetworkopen/fullarticle/2824353.

167 **under the category of Software:** "Artificial Intelligence and Machine Learning in Software as a Medical Device," US Food and Drug Administration, January 6, 2025, https://www.fda.gov/medical-devices/software-medical-device-samd/artificial-intelligence-and-machine-learning-software-medical-device.

168 **University of Pennsylvania radiologist:** Matthew Perrone, "Will AI Replace Doctors Who Read X-Rays, or Just Make Them Better Than Ever?," Associated Press, May 14, 2024.

168 **2024 study supported this view:** Hui Liu et al., "Artificial Intelligence and Radiologist Burnout," *JAMA Network Open* 7, no. 11 (2024): e2448714, https://doi.org/10.1001/jamanetworkopen.2024.48714.

169 **two hundred healthcare organizations:** Monique Rasband and Jonathan Christensen, "Imaging AI 2024," KLAS Research, November 27, 2024, https://klasresearch.com/report/imaging-ai-2024-multiple-solutions -gaining-traction-in-a-crowded-market/3664.

170 **"start treatment right away":** Grace Cordovano, interview by author, October 30, 2024.

173 **"Evolution of Who Knows What":** Dave deBronkart, "The Evolution of Who Knows What: A Cluetrain Manifesto for Empowered Patients," *e-Patient Dave* (blog), May 30, 2023, https://www.epatientdave.com/2023 /05/30/the-evolution-of-who-knows-what-a-cluetrain-manifesto-for -empowered-patients.

174 **"gave us access to information":** Dave deBronkart, interview by author, September 27, 2024.

174 **"We are pretty good":** Smith, interview.

175 **"Gimme My Damn Data":** Dave deBronkart, "Let Patients Help!" *TEDxMaastricht*, April 7, 2011, YouTube, https://www.youtube.com /watch?v=2vejkD0Rl3o.

175 **lamented the late Atul Butte:** Atul Butte, interview by author, June 4, 2024. Butte tragically passed away in June 2025.

176 **"go figure it out themselves":** Elizabeth Dwoskin, Daniel Gilbert, and Tatum Hunter, "Doctors Couldn't Help: They Turned to a Shadow System of DIY Medical Tests," *Washington Post*, June 9, 2024.

176 **"I think AI for patients":** Peter Lee, email to author, June 18, 2025.

177 **health journalist Carey Goldberg recounted:** Carey Goldberg, "Patient Portal—When Patients Take AI into Their Own Hands," *NEJM AI* 1, no. 5 (2024), https://doi.org/10.1056/AIp2400283.

Chapter 5 | Institutions and Innovations

180 **take more hours than exist:** Justin Porter et al., "Revisiting the Time Needed to Provide Adult Primary Care," *Journal of General Internal Medicine* 38, no. 1 (2023): 147–55, https://doi.org/10.1007/s11606-022-07707-x.

180 **are either treading water:** Shelby Livingston, "Amazon, CVS, and Walgreens Went All In on Primary Care: Their Bets Are All Bleeding Money," *Business Insider*, March 6, 2024, https://www.businessinsider .com/cvs-walgreens-amazon-primary-care-acquisition-strategy-2024-3.

181 **it shuttered all of them:** Siddharth Cavale and Granth Vanaik, "Walmart to Shut All Health Clinics in US over Lack of Profitability," *Reuters*, May 1, 2024.

181 **company at more than $1 billion:** Noor Zainab Hussain, "Exclusive: Forward Health Valued at over $1 Billion in Latest Funding from SoftBank, Others—Source," *Reuters*, March 11, 2021.

182 **a self-service clinical kiosk:** Jennifer A. Kingson, "New AI-Powered

Doctor's Office Allows Patients to Draw Blood, Take Vitals," *Axios*, December 8, 2023, https://www.axios.com/2023/12/08/carepod-forward -doctors-office-telehealth-telemedicine.

182 **Aoun, who cultivated:** Adrian Aoun, "HLTH Panel," *Forward*, October 21, 2021, YouTube, https://www.youtube.com/watch?v=9gTpLFsJZ3A.

182 **"An ATM doesn't do everything":** Heather Landi, "Primary Care Player Forward Unveils AI-Based, Self-Serve CarePods Backed by $100M Series E Round," *Fierce Healthcare*, November 15, 2023, https://www.fiercehealthcare .com/health-tech/primary-care-player-forward-unveils-ai-based-self -serve-carepods-backed-100m-investment.

182 **logistical and operational challenges:** Rob Price and Rebecca Torrence, "Forward's Leaders Are Already Recruiting for a New Startup," *Business Insider*, November 22, 2024, https://www.businessinsider.com/forwards -execs-are-already-recruiting-for-a-new-startup-2024-11.

183 **"For me, the lesson is":** Heather Landi, "Forward Founder Says He's Launching New Venture After Winding Down Primary Care Startup: Report," *Fierce Healthcare*, November 27, 2024, https://www.fiercehealth care.com/health-tech/forward-founder-says-hes-launching-new-venture -after-winding-down-primary-care-startup.

183 **was that of Babylon Health:** Ingrid Lunden, "The Fall of Babylon: Failed Telehealth Startup Once Valued at $2B Goes Bankrupt, Sold for Parts," *TechCrunch*, August 31, 2023, https://techcrunch.com/2023/08/31/the -fall-of-babylon-failed-tele-health-startup-once-valued-at-nearly-2b -goes-bankrupt-and-sold-for-parts.

183 **also began making substantial inroads:** Matthew Field, "How Out of Control Spending and a Botched US Expansion Left NHS Partner on Brink of Collapse," *The Telegraph*, August 25, 2023.

183 **15 percent of cases:** Parmy Olson, "This Health Startup Won Big Government Deals—but Inside, Doctors Flagged Problems," *Forbes*, December 17, 2018.

184 **gave Babylon a spin:** Bob Kocher, interview by author, June 18, 2024.

185 **"is a losing proposition":** Neal Khosla, interview by author, June 17, 2024.

186 **founder of Private Medical:** Jordan Shlain, interview by author, January 6, 2025.

188 **Mayo's Henry Plummer introduced:** Axel Gumbel, "From Paper to Digital: The Medical Record at Mayo Clinic," *Mayo Clinic*, accessed May 15, 2025, https://history.mayoclinic.org/stories/from-paper-to-digital-the -medical-record-at-mayo-clinic.

190 **Farrugia came to believe:** Gianrico Farrugia, interview by author, October 31, 2024.

191 **"think it was too complicated":** John Halamka, interview by author, November 1, 2024.

192 **"monk-like asceticism," he wrote:** John Halamka, "The Yin to My Yang," *Dispatch from the Digital Health Frontier* (blog), March 18, 2010, https://geekdoctor.blogspot.com/2010/03/yin-to-my-yang.html.

193 **"started with Mayo Clinic data":** Steve Bethke, interview by author, October 31, 2024.

195 **partnership with Epic and Abridge:** Heather Landi, "Abridge Teams Up with Epic, Mayo Clinic to Develop Gen AI Tools for Nurses," *Fierce Healthcare*, July 23, 2024, https://www.fiercehealthcare.com/ai-and-machine-learning/abridge-teams-epic-mayo-clinic-develop-gen-ai-tools-nurses.

195 **even Mayo is having problems:** Jim Rogers, interview by author, October 31, 2024.

196 **"after looking at the slide":** Andrew Norgan, interview by author, November 1, 2024.

196 **estimates of patients' ejection fraction:** Zachi I. Attia et al., "Screening for Cardiac Contractile Dysfunction Using an Artificial Intelligence–Enabled Electrocardiogram," *Nature Medicine* 25 (2019): 70–74, https://doi.org/10.1038/s41591-018-0240-2.

196 **future risk of atrial fibrillation:** Zachi I. Attia et al., "An Artificial Intelligence–Enabled ECG Algorithm for the Identification of Patients with Atrial Fibrillation During Sinus Rhythm: A Retrospective Analysis of Outcome Prediction," *The Lancet* 394, no. 10201 (2019): 861–67, https://doi.org/10.1016/S0140-6736(19)31721-0.

196 **(as opposed to chronological) age:** Adetola O. Ladejobi et al., "The 12-Lead Electrocardiogram as a Biomarker of Biological Age," *European Heart Journal: Digital Health* 2, no. 3 (2021): 379–89, https://doi.org/10.1093/ehjdh/ztab043.

196 **recipient of a heart transplant:** Ilke Ozcan et al., "Artificial Intelligence–Derived Cardiac Ageing Is Associated with Cardiac Events Post–Heart Transplantation," *European Heart Journal: Digital Health* 3, no. 4 (2022): 516–24, https://doi.org/10.1093/ehjdh/ztac051.

196 **when patients are identified:** Casey Ross, "At Mayo Clinic, AI Engineers Face an 'Acid Test': Will Their Algorithms Help Real Patients?," *STAT*, December 18, 2019, https://www.statnews.com/2019/12/18/mayo-clinic-artificial-intelligence-acid-test.

197 **As Mayo electrophysiologist:** Samuel Asirvatham, interview by author, October 31, 2024.

197 **AI-EKG analysis, this stethoscope:** Attia et al., "Screening for Cardiac Contractile Dysfunction."

199 **I asked Aaron Neinstein:** Aaron Neinstein, interview by author, June 5, 2024.

200 **major study, the Flexner Report:** Abraham Flexner, *Medical Education in the United States and Canada: A Report to the Carnegie Foundation for the*

Advancement of Teaching (Carnegie Foundation for the Advancement of Teaching, 1910).

204 **"All the time-motion studies reveal":** Marc Triola, interview by author, September 16, 2024.

206 **published these results in 2023:** Marc M. Triola et al., "Artificial Intelligence Screening of Medical School Applications: Development and Validation of a Machine-Learning Algorithm," *Academic Medicine* 98, no. 9 (2023): 1036–43, https://doi.org/10.1097/ACM.0000000000005202.

206 **so-called precision education:** Marc M. Triola and Jesse Burk-Rafel, "Precision Medical Education," *Academic Medicine* 98, no. 7 (2023): 775–81, https://doi.org/10.1097/ACM.0000000000005227.

209 *New York Times* **opinion writer:** Ezra Klein, "What If Dario Amodei Is Right About A.I.?," *The Ezra Klein Show* (podcast), *New York Times*, April 12, 2024, https://www.nytimes.com/2024/04/12/opinion/ezra-klein-podcast -dario-amodei.html?showTranscript=1.

210 **a young physician-informaticist:** Jesse Burk-Rafel, interview by author, September 16, 2024.

210 **I spoke to Nina Singh:** Nina Singh, interview by author, October 3, 2024.

211 **told the audience:** Ashley Stewart and Blake Dodge, "Oracle's Deadly Gamble," *Business Insider*, May 20, 2024, https://www.businessinsider .com/oracle-cerner-health-larry-ellison-28-billion-deadly-gamble -veterans-2024-5.

212 **in a tense congressional hearing:** Blake Dodge, "Oracle Cofounder Larry Ellison Says He Wants to Transform Healthcare: First His Company Will Have to Tackle a Billion-Dollar Mess," *Business Insider*, July 28, 2022.

212 **"was built in somebody's garage":** Seema Verma, conference presentation, September 25, 2024.

213 **described it to me:** David Feinberg, interview by author, December 5, 2024.

214 **worth a brief retelling:** Katie Jennings, "The Billionaire Who Controls Your Medical Records," *Forbes*, May 31, 2021.

215 **Faulkner later recalled:** Erik Lorenzsonn, "Cap Times Idea Fest: Judy Faulkner Reflects on How a Culture of Fun, Creativity, Focus Has Shaped Epic Systems," *Cap Times*, September 15, 2019.

215 **recounted in a 2021 interview:** Jennings, "The Billionaire Who Controls."

216 **theme was, of course, AI:** "Storytime at Epic UGM 2024," *Digital Health Wire*, August 22, 2024, https://digitalhealthwire.com/newsletter/epic -ugm-recap-clariums-ai-supply-chain.

216 **"You ain't seen nothing yet!":** Marc Eisen, "Epic Dominates the Marketplace," *Isthmus*, September 5, 2024.

217 **a 2024** *Forbes* **profile:** Seth Joseph, "Epic's Market Share: Who Should Control the Levers of Healthcare Innovation?," *Forbes*, February 26, 2024.

218 **"the majority of them won't"**: Jennings, "The Billionaire Who Controls."

218 **profile outlined seven Epic tactics:** Seth Joseph, "Competitive or Exclusionary? Epic's Seven Business Practices That Raise Questions," *Forbes*, February 26, 2024.

218 **later rebranded to "Workshop":** Alex Knapp and Katie Jennings, "InnovationRx: New Ways to Connect with Epic," *Forbes*, January 17, 2024.

219 **"I have fifty vendors":** Joseph, "Epic's Market Share."

220 **"we're building an AI platform":** Heather Landi, "How Epic's AI Moves Could Shake Up the Healthcare AI Market," *Fierce Healthcare*, August 18, 2025, https://www.fiercehealthcare.com/ai-and-machine-learning/how -epics-ai-moves-could-shake-health-tech-market.

220 **Epic was engaged in monopolistic:** Heather Landi, "Epic's Countermove: Calls for Carequality, Particle Health to Go Public with Patient Privacy Dispute," *Fierce Healthcare*, September 27, 2024, https://www.fiercehealthcare .com/ai-and-machine-learning/epics-countermove-calls-carequality -particle-health-go-public-patient.

220 **Epic punched back:** Heather Landi, "Epic, Particle Health Dispute Exposes Broader Challenges with Sharing Patient Data, Health IT Experts Say," *Fierce Healthcare*, April 15, 2024, https://www.fiercehealthcare.com /health-tech/epic-particle-health-dispute-exposes-broader-issues-accessing -and-sharing-patient-data.

221 **"scheme to destroy":** Heather Landi, "CureIS Healthcare Hits Epic with Lawsuit for Alleged 'Scheme to Destroy' Its Business," *Fierce Healthcare*, May 17, 2025, https://www.fiercehealthcare.com/health-tech/epic-hit -lawsuit-cureis-healthcare-alleged-scheme-destroy-its-business.

221 **"a need for broader reform":** Robert Kuttner, "An Epic Dystopia," *The American Prospect*, October 1, 2024.

221 **"now our execution is insane":** Feinberg, interview.

223 **record is actually Sabre:** Max D. Hopper, "Rattling SABRE—New Ways to Compete on Information," *Harvard Business Review* (May–June 1990).

223 **the prominent healthcare investor:** Bryan Roberts, interview by author, June 12, 2024.

Chapter 6 | Payment, Policies, and Politics

226 **Gartner Hype Cycle:** "Hype Cycle of the Top 50 Emerging Digital Health Trends," *The Medical Futurist*, accessed May 15, 2025, https://cdn .medicalfuturist.com/wp-content/uploads/2021/10/2023_hype_cycle _infographic_small.png.

226 **analytics company, said in 2024:** Cade Metz, Karen Weise, and Tripp Mickle, "A.I. Start-Ups Face a Rough Financial Reality Check," *New York Times*, April 29, 2024.

227 **CEO Sam Altman in 2024:** Christiaan Hetzner, "OpenAI's Sam Altman Doesn't Care How Much AGI Will Cost: Even If He Spends $50 Billion a Year, Some Breakthroughs for Mankind Are Priceless," *Fortune*, May 3, 2024, https://fortune.com/2024/05/03/openai-sam-altman-microsoft -agi-artificial-general-intelligence-costs.

227 **quipped tech journalist Casey Newton:** Kevin Roose and Casey Newton, *Hard Fork*, podcast, episode 95, "Google's Monopoly Money + Is the A.I. Bubble Popping? + The Hot-Mess Express," *New York Times*, August 9, 2024, https://www.nytimes.com/2024/08/09/podcasts/hardfork-google -antitrust-ai-bubble.html?showTranscript=1.

228 **Viz LVO, an AI tool:** Ameer E. Hassan, Victor M. Ringheanu, and Wondwossen G. Tekle, "The Implementation of Artificial Intelligence Significantly Reduces Door-In-Door-Out Times in a Primary Care Center Prior to Transfer," *Interventional Neuroradiology* 29, no. 6 (2023): 631–36, https://journals.sagepub.com/doi/full/10.1177/15910199221122848.

228 **Medicare increased its reimbursement:** Ruth Reader et al., "Senate Moves to Regulate Social Media," *Politico*, July 30, 2024, https://www .politico.com/newsletters/future-pulse/2024/07/30/officials-go-ahead-and -try-ai-00171675.

228 **many radiologists are offering them:** Knvul Sheikh, "A.I. Could Spot Breast Cancer Earlier: Should You Pay for It?," *New York Times*, April 8, 2024.

229 **study of nearly 750,000 patients:** Radiological Society of North America (RSNA), "Women Pay for AI to Boost Mammogram Findings," press release, December 5, 2024, https://press.rsna.org/timssnet/media/pressreleases /14_pr_target.cfm?ID=2540.

229 **was a Boston-based company:** Ruth Reader and Ben Leonard, "Sorry, the Government's Not Paying for Your Therapy App," *Politico*, May 14, 2023, https://www.politico.com/news/2023/05/14/online-medicine-government -funding-00096023.

229 **clearly a delicate balance:** Ravi B. Parikh and Lorens A. Helmchen, "Paying for Artificial Intelligence in Medicine," *NPJ Digital Medicine* 5, no. 63 (2022), https://doi.org/10.1038/s41746-022-00609-6.

229 **wrote health economists:** Anna Zink, Michael E. Chernew, and Hannah T. Neprash, "How Should Medicare Pay for Artificial Intelligence?," *JAMA Internal Medicine* 184, no. 8 (2024): 863–64, https://doi.org/10.1001 /jamainternmed.2024.1648.

230 **a physician and strategist:** Brian Silverstein, interview by author, July 12, 2024.

230 **Ami Parekh, chief medical officer:** Ami Parekh, interview by author, August 3, 2024.

231 **Taneja, CEO of General Catalyst:** Hemant Taneja, interview by author, October 15, 2024.

232 **its purchase of Summa Health:** Madeline Ashley, "General Catalyst to Acquire Summa Health for $485M," *Becker's Hospital Review*, November 7, 2024, https://www.beckershospitalreview.com/hospital-transactions -and-valuation/general-catalyst-to-acquire-summa-health-for-485m.html.

233 **he no longer attends HIMSS:** John Halamka, interview by author, November 1, 2024.

234 **"in the bowels of Google":** Robert Califf, interview by author, December 23, 2024.

235 **New York City passed:** Katharine Liao and Scott Held, "New York Update: NYS Amends WARN Regulations and NYC Provides Guidance on New Law Concerning Use of AI in Hiring (US)," *National Law Review*, July 11, 2023.

236 **this story with Micky Tripathi:** Micky Tripathi, interview by author, September 25, 2024. In early 2025, Tripathi announced that he was assuming a new role as chief AI implementation officer at the Mayo Clinic.

237 **has thrown an enormous wrench:** Enrico Coiera and David Fraile-Navarro, "AI as an Ecosystem—Ensuring Generative AI Is Safe and Effective," *NEJM AI* 1, no. 9 (2024), https://doi.org/10.1056/AIp2400611.

237 **one thousand AI-enabled:** "Artificial Intelligence and Machine Learning (AI/ML)–Enabled Medical Devices," US Food and Drug Administration, December 20, 2024, https://www.fda.gov/medical-devices/software -medical-device-samd/artificial-intelligence-and-machine-learning-aiml -enabled-medical-devices.

237 **Christina Silcox, a Duke University:** Christina Silcox, interview by author, January 7, 2025.

238 **Califf and colleagues wrote:** Haider J. Warraich, Troy Tazbaz, and Robert M. Califf, "FDA Perspective on the Regulation of Artificial Intelligence in Health Care and Biomedicine," *JAMA* 333, no. 3 (2024): 241–47, https:// doi.org/10.1001/jama.2024.21451.

239 **the agency's guidance shifted:** "Clinical Decision Support Software," US Food and Drug Administration, September 28, 2022, https://www.fda.gov /regulatory-information/search-fda-guidance-documents/clinical-decision -support-software.

239 **Sendak and colleagues analyzed:** Mark P. Sendak et al., "Strengthening the Use of Artificial Intelligence Within Healthcare Delivery Organizations: Balancing Regulatory Compliance and Patient Safety," *Journal of the American Medical Informatics Association* 31, no. 7 (2024): 1622–27, https://doi.org/10.1093/jamia/ocae119.

240 **regulatory affairs, Bakul Patel:** David Blumenthal and Bakul Patel, "The Regulation of Clinical Artificial Intelligence," *NEJM AI* 1, no. 8 (2024), https://doi.org/10.1056/AIpc2400545.

242 **Predetermined Change Control Plan:** "Marketing Submission

Recommendations for a Predetermined Change Control Plan for Artificial Intelligence–Enabled Device Software Functions," US Food and Drug Administration, December 3, 2024, https://www.fda.gov/regulatory -information/search-fda-guidance-documents/marketing-submission -recommendations-predetermined-change-control-plan-artificial -intelligence.

242 **its Conditions of Participation:** Michelle M. Mello and I. Glenn Cohen, "Regulation of Health and Health Care Artificial Intelligence," *JAMA* (2025), https://jamanetwork.com/journals/jama/fullarticle/2831831.

243 **thirty-five-thousand-foot view:** Michelle Mello, interview by author, July 25, 2024.

243 **network of "assurance labs":** Emma Beavins, "CHAI Members Hash Out Remaining Questions About AI Assurance Labs," *Fierce Healthcare*, November 7, 2024, https://www.fiercehealthcare.com/ai-and-machine -learning/questions-remain-about-ai-assurance-labs.

243 **come with a "model card":** Emma Beavins, "CHAI's AI Nutrition Label Is Now Open Source," *Fierce Healthcare*, January 9, 2025, https://www .fiercehealthcare.com/ai-and-machine-learning/hlth24-heres-first-look -draft-nutritional-label-health-ai.

243 **a partnership with CHAI:** Erin Schumaker and Ruth Reader, "NIH's 'Forward-Funding Scheme,'" *Politico*, June 11, 2025, https://www.politico .com/newsletters/future-pulse/2025/06/11/nih-forward-funding-scheme -00398712.

244 **sees promise in CHAI's approach:** Scott Gottlieb, "Congress Must Update FDA Regulations for Medical AI," *JAMA Health Forum* 5, no. 7 (2024), https://jamanetwork.com/journals/jama-health-forum/fullarticle /2821274.

244 **Glenn Cohen agrees:** Glenn Cohen, interview by author, August 6, 2024.

244 **Punit Soni, CEO of Suki:** Ruth Reader et al., "Opioids, AI and a Plan to Save Lives," *Politico*, March 12, 2024, https://www.politico.com/newsletters /future-pulse/2024/03/12/opioids-ai-and-a-plan-to-save-lives-00146440.

244 **congressmen raised concerns:** Casey Ross, "Republican Lawmakers Criticize FDA's Partnership with CHAI on Regulating AI in Medicine," *STAT*, June 18, 2024, https://www.statnews.com/2024/06/18/chai-fda -lawmakers-criticize-regulation-ai-medicine.

244 **bristles at these accusations:** Halamka, interview.

245 **Hardeep Singh have outlined:** Dean F. Sittig and Hardeep Singh, "Recommendations to Ensure Safety of AI in Real-World Clinical Care," *JAMA* 333, no. 6 (2024), https://doi.org/10.1001/jama.2024.24598.

246 **warned in his sobering book:** Mustafa Suleyman, *The Coming Wave: Technology, Power, and the 21st Century's Greatest Dilemma* (Crown, 2023).

Chapter 7 | Implications, Recommendations, and Predictions

249 **Gallup survey published in 2025:** Ellyn Maese, "Americans Use AI in Everyday Products Without Realizing It," *Gallup*, January 15, 2025, https://news.gallup.com/poll/654905/americans-everyday-products-without-realizing.aspx.

250 **a chief health AI officer:** Ashley N. Beecy et al., "The Chief Health AI Officer—an Emerging Role for an Emerging Technology," *New England Journal of Medicine AI* 1, no. 7 (2024), https://doi.org/10.1056/AIp2400109.

251 **Digital Transformation (DoC-IT for short):** See Division of Clinical Informatics and Digital Transformation home page at https://docit.ucsf.edu.

251 **mindful of the Productivity Paradox:** Robert M. Wachter and Erik Brynjolfsson, "Will Generative Artificial Intelligence Deliver on Its Promise in Health Care?," *JAMA* 331, no. 1 (2023): 65–69, https://jamanetwork.com/journals/jama/fullarticle/2812615.

251 **a leading health tech entrepreneur:** Heather Landi, "JPM25 Day 3: Why 2025 Will Be a Hot Year for M&A; Talkspace Rolls Out New AI-powered Tool for Therapists," *Fierce Healthcare*, January 15, 2025, https://www.fiercehealthcare.com/providers/jpm25-day-3-why-2025-will-be-hot-year-ma-talkspace-rolls-out-new-ai-powered-tool.

252 **I recently watched a demo:** Aaron Neinstein, interview by author, January 26, 2025.

252 **leads DoC-IT at UCSF, explained:** Julia Adler-Milstein, interview by author, January 27, 2025.

253 **a demo of Epic's version:** Phil Lindemann, interview by author, February 4, 2025.

256 **a small virtual AI hospital:** Jingwei Li et al., "Agent Hospital: A Simulacrum of Hospital with Evolvable Medical Agents," preprint, *arXiv*, January 17, 2025, https://doi.org/10.48550/arXiv.2405.02957.

Index

Aaron, Hank, 55
Abridge, 74, 101–4, 218, 251
academic medical centers (AMCs), 201, 204
accreditation, 237, 242, 243
Adams, Garrett, 116*n*, 117
Adler-Milstein, Julia, 252–53
Adobe, 191
adoption curve, 69–70, 73–74, 260
    driverless cars, 70–74
Aga Khan University, 193
agentic AI, 172, 253–54, 220, 261
AI bubble, 226–28
AIDS, 162–63
AI (artificial intelligence), origins of term, 16
Airbnb, 76
Air France Flight 447, 87
AI slop, 59–60
AI Snake Oil (Narayanan and Kapoor), 132–34
"AI winter," 17, 22, 249
Alagappan, Muthu, 85
alarm fatigue. *See* alert fatigue

Albom, Mitch, 152
alert fatigue, 8, 137–39, 141
alerts, 4, 8, 11, 147
    sepsis, 141–43
"algorithmic absurdity," 132–33
algorithmic drift, 44–45, 237, 245
"algorithmovigilance," 45
Alphabet, 73, 227*n*. *See also* Google
Alseidi, Adnan, 154, 156–57, 158–59
Altman, Sam, xxvii, 63, 136, 227
Alzheimer's disease, 139–40
Amazon, 74, 180, 199, 226, 227*n*, 254
Amazon Care, 175
Ambience, 74, 103–6
ambient clinical intelligence, 97–109. *See also* digital scribes
American Board of Internal Medicine, 50
American Board of Surgery, 152–53
American Prospect, 221
American Recovery and Reinvestment Act of 2009 (stimulus package), 3–4
analog health records, 2–3
Anderson, Richard, 94

Index